BARRY SHEENE

BARRY SHEENE
1950-2003

THE BIOGRAPHY

STUART BARKER

CollinsWillow

An Imprint of HarperCollins*Publishers*

First published in 2003 by
CollinsWillow
an imprint of HarperCollins*Publishers*
London

© Stuart Barker 2003

1 3 5 7 9 8 6 4 2

A CIP catalogue record for this book
is available from the British Library

ISBN 0 00 716180 8

Printed and bound in Great Britain
by Clays Ltd, St Ives plc

The HarperCollins website address
is www.fireandwater.com

CONTENTS

For my parents, Jim and Josie Barker,
for starting this whole thing.

ACKNOWLEDGEMENTS

Thanks to the following for their assistance in compiling this book: Mark Bosworth, Colin Breeze, Angela 'Pooster' Coe, John 'Moon Eyes' Cooper, Mick Grant, Martin Hadwen at Motor Racing Archive, Ann Haslam, Ron Haslam, Chip Hennen, Pat Hennen, Steve Hislop, Niall Mackenzie, Randy Mamola, Don Morley, Chas Mortimer, Chris 'Mossy' Moss, Rob 'Bertie' Simmonds, Simon Tonge, John Watterson, Felicity 'Flick' Webb, and James Wilson at Set-Up Engineering.

A special thanks to Michael Doggart, Tom Whiting, Tarda Davison-Aitkins, Rachel Nicholson, Caroline Hotblack and all at HarperCollins*Publishers* for making this book possible, and thanks also to those who didn't wish to be named for various reasons. You know who you are.

INTRODUCTION

'I'm not going to let fucking cancer get in the way of me enjoying myself.'

It was like nothing had ever changed. The famous Donald Duck logo on the black and gold crash helmet could just be made out as the tall, gangly rider tucked in behind the bike's screen, reducing wind drag to gain a fraction of a second over his pursuer. The equally famous number seven, crossed through European-style, was emblazoned on the bike's bodywork as it had been almost 30 years before. It had always been lucky for him. Maybe it could be again.

His 51 years counted for nothing when he was on a motorcycle; it was as much a part of him as the plates, pins and 27 screws that held his legs together. The smooth but aggressive riding style, the determined and sustained attack, could all have belonged to a 20-year-old kid with a fire in his belly and a burning desire to win against the odds. Any odds.

Behind him, the 1987 500cc motorcycle Grand Prix world champion Wayne Gardner tried everything he knew to close the 1.3-second gap. But despite being 10 years younger and having a bike which was 20mph faster than the man out front, there was nothing he could do to get past. The distinctive riding style of the race leader hadn't changed since he'd started racing bikes in 1968, and his desire to win appeared to be no less now than it was then. It was as if he still had something to prove.

The crowd, as ever, yelled their delight at the on-track bravado of the man in black, urging him on, willing him to make that decisive break, wanting him, needing him to dig deeper to secure a victory. Many of them had been teenagers when they first thrilled to their hero's titanic battles with the best riders in the world, most of the races televised on ITV's Saturday-afternoon *World of Sport* programme – warm, comforting memories of a childhood long gone. There were thousands in attendance who wouldn't even have had an interest in motorcycles had it not been for the influence of the man who was out there throwing his bike hard over from side to side, skimming his knees off the tarmac with a grace and style all of his own and gunning his steed down the straights as fast as the laws of physics would allow.

For the vast majority of the crowd, there was only one rider in the race; they would love him, applaud him and later mob him whether he came first or last. But Barry Sheene wasn't accustomed to coming last. Even after 18 years of retirement from the sport that made him an international superstar, a multi-millionaire and one of the true icons of the seventies, he was out there proving he still had what it took to win races.

The more imaginative among the packed grandstands and trackside enclosures could have transported themselves, mentally if not physically, back to the halcyon days of the seventies when Sheene was on top of the world as the most famous motorcycle racer in history, a pin-up glamour boy for millions of teenage girls and a *Boys' Own* hero for an entire generation of lads. Dads and mums alike now took great pleasure in pointing out to their own kids the very man who had quickened their young pulses nearly three decades earlier.

But even the most nostalgic of spectators were forced, however reluctantly, to admit that things *were* different this time round. For starters, it was 2002, not 1976. And this was not a 500cc Grand Prix World Championship race, it was a classic bike race being staged at the Goodwood Revival event organized by Sheene's close friend, the Earl of March. Sheene's bike, a classic sixties Manx Norton, was a far cry from the vicious 130bhp, 170mph monsters he used to tame on race tracks around the world for the pleasure of millions. But the fans didn't care. It was still Barry Sheene out there, he was still racing a bike, he was still winning, and that was all that mattered.

The most significant change of all, the thing that really brought a lump to the throats of so many and which made Sheene's eventual victory over Gardner even more remarkable and emotional, was the recently divulged fact that Barry had cancer. This was the first time he had appeared in public since being diagnosed. The poignancy of his win was not lost on the 80,000-strong crowd who realized they were probably witnessing Sheene's last-ever race.

Barry had been diagnosed with cancer of the oesophagus and upper stomach just a few weeks earlier, and there were more than a few tears shed as he crossed the line, removed his helmet and waved to the masses on his victory lap. He had come a long way to get to Goodwood in the sleepy West Sussex countryside – from the other side of the world, in fact. An 18-hour direct flight from Australia is gruelling enough for most passengers, never mind one suffering from cancer. But to ride flat-out against some supremely talented opposition, including former world champions Gardner and Freddie Spencer, and to eventually take the race win gave all his fans reason to believe that this time cancer had picked the wrong body. Sheene was a fighter and a winner; he had proved it many times before. Surely, if anyone could beat the most dreaded of diseases, it was he.

When news of his illness broke, Sheene shocked fans around the world by announcing he would not be undergoing invasive surgery or chemotherapy to treat his condition. Instead, he would rely on alternative cures and a special frugal diet. Sheene had already lost a stone off his slight frame by the time he appeared at Goodwood, and orthodox oncologists warned that he risked malnutrition by continuing with the diet. But Sheene has always done things his own way, and he was adamant when interviewed by *Motor Cycle News*: 'I'm not going to be fighting this in the conventional way. I won't subject my body to chemotherapy. I'm putting my faith in the natural way.'

Typically for a man who had made a living out of cheating death, Barry put a brave face on his illness and already had his quips and quotes worked out for the media. 'I don't like cancer, but it's growing on me'; 'If I don't beat this my wife's going to kill me.' These were just two of the lines he bandied about like a stand-up comic living in denial of the very real risk to his life. Sheene also insisted that he wasn't 'going to let fucking cancer get in the way of me enjoying myself' and admitted that his second thought upon hearing his diagnosis was that he might have to miss the Goodwood event. It hadn't taken long for him to re-establish control, pack a suitcase and catch a flight; he wasn't about to let down his fans. Anyway, it wasn't as if fighting for survival was something new to Sheene. In the past he had astounded some of the most respected doctors and surgeons in the world with his ability to recover from serious injuries in unheard-of time spans.

Well-publicized X-rays of his shattered legs from two horrific high-speed crashes played as much a part in making him a household name as any of his victories on the race track. In 1975, his rear tyre blew out at 178mph on the notorious banked section of the Daytona Speedway in Florida. The crash, captured by a television documentary crew who were following Sheene at the time, was shown on TV news programmes around the world, and the incident made Barry famous overnight. His leg was broken so badly it was twisted up behind him, out of sight, making him think he had lost it. He also lost shocking amounts of skin and broke his forearm, wrist, six ribs and a collarbone, as well as suffering compression fractures to several verte-brae. On top of that, damage to his kidneys meant he urinated blood for several weeks. Despite the serious nature of his injuries, Sheene did not lose his 60-a-day passion for strong, unfiltered cigarettes – he preferred the French brand Gauloises, but would happily smoke any brand that was being offered around – and insisted on being wheeled out of the hospital on his bed from time to time so that he could smoke. The hole he drilled in the chin bar of his crash helmet so that he could have a puff on the starting grids at race meetings remains the stuff of legend in bike-racing circles, but no one was laughing any more. Sheene's heavy smoking habit, which had started when he was just nine years old, was one factor cited as a possible cause of his cancer.

The Daytona disaster was the kind of accident that would take 'normal' people months, if not years, to recover from. Many would never overcome the psychological scars of remembering every bone-crushing, skin-shredding second of their crash, and would certainly never contemplate getting back on a motorcycle again, but then most people aren't Barry Sheene. He was racing again just seven weeks later with an 18-inch pin in his left thigh bone, and went on to win his first World Championship the following year.

Crashes are common in bike racing, but big ones like Sheene's Daytona incident are rare – at least, it's rare to survive them. Broken arms or legs are frequent injuries, as are abrasions, damaged tendons and general cuts and bruising, but few people live through, or are unfortunate enough to have in the first place, crashes at such extreme speeds. Sheene had not one but two. The second happened seven years and two World Championships later (Barry retained the title in 1977 and was awarded an MBE for doing so) at the Silverstone circuit in England, and it was every bit as bad, if not worse, than the first. Sheene struck a crashed bike which was lying on the circuit just above a blind rise and its fuel tank instantly ignited causing a massive explosion. He had been travelling at around 165mph at the moment of impact. Moments later, another bike hit the wreckage causing another explosion; the resulting carnage resembled the aftermath of a terrorist bombing. Sheene's already fragile legs had been smashed again, this time more gravely than before, and he also suffered injuries to his head, chest and kidneys.

But while his body was in bad shape, his mental attitude remained as gritty as ever. He told gathered reporters from his hospital bed that 'Broken bones are a mechanical problem. You can fix them.' Sheene's surgeon, Nigel Cobb, inserted plates, pins and a total of 27 screws into his famous patient's legs and triggered a barrage of schoolboy gags about Barry Sheene and airport metal detectors. But his rate of recovery, once again, was phenomenal.

If Barry Sheene had been a star before his Silverstone crash, he was a superstar after it – and, it appeared, an invincible one. No bike racer before or since has commanded anywhere near the same amount of media coverage as Sheene. It is inconceivable in the current climate of the sport to imagine a national newspaper running a front-page story on a bike racer just because he'd met a new blonde girlfriend, and how many other bikers could have starred alongside boxer Henry Cooper in a terrestrial TV advert for a body scent encouraging users to 'splash it all over'? How many racers counted members of the Beatles as close personal friends and dined with Hollywood legends such as Cary Grant? None.

As well as being a world champion racer, Barry Sheene was a marketing phenomenon, gaining exposure for his growing attachment of sponsors in areas even they couldn't have imagined. He co-hosted ITV's *Just Amazing!* show in the eighties and was the star attraction at the 1982 BBC Sports Personality of the Year awards when he rode his new Suzuki onstage and announced he'd be leaving Yamaha to join Suzuki for the following season. He starred as himself in the (very bad) movie *Space Riders*, and appeared on every major television show of his time from *Parkinson* to *Swap Shop*, *Jim'll Fix It* to *Russell Harty*. But perhaps the most enduring legacy of Barry's fame is that he's still the only biker the general public as a whole have heard of. Ask any one of them to name a motorcycle racer and they'll invariably say Barry Sheene. The same thing happens whenever anyone, young or old, is attempting to go too fast or to do something stupid on a two-wheeler, be it a motorcycle or a pushbike. The response from policemen and dads alike is always the same: 'Who do you think you are, son, Barry Sheene?'

Everyone appreciated a British sportsman who was capable of beating the world in an era when such a thing wasn't (and, sadly, still isn't) commonplace. Sheene remains the last British rider to win a Grand Prix World Championship despite the fact that he last held the title 25 years ago. Even more than his ability to win, the public applauded his guts and bravery as he came back not once but twice from injuries that would have ended any other sportsman's career. After his Silverstone crash, Sheene was extremely lucky to be able to walk again, let alone be fit enough to win motorcycle races.

It was this fighting spirit, this never-say-die attitude, which gave hope to millions when Barry announced he was ready to battle cancer and wouldn't be beaten in the fight. With typical bravado, he commented shortly after being diagnosed that it was 'a complete pain in the arse', and vowed to deal with it.

It was a great irony that a man who had spent 16 years risking his life on a motorcycle should retire from the sport still in one piece only to face death from a creeping, silent and devastating opponent from within. The irony was not lost on those who remembered that Britain's other great champion motorcyclist, Mike Hailwood, was killed in retirement by an errant lorry driver while returning in his car from his local fish and chip shop. Sheene's former rivals, as well as his constant supporters, were without exception shocked by the news of his cancer, and all of them rallied round to offer words of support and encouragement. Old differences were forgotten. The only thing that mattered was for Sheene to concentrate on beating his disease.

Barry Sheene was the first, and arguably the last, truly mainstream motorcycle racer who could genuinely lay claim to being a household name. In truth, there was no need for him after 1982 to continue to risk life and limb on a 180mph motorcycle when he was already a multi-millionaire with a twelfth-century, 34-bedroom mansion in Surrey, his own helicopter and a guaranteed career outside racing whenever he decided to call it quits. But that's what made him Barry Sheene: his determination to be the best, to be the fastest, never to give up, to push a 130bhp motorcycle past its limits and bring it back safely again. Sometimes he didn't bring it back safely; sometimes the bike would savagely bite back and spit Sheene off like an angry rodeo steer ditching its rider. But Sheene always got back on. He always returned to show the bike, and his public, who was boss.

But at the age of just 51, Sheene had a new and even more deadly opponent than a badly behaved, viciously powerful motorcycle, a more lethal foe than speed itself, and a more cunning enemy than any he had faced off before. He had cancer. Without doubt, it would prove to be the toughest battle of his impressive but painful career, but on that day at Goodwood there seemed to be no one in the world with a mindset more suited to combating the biggest killer of modern times. He had cheated death many times before. All he had to do was cheat it one more time.

CHAPTER 1

COCKNEY REBEL?

*'For me, school was like a bad dream. Every
minute of every day was murder.'*

If you're going to be a motorcycle racer, you're going to have
to get used to pain, discomfort and hospital food. Barry
Sheene had a very early introduction to all three. Almost
from the moment he was born he suffered from infantile
eczema which caused him, and his mother Iris, years of sleep-
less nights as Barry tossed around in his cot scratching and
clawing at every part of his tiny body seeking a moment's
respite from the maddening, all-enveloping itch. As anyone
who's ever had the misfortune to suffer from severe eczema
will testify, it's not a very pleasant condition. Barry's torment
increased at the age of two when he also developed chronic
asthma. The infant Sheene therefore had to endure the
double misery of an infernal itch while struggling for breath
at the same time. Almost from the moment he was born, he
learned about tolerance to pain, about how to overcome illness, about how never to give up in the struggle back to
health. These experiences would stand him in good stead.

Sadly, 11 September is a date that will now always be remembered for the wrong reasons following the terrorist attack on New York's World Trade Center in 2001, but in 1950 the date was significant in the Sheene family's London household because it was when Frank and Iris welcomed into the world their second child, having already given birth to a daughter, Margaret. Barry Stephen Frank Sheene was born at 8.55 p.m. on a Monday evening and was later taken home to a four-bedroom flat in Queens Square, Holborn, just off Gray's Inn Road in London WC1.

Much has been made of whether or not Sheene, having been born and raised in WC1, can actually lay claim to being a genuine cockney. Traditionally (and according to the *Collins Dictionary* definition), the only qualification required for the title is to be 'born within the sound of the bells of St Mary-le-Bow church', or the 'Bow Bells' as they are more commonly referred to. Since weather conditions, white noise and the relative abilities of one's hearing will naturally affect the range of the bells, it appears to be a moot point in Sheene's case. There is no strict dividing line painted around London to define which streets are 'cockney' and which are not, but it's probably fair to say that those living further east in the city disputed Sheene's claim while the rest of the world happily accepted it. Still, Sheene was proud of his cockney roots and no one is in a position to deny him those roots with any authority.

Sheene's father Frank, or Franco as he has always been affectionately called by his son, was the resident engineer at the Royal College of Surgeons. The family's flat went with the job, as did a fully equipped workshop out back which was to prove of significant importance to the young Barry in the years that followed. The family was neither wealthy nor poor; Barry would later describe his family's socio-economic status as 'slightly above average'. Iris worked at the college as a housekeeper to top up the family income and Frank brought in some handy extra cash working as a mechanic and bike tuner in the evenings. By the mid-sixties he had earned such a good reputation as a two-stroke tuner that world champions including Bill Ivy and Phil Read came knocking on his door. The former was a hero to Barry, but he was sadly killed in a racing accident when Barry was still young. The latter would start out as a friend before falling out with Barry in 1975 over an alleged bribe attempt, more of which later.

Work became plentiful for Frank, and his skills were highly valued by any racer who had the money and wanted his motorcycle to go faster. It was Frank's skill with all things mechanical that saved his son's manhood after a nightmare incident when Barry was just four years old; eczema and asthma notwithstanding, his well-being suffered a further setback, as Michael Scott related in his 1983 book *Barry Sheene: A Will to Win*. According to Iris Sheene, Barry had been playing with a clockwork toy train while being bathed in the kitchen sink when he suddenly let out a terrible scream. When a panicked Iris turned to see the cause of the commotion, she noticed that the bodywork of the train was missing (probably due to Barry's early curiosity for all things mechanical) but the cogs and mechanisms had caught his foreskin and were still churning away, tearing into the sensitive flesh of her child's genitalia. A traumatized Barry was rushed to a nearby hospital where his father exercised all his skill in dismantling the train's workings while desperately holding back the tightly loaded spring that was the cause of his son's agony. Eventually Frank worked the train loose at the expense of much blood and some tissue, but Barry would have much to thank his father for in later years when he came of age. Had it not been for his father's skill and quick thinking, Barry Sheene the playboy might never have been. It was a fortunate escape, and by no means Barry's last.

Frank began to pass on his considerable mechanical knowledge to his son from a very early age. Before her death from a brain tumour in 1991, Iris recalled, 'When he [Barry] was only eighteen months old, I can remember him wandering around in his dungarees with a spanner in his hand.' There was to be an early introduction to race meetings, too: from the age of four Barry was being dragged around bike events, soaking up the addictive sights and smells of paddocks all over England and, on occasion, overseas as well. Frank had raced a variety of motorcycles as an amateur for many years, both before and after the war (he won a trophy on the famous Brooklands circuit just before war broke out). He was a competent and enthusiastic club racer but never really World Championship material. Nor did he have the longing to be a world champion; his interest lay more in the preparation and tuning of machinery, and he was most certainly world class at that. Further cementing the Sheene family's ties with motorcycle racing was Frank's brother Arthur, himself an extremely capable speedway rider for Coventry and a loyal member of 'Team Sheene' once Barry took up racing.

Unlike his son, Frank was a keen supporter of the Isle of Man TT races which at that time was still the most important bike event in the world. It was when he took five-year-old Barry to the island for what was already his second TT trip that the youngster found himself having health traumas yet again, and this time it really did look bad. Set as it is in the middle of the Irish Sea, the Isle of Man's wet and misty climate is not particularly suited to asthma sufferers. Barry suffered such a severe attack that he quite literally turned blue. He was rushed to Nobles Hospital where he was detained for three days until his breathing returned to normal. It was the start of an unhappy relationship with the Isle of Man which would have far-reaching consequences in later years.

But Sheene was always quick to spot an opportunity, extremely adept at turning ill fortune to his advantage. Rather than seeing his asthma as a disability, he found ways to make it work for him. For starters, it was a good excuse for getting out of school sports, of which he was never fond; it was an even better excuse for playing truant, and he regularly told teachers he had asthma clinics to attend. To be fair, sometimes he did have legitimate appointments, but there were many more occasions when he didn't. His truancy habit was made considerably easier to sustain when Sheene found a pile of pre-stamped appointment cards on one particular visit to a clinic. Spotting a golden opportunity, he promptly pocketed the lot, got a friend to sign them, and from then on enjoyed what amounted to a healthy supply of get-out-of-school-free cards. They were not wasted.

   Sheene's hatred of school has been well documented. It's not that he didn't have an aptitude for learning – as he would later prove by teaching himself five languages and learning to pilot a helicopter – it was just that he didn't like it. And when Barry Sheene didn't like doing something, he didn't do it. He didn't like the work, he didn't like the discipline, and most of all he didn't like the teachers. 'For me, school was like a bad dream,' he said. 'Every minute of every day was murder. I hated being told what to do and when to do it by a bunch of teachers who always wanted to try to insult me or belittle me.' Sheene didn't respond well to being told what to do. If he was given a free rein, as he was in Frank's workshop, he displayed a fantastic ability to learn, but he resented the apparently pointless rigidity of the school environment. That stubborn streak would remain with him throughout his life, and it helped him amass a fortune as a property developer in Australia when he stopped racing motorcycles. Barry's headmaster at St Martin's in the Fields once told Iris that her son could have been top boy if he had only put his mind to it, but Barry simply wasn't interested. He had decided at a very early age that he would do things his own way or not at all. That same headmaster sent his former pupil a letter of congratulations when he won the 500cc World Championship in 1976, a fact of which Barry was under-standably proud. It was, after all, a written acknowledge-ment of achievements attained without the aid of formal education.

Sheene brought up the subject of his schooldays again in 1978 when he appeared on the *Parkinson* show. Speaking of one teacher whom he had particularly disliked (he diplomatically stopped short of naming him) he said, 'I was caught for *This Is Your Life* the other night. I thought, "I hope they don't bring that teacher on because it would be the first punch-in." I feel bitter about it. I think it is one of the things that's driven me on, because in the back of my mind there's always this guy saying you will never make anything of your life.'

At one point, it looked more likely that Barry Sheene would become famous as a musical star rather than as a bike racer as he landed a job as an extra in the musical *Tosca* in Covent Garden, not far from his house. Sheene had been spotted fighting by a teacher who was looking for extras and she'd asked him if he could sing as well as fight. He replied that he could 'at a push', auditioned for the part of a scrapping, singing youth, and ended up sharing the stage with world-renowned opera singer Maria Callas. Sheene explained, 'She [the teacher] was recruiting lads as extras . . . and another young boy and I were auditioned and given small parts in the first act to scrap in a churchyard scene. Being cast as a singing, fighting hooligan wasn't altogether at odds with the way I behaved in real life! Sharing the stage with Tito Gobbi and Maria Callas at such a famous place became one of my most vivid childhood memories. I even had to sing. Best part of it was it meant getting off school.'

To escape the misery of school when he wasn't treading the boards, Barry would often sneak off behind the bike sheds to chain-smoke cigarettes. It seems incredible that someone with chronic asthma would want to smoke, but Barry had taken up the habit when he was just nine years old. Most parents would have been horrified to catch their child smoking, although to be fair on Mr and Mrs Sheene attitudes towards smoking have changed markedly since the fifties and sixties; when Frank caught Barry at it when he was 11, he simply handed him two Woodbines (extremely strong, non-filter cigarettes) and said that if Barry could finish them off he was free to smoke. Fifteen minutes later, Barry was free to smoke. He was soon openly sharing his cigarettes with his family. Years later, his greatest joy having returned to the paddock was his first post-race cigarette. 'For no other reason than for the sheer pleasure it brings, my first priority upon dumping the bike in the pits is to have a cigarette,' he said. 'I might have had my last drag on the start line [through the hole drilled in his helmet's chin bar] but I crave one immediately I've finished the race, not as a means of calming the nerves but simply because it has been over an hour since my last one. For a heavy smoker like myself, that's a long time!'

Drinking, however, was never one of his vices, although he was as prone to getting carried away on nights out as the next man, and he did once take sadistic pleasure in getting a schoolfriend drunk during a lunch break in what has become one of the most often-repeated stories from Sheene's childhood. Barry plied his hapless chum with a concoction of spirits from his father's drinks cabinet before dragging him back to the classroom to observe the effects. His friend was so intoxicated that he needed to be rushed to hospital to have his stomach pumped. Sheene, not surprisingly, thought he was in for big trouble when his parents were called in to school to see the headmaster, but Frank was his usual laid-back self, dropping cigarette ash all over the headmaster's pristine carpet as he explained his son's actions by resignedly announcing that 'Boys will be boys.'

Barry first got drunk at the Isle of Man TT in 1960 when he was only 10 years old after guzzling two glasses of champagne given to him by Gary Hocking, who had just finished second in the Junior TT. The experience was enough to put him off touching another drop of alcohol until he was 16. Even after that he claimed he never became a heavy drinker, although he did later develop a passion for fine wines and took great pride in his well-stocked cellar.

Girls were another matter altogether. Perhaps because he'd come so close to losing his manhood as a child, Barry seemed determined to put it to good use as soon as the opportunity presented itself. It finally did over a snooker table in the crypt of a local church when Barry was 14, with a girl whose name he could never remember. From that point on he never looked back. He'd eventually become so famous for his womanizing that he would make front-page news after being photographed leaving a night-club with a new date, and he would also be selected as a judge for the Miss World contest.

But whatever mischief Barry got up to in his youth, he never rebelled against his parents. The Sheene family was a very tight-knit unit and it stayed that way throughout Barry's racing career, with Frank helping on the bikes and

Iris keeping hot food and drinks flowing for the family and their guests. Barry never treated his parents with anything other than full respect, though he often fought with his elder sister Maggie. 'Team Sheene' would become legendary round the paddocks of the world, Frank and Iris providing all the back-up their boy needed when he was racing bikes. The trio were practically inseparable.

Unlike some parents who attempt to live out their own unfulfilled dreams through their children, Frank never pushed Barry into riding motorcycles, but then he didn't have to. When he offered the five-year-old Barry a motorcycle, the youngster jumped at the chance, like most boys would. The bike was a damaged 50cc Ducati that Frank had rebuilt, and Barry spent hours riding around the spacious back yard of the Royal College of Surgeons on the little four-stroke single, driving the neighbours to distraction. The machine actually had two gears, but Barry, not knowing how to change gears, only ever used one. It was still good enough to reach speeds of around 50mph.

Ironically, it wasn't hurtling around on a motorcycle which caused Barry's first serious injury; it was a pushbike accident at the age of eight which resulted in a broken arm. After the arm was plastered, Sheene told his mother that he'd always wanted to break his arm (again, like most schoolboys) and was well chuffed with his plaster trophy.

The little Ducati was eventually replaced by a 100cc Triumph Tiger Cub which Barry took to race meetings so he could potter around in the nearby fields, of which there wasn't an abundance in central London. He had tried riding the Tiger round the roads near his home but a couple of run-ins with the law had put an end to that, even though the coppers had taken it easy on Barry as they regularly utilized Frank's services for repair work. When he wasn't riding his own bike, Barry would take his dad's race bikes out for short test runs at disused airfields or racing paddocks, all the time developing his skill for analysing how the bikes were running. Sheene's developmental and analytical skills became finely honed during these years, and they played a big part in his success. But that was no real surprise when one considers that he could strip and rebuild an engine by the age of 12 and was riding real racing motorcycles when his class-mates were still mastering the art of pedalling. Barry recalled getting plenty of snotty looks as a kid when he suggested to puzzled and frustrated riders in the paddock what might be wrong with their bikes just by listening to them being revved. But those who were modest enough to take his advice usually found (probably to their amazement) that the advice was good. Indeed, Sheene became quite the little paddock consultant for any rider whose ego was willing to accommodate the fact that a child knew more about engine mechanics than he did.

Frank Sheene's bikes were among the best in the country in the sixties and were in demand by many of the top racers of that era, and Barry was fast catching his father up on technical know-how. So much so that by the time he was 14 he was a good enough mechanic to be offered a job looking after race bikes, even though it didn't pay. But for someone who hated school as much as Barry did the opportunity must have felt like a dream come true: he was asked if he would like to spend a month working as a mechanic in Europe for American Grand Prix racer Tony Woodman. Needless to say, he didn't have to be asked twice. Frank, fully approving of what he saw as a unique chance for his son to see something of the world and to gain work experience while other kids were stuck in school only reading about foreign lands, gave his son £15 for the month to cover all expenses from food, drink and cigarettes to ferry fares. It was a very modest sum, even in 1964, but Barry, showing a thriftiness that would later become a hallmark, managed to return from the trip with change in his pocket. His parents signed him off school for a month, blaming another bout of illness.

There were few luxuries available and food was scarce, but it was an incredible experience for a boy of 14 and an invaluable insight into the Grand Prix world he would soon come to dominate. And the fact that Woodman was not there just to make up the GP numbers but was a genuine contender made Sheene's position even more remarkable, a real testament to the skills he had acquired. The trip, which embraced visits to the Salzburgring and the Nurburgring for the Austrian and German GPs, went well. Barry could not have had much interest in returning to school after such an eye-opener, but he still had one year to complete before being officially allowed to leave so he got on with it as best he could. Woodman, incidentally, was later paralysed after breaking his back in the North West 200 road races in Northern Ireland. It was a harsh reminder, if Sheene needed one, that racing motorcycles is a risky business, but at that point Barry showed no signs of wanting to race anyway. Like his father, he was more than happy working on bikes instead of riding them.

His final year at school completed, Sheene was at last free to try his luck in the world at large. He left formal education without a single qualification to his name and in the knowledge that the only thing he'd topped at school was the absenteeism list. But one good thing, aside from Barry's utter relief, came from leaving school: his asthma attacks all but disappeared. They had always been made considerably worse when Barry was stressed or emotionally upset, and he felt there was no mystery attached to their clearing up almost as soon as he left school: it was a sure measure of how much he had dreaded that establishment. He couldn't have been happier when it was time to turn his back on it for good.

It seemed obvious from his early-learned hatred of authority that Barry wasn't going to settle comfortably into just any old job under any old boss. As he said, 'I had never experienced working for someone other than Frank and I wasn't quite sure how I would take to someone giving me orders.' But with no formal qualifications, he wasn't going to be offered many decent jobs either. Deep down, however, both Sheene and his parents knew that his profound mechanical knowledge would somehow see him through. Frank had taught him all he needed to know about stripping and rebuilding engines, about how to squeeze every last ounce of power out of a motorcycle. Surely that knowledge alone would stand him in good stead?

But being a mechanic didn't seem to be top of Barry's job-hunting list. In fact, initially he didn't have a clue what he wanted to do, and he soon found himself drifting in and out of jobs like most young people trying to find their feet in the world. Eventually he landed a job in a car spares warehouse unloading parts into different bins. The work was neither glamorous nor stimulating, and it paid a measly £5 a week, of which Barry pocketed just 75 shillings after paying tax and national insurance. Needless to say, he didn't stick at the job for long. Within a few months he had moved on to a new position which was infinitely more exciting and one small step closer to his destiny: he became a motorcycle despatch rider.

Having failed his bike test first time round because the number plate fell off his machine (in his 1976 book *The Story So Far*, Sheene wrote that he took his test on a 75cc Derbi, but in 2001 he claimed it was on a BSA Bantam), Barry passed at his second attempt, although he told *Bike* magazine years later that 'In no way did it [the bike test] prepare me for the road. Absolutely not. In the same way that shagging your girlfriend in a Transit van does nothing to prepare you for married life.' Having passed, Sheene was handed a BSA Bantam (which perhaps explains his confusion over which bike he had passed his test on) with which to deliver proofs and copy around London for an advertising agency. His wages jumped up to a healthier £12 a week, and more importantly for the girl-mad young Sheene, he got to meet lots of glamour models.

Needless to say, no motorcycle could be taken back to the Sheene household without Frank giving it the once-over, and the British-built Bantam was no exception. Frank soon had it tweaked and tuned to reach a top speed of

80mph, which, through London traffic at any rate, was about as fast as even Barry Sheene dared to go.

Barry enjoyed his stint as a courier, and no doubt it helped to hone his riding skills since travelling through heavy London traffic at speed is no easy task. But at the time money was more important than job satisfaction, and when a friend offered him more cash for sprucing up second-hand cars for his showroom, Barry gladly accepted.

After eighteen months of valeting cars it was time for another change, and Sheene took to driving a truck around London delivering antique furniture, quite often to television stage-sets. He had to lie about his age to get the job and had to show his prospective employers his dad's driving licence which included the all-important HGV stamp, but somehow it worked and Barry found himself employed as a truck driver. The only problem was, he couldn't drive a truck. This shortcoming was compounded when his new boss asked him for a lift in the truck straight after the interview. Sheene thought fast and insisted he had to have some time to check the truck over in the yard before he drove it, him being so safety conscious and all. His boss seemed suitably impressed and sought alternative transport, leaving his relieved new employee to drive round and round a nearby car park, familiarizing himself with the skills required to drive a heavy goods vehicle. Sheene took to the task easily, passed his month's probation without any problems, and was once more to be seen despatching goods around London, albeit at a much more sedate pace.

Barry had been a competent driver, of cars if not HGVs, long before he passed his driving test first time round at the age of 17 in his father's Rover 105. At just eight years of age he was driving an Austin Ten round the back yard at the Royal College of Surgeons. He was so small that Frank had had to fix lumps of wood onto the foot pedals. But cars never held a great appeal for Barry. To his mind, they were simply more useful for pulling women than anything else, so the style of his four-wheeled transport was more important than its performance. Most 17-year-old boys would have been delighted to be given a Thames van by their fathers, as Barry was, but he bemoaned the fact that it 'wasn't too flash for pussy-pulling'.

Although the young Sheene had his uses for cars, it was bikes that he was instinctively drawn to. After all, he'd been surrounded by them and their racers since birth, and even though in the early part of his youth he harboured no ambitions of being a racer, it seemed almost inevitable that he would at least try his hand at it eventually, if only out of curiosity.

The seeds of Barry's racing career were sown, albeit indirectly, during a trip to Spain when he was eight years old. In 1958 Frank took his son to see the then-famous Barcelona 24-Hour race at Montjuich Park, and during the trip Frank introduced himself to Francesco Bulto, the head of Spanish bike manufacturer Bultaco. The two soon became friends, and it was this friendship that eventually led to Barry's racing debut. Through Señor Bulto, Frank managed to secure a place on the first racing Bultaco to come into Britain, and he actually won a race on it first time out at the now defunct Crystal Palace circuit. Frank was suitably impressed with the capabilities of the machinery, and from that point onwards he received two new factory models at the beginning of each year to set up for other riders to race. During that 1958 trip, Bulto had allowed Barry to sit on one of his bikes and showed him how to change gears for the first time. He also reportedly told Barry that one day he would ride a factory Bultaco for him. Although he was no doubt simply humouring the child, his prediction came true fewer than ten years later when Barry made his racing debut at Brands Hatch on one of Bulto's factory machines.

Throughout his childhood and youth, Barry had accompanied his dad to race meetings almost every weekend during the summer; if Frank wasn't going to be attending a race or a practice day for whatever reason, young Barry would scrounge a lift from one of the many racers he had got to know in the paddock. Before he ever turned a wheel in anger, Barry Sheene was a paddock institution who could be seen either offering technical advice to riders or just generally mucking in by carrying tyres, working stopwatches or cleaning bikes. He was, quite literally, born to the paddock.

He had, for example, worked on Chas Mortimer's bikes when Mortimer was racing them for Frank. Chas went on to win eight Isle of Man TTs and had a successful career in GPs and in British championships, as well as being Sheene's team-mate at Yamaha in Grands Prix in 1972. 'Barry worked for me as my mechanic when I rode for his father Frank in, I think, 1967,' Mortimer recalled. 'I did a few meetings in the UK on his 125 and 250cc Bultacos. Barry was quite good with the spanners even then, he always has been. I remember he used to run my bikes in for me when he was a young, long-haired youth living in Holborn. Franco and Barry used to work on the bikes in the workshop there; well, Barry would work on the bikes and Franco would be doing the talking, the team manager bit.' Mortimer thought that the fundamentals of the characteristics which later made Sheene famous were already in place in the late sixties. 'Barry was always quite outspoken, he was quite a precocious boy. He got his reputation with the women from right early on, and I remember when he was 14 he was smoking 30 fags a day – breaking the filters off the ends, of course.'

Multiple British champion John 'Moon Eyes' Cooper – so called because of the trademark eyes painted on his helmet – also remembered Sheene around the racing scene as a youngster. 'I've known Franco for about 50 years,' he said. 'I never rode his bikes but he was always about the paddocks, riding at first then tuning bikes for other riders. Barry was always around too. When he was about 15 he used to come and stay at my house with a racer called Dave Croxford because he was helping Dave a bit at the races.' Croxford was just one of a long list of riders who raced Frank Sheene's bikes, and the young Barry would not only help him with the spanners, he would also be constantly absorbing valuable information from everything he saw and heard around him. 'I'd watch the blokes on dad's bikes [and] note how they would handle them,' he explained, 'listen for anything that sounded off-song. I certainly knew how an engine worked even then. While other lads would know who played outside-left for Arsenal, I could explain the principles of a two-stroke motor.'

In early 1968, Sheene experienced an even more direct involvement with racing, this time on the other side of the armco. Frank had just received his usual allotment of Bultacos – a 125cc machine and a 250cc bike – for the coming season. After stripping and rebuilding them to his own particular specifications, as every bike tuner does, he asked Barry to run them in for him at Brands Hatch. He knew his son would be mechanically sympathetic during the running-in process and he also knew that as Barry wouldn't be out to prove anything on the track there was little chance of him crashing the precious bikes before they were even raced. Besides, there was no one else available at the time. Little could the pair have known that that inauspicious track debut would lead to one of the most glittering careers in motorcycling history.

Although Barry insisted that his dad never forced him into his track debut, it's tempting to think he must have been at least a little curious to see how his boy would go round a circuit even if Barry didn't seem too desperate to find out for himself. He hadn't shown much competitive spirit at school or in his early jobs, so why should things be any different now?

Barry's competitive career had actually started in trials riding some years before. Trials is a sport where riders negotiate near-impossible obstacles such as logs, barrels and rock faces at very low, often dead-stop speeds. The emphasis is on precise throttle control and balance, and as such it's a good way for riders to hone their skills. The only problem was that it didn't involve speed, and Sheene liked his speed. Despite this, Barry had shown promise in the early stages of most of the events he entered, but he struggled to maintain enough interest and concentration in the sport to make further progress. He was more engaged by the ground between the marked-out sections on the course where he could indulge in sudden bursts of speed and practise the wheelies he'd later become renowned for. In the end, it just wasn't the sport for him. Road racing, however, was to prove a different matter entirely; it was to be the sport for which Barry had an innate aptitude.

Running in a racing motorcycle, like running in anything else, is a progressive business. It's all about getting some steady miles on the clock to ensure everything is bedded in correctly before the machine is thrashed near to death by whoever races it. Even so, there was an inherent danger in the exercise for Sheene because every one of Frank's new Bultacos in the past had seized on their initial outings. In other words, the engines had locked solid in mid-flight, and that usually ends with the rider being thrown off the bike unless his reactions are quick enough to allow him to pull the clutch in and freewheel to a standstill. This time round, the bikes didn't seize. Barry found he'd actually enjoyed himself riding round the same track on which he'd watched his heroes racing for so many years. Brands Hatch, situated to the south-east of London, was Sheene's 'home' track. He'd been there countless times and was familiar with the famous corners like Paddock Hill Bend, Druids and Clearways.

As things turned out, the day's testing went so smoothly that Frank asked Barry to do some further bedding-in the following week. By that point the bikes had some miles under their belts and Barry was able to pick up the revs and push a good bit harder. He was also much more familiar with the track layout, the correct lines to take and the whole race-track environment, all of which is very alien to beginners. Being let loose on a circuit where there's no cars, trucks or buses coming the other way, no speed limits, no mirrors on your bike and no restrictions or guides as to where you should position yourself on the road takes a bit of getting used to, even if you are Barry Sheene. But by the second weekend of testing, Barry was looking like he'd been born to it, and the fact didn't go unnoticed. Reports from trackside marshals started to filter back to Frank that his son was looking a bit handy out there on the Bultacos; in fact, he looked faster than many racers those same marshals had seen. Maybe Barry should try his hand at racing? Frank related the news to his son, and Barry admitted to letting the praise go to his head. He readily agreed that maybe the time was right to carry on the family racing tradition and get out on the track in anger for the first time.

It was March 1968 and Sheene was 17 years old when he lined up on the starting grid, his gangly figure dwarfing the little 125cc Bultaco, for his first ever race. By today's standards that's pretty old – Valentino Rossi, for example, was a world champion at the same age in 1997 – but back in the late sixties it was more in keeping with the norm. It was an impressive debut by anyone's standards. Sheene had worked his way up to second place in the race and was threatening the leader Mike Lewis when it all went wrong: the Bultaco seized, as it had never done during the running-in period, and spat its rider off over the handlebars. It wasn't Barry's fault in any way, but his detractors have often sniggered over the fact that Sheene crashed in his very first race. Indeed, that first race established a pattern that was to become all too familiar for Barry Sheene: being on the edge of glory just moments before a fall.

James Wilson was having only the second outing of his racing career that day on a 204cc Elite-engined Ducati. He recalled, 'I remember I went up the inside of Sheene at Druids on one lap then went down through Southbank, and then bang, my clutch went and Barry came flying past me. His Bultaco was very quick, but then he locked up as well and crashed, although it wasn't a bad one. The van took us back to the paddock together and we nattered in the van quite a bit. There was none of this "I'm a hero" kind of stuff. I knew about Barry from the paddock; he was the guy with the long blond hair who was always having a laugh and smoking a fag. He looked like a bloody good rider even back then; he really stood out. I mean, I stood out as well, but I had no help at all while Barry had his mum and dad, his sister and a van filled with all the right stuff. He didn't have loads of money but he had enough, and he had a wealth of experience because of his family background. I was envious, not jealous, of the help Barry had. I knew then that he was going somewhere because he could ride and he had the right back-up as well.' Wilson also remembered Sheene drawing attention to himself in the paddock that day, one of the few times anyone can remember him being violent. 'I remember he punched the lights out of somebody that day because they owed money to Franco. I don't know if he ever got the money but I doubt if the guy ever went near Barry again.'

Money aside, Frank Sheene must have been wondering what he'd got his son into when he learned that Barry had banged his head quite badly, lost some skin off his hands and cut his lip. Protective racing gear in the late sixties was extremely primitive compared to modern helmets, leathers, gloves and boots; a rider would probably be completely unscathed if he had a similar crash today. As it was, Sheene displayed admirable courage by ignoring his injuries and any psychological effects of the crash, and by refusing to be carted off by the circuit ambulance to hospital for a check-up. Instead he lined up to take part in the 250cc race on his other Bultaco.

Frank hadn't wanted Barry to go back out again, but, showing the guts and determination that would eventually make him famous, he went out and finished third in the first event he ever completed. In a way, that first race day was a microcosm of Sheene's career. He rode well, crashed, ignored his injuries and came back to finish strongly, both defiant and jubilant. He proved right from the start that he wasn't a quitter.

A rostrum position for his first-day's racing was a great achievement, but an even better result wasn't very far away. Just one week later, and again at Brands Hatch, Barry took his first race win, and he did it in style by an incredible 12 seconds. And the best was yet to come. Frank had a special 250 Bultaco he had bored out to a larger 280cc capacity, and he wanted to know how it would compare against the machines in the 350 race. As things turned out, the bike didn't compare – it totally dominated.

Beaming with pride, Frank watched his son, and his project bike, finish half a lap ahead of the rest of the field, Barry romping home to take his second victory of the day.

Sheene junior was ecstatic. He might have been shaking with excitement after his first race win, but second time round he was completely overjoyed. Having proved to any doubters that his first victory was no fluke, he suddenly found himself the centre of attention in the paddock as members of the press and fellow racers gathered round to congratulate him. Keener paddock observers realized that the gangly Londoner wearing a cheeky smile from ear to ear was a star in the making. Those who didn't take notice soon would, because Barry Sheene had finally arrived and motorcycle racing would never be the same again.

CHAPTER 2

THE RACER: PART ONE

*'He was it. He was the main man who everyone
had to beat.'*
RON HASLAM

After scoring such a resounding double victory in only his
second-ever race meeting, in April 1968 Barry Sheene
surprised many people by opting out of racing for a few
months. Still unconvinced that racing was the proper
career path to follow, he decided to take in a second tour
of Europe, this time spannering for a rider called Lewis
Young. Young was riding Bultacos, which by now Barry
knew inside out, and he wisely came to the conclusion that
a season following the Grand Prix circus around Europe
would teach him more about the motorcycle racing business
than a few weekends spent hurtling round British circuits.
It might have seemed at the time an odd move to make, but
it proved to be a well-judged one. This time, Barry really
laid the foundations for his future career by getting to
know all the circuits, the travelling routines and the way of
life in the paddock, as well as gaining countless contacts all

of whom would play a part in his future. The experience was heady and intoxicating, and by the time he returned to England that autumn not only was he 10kg lighter after eating so sparsely and irregularly, he had also decided to race again. Having seen some of the lesser lights who were competing in the Grands Prix, Barry had become convinced that he could beat most of them.

The year 1969 was Barry Sheene's first full season of racing, and for the job in hand he had three Bultacos (125, 250 and 350cc), all immaculately prepared by himself and Frank (his Ford Thames van wasn't quite so immaculate, but it was good enough for the job). By the end of it he was being celebrated as the best newcomer of the season, having finished second to and 16 points behind established British rider Chas Mortimer in the 125cc British Championship. 'I seem to remember that I won the 125 British Championship quite early on that year,' Mortimer recalled, 'then I went on to do some Grands Prix while Barry finished off the championship.'

That season very nearly became Sheene's first and last when his hero and friend Bill Ivy was killed during practice for the East German Grand Prix in July. Sheene was devastated and suffered a massive asthma attack upon hearing the news. He hadn't had a relapse since leaving school, and he never had another again. He seriously considered packing in the racing game after Bill's death, but eventually managed to come to terms with the tragedy, as all motorcycle racers must do; it had to be chalked down as an accident and life had to go on. Sheene persisted, and went on to become Bill's natural successor in the paddocks of the world, the cheeky cockney rebel with a playboy lifestyle and a gift for flamboyancy. Ivy would have been proud of him.

It was his natural flamboyancy that led Sheene to design the most famous crash helmet in motorcycle racing history, and it grabbed lots of attention during the 1969 season. While most other riders wore very basic designs on their helmets, if any at all, Barry had Donald Duck emblazoned on the front of his in a bid to attract attention to himself. It worked, and as the design developed over the years it became the most recognizable in the sport. The completed item featured a black background with gold trimmings, the famous number seven on the sides (more of which later) and, for the first time ever in the sport, the rider's name on the back. 'It wasn't intentional,' Sheene explained. 'My helmet had gone away to a chap I knew to be painted and it came back with my name emblazoned on the rear. That's neat, I thought, and I know I turned many heads when I unveiled it for the first time.' Over the next few decades it became almost compulsory for riders to have their names on the backs of their helmets, and Barry claimed he was the originator of the fashion.

And his fashion sense didn't stop at helmet designs; he also helped instigate the long-overdue decline in the use of all-black leathers which had so tarnished the image of motorcycle racing. In the twenty-first century motorcycle racing is one of the most colourful sports on the calendar, but it wasn't always the case, far from it in fact, and Sheene played a large part in the technicolour transformation. In 1972 he ordered a set of white leathers, again largely as a gimmick to get noticed but also as a way of improving the sport's then drab, greasy image of rough men in black leathers riding noisy, smelly motorbikes. He wasn't the first rider to brighten up the sport, however, and not everyone was blown away by his garb, as Chas Mortimer testified. 'I don't particularly remember Barry's Donald Duck helmet and white leathers standing out in those days. I mean, I had white leathers then too. Rod Scivyer was the first person to wear them in about 1967 or 1968.' Sheene would later ditch the white colour scheme believing it was a step too far, but he would go on to wear other brightly coloured leathers such as the famous blue and white Suzuki garments and the even more famous red and black Texaco outfit.

With the trauma of Bill Ivy's death behind him, Sheene set about preparing for the 1970 season with a team set-up and determination as yet unseen. The icing on the cake was the purchase of an ex-factory 125cc Suzuki from retired rider Stuart Graham. It cost a whopping £2,000, which was an enormous sum at the time and certainly out of Barry's reach without the help of his dad. Barry used every penny he had to secure the bike – he was still driving a lorry for up to 14 hours a day to raise funds – and borrowed the rest from Frank, though he insisted he paid every penny back.

He made a point of letting everyone know that he repaid his father because he had always been acutely aware of the perception that he was born with a silver spoon in his mouth when it came to racing. After all, he'd had two factory Bultacos for his first outing, a world-class tuner in his dad and, through his father's connections, advice from some of the best riders in the world. Ron Haslam, who began to challenge Barry's supremacy on the domestic scene in the mid-seventies, recalled Barry's machinery advantage. 'He was it. He was the main man who everyone had to beat. I was helping my brother [Terry Haslam, who was killed racing in 1974] who was beating him sometimes even though he didn't have all the tackle Sheene had. Sheene had factory bikes from the start so it was such a big thing for my brother to beat him on lesser machinery.' Ron himself struggled against Barry on 'lesser machinery' on many occasions; whenever he came out on top it was always sweetly satisfying. 'Sheene was like any rider in that he thought he was the best, as I did. You have to think that. He had superior equipment but he was still beatable, and I always believed I could beat him.'

Barry knew that his little ten-speed Suzuki was fast enough to run at World Championship level, and that's exactly where he intended to be for his third year of racing – a feat almost unheard of in the modern Grand Prix world. Having won his first race on the Suzuki at Mallory Park, Sheene became so dominant on it in Britain that year that he later left it at home and raced the Bultaco instead. It appeared to be an extremely sporting gesture but was, in essence, more of a shrewd financial move: the Suzuki was much too precious to risk in British rounds when it wasn't needed, and Barry couldn't afford to be faced with astronomical spares bills should he crash the bike or damage it in any way. The Suzuki was, however, the weapon of choice for the last Grand Prix of the season in Spain, which also happened to be Barry's first. He had already wrapped up the 1970 125cc British Championship for his first-ever title and decided he needed to up the stakes as far as the competition went if he was to continue on his steep learning curve.

John Cooper remembered watching – sometimes from trackside, sometimes on the track – as the young Sheene progressed. 'Initially Barry was like everyone else. He came up through the ranks in 125s and 250s, but he was always a good rider. At one point I had a 250cc Yamsel [a Yamaha engine in a Seeley frame] and he had a 250 and 350cc Yamaha so we often raced each other and he used to say to me, "I wish you'd bloody pack up and give me a chance."' Sheene didn't get his chance until 1973 when Cooper retired after almost 20 years of racing. 'Barry's career just overlapped mine. When I finished racing he became really good. But he did ride my Yamsel a few times in the early seventies if I wasn't using it just because it was a particularly good bike. He couldn't beat me when I was on it really because his bikes were fairly standard at the time, but then he got the works Suzuki 500 and by then I had packed up and Barry just went from strength to strength.'

One week before that Spanish Grand Prix, Barry entered a big Spanish International event and actually managed to beat the current World Championship leader, the Spaniard Angel Nieto, to the great displeasure of the partisan crowd. It's worth noting that big one-off international race meetings for bikes have now all but disappeared, but in the seventies there were many big-money meets which attracted all the best riders, and a win in one of those was equivalent to a

Grand Prix win by virtue of the fact that all the GP competitors were entered in the race. They were also financially profitable, as Sheene explained in the 1975 *Motor Cycle News* annual. 'At a Grand Prix, I could make between £200 and £500 for one start, but at a non-championship meeting in France, say, I could ask for over £2,000 – and get it.' The risk of injury in non-world championship events eventually heralded their demise in the eighties; for sponsors, manufacturers, riders and teams, the World Championship had to come first and they actively discouraged their contracted riders from taking part in any other events.

Sheene's Spanish win was just what he needed before making his Grand Prix debut, and only a small misjudgement in the setting up of his bike robbed him of the chance of winning that race too. He had been only half a second slower than Nieto in practice despite never having ridden the Montjuich Park circuit before, but his bike was slightly undergeared and Nieto won by eight seconds, with Barry a huge 40 seconds ahead of the third-placed rider Bo Jansson. It was a sensational debut, and also the start of a great friendship between Sheene and Nieto, who would play a big part in helping Barry learn Spanish. He later learned to speak Italian and French as well, to varying levels of fluency, allowing him both to read what was written about him in the bike press of those countries and to conduct interviews with their media – always a popularity booster when very few Brits bothered to learn a second language. Sheene's Japanese was not as good, but it too proved invaluable over the years when dealing with his

Japanese employers Suzuki and Yamaha and their respective mechanics.

Sheene also had his first ride in the premier 500cc class at the Spanish Grand Prix that weekend, although his debut cannot be taken too seriously. Up against the mighty 500cc MV Agustas, Barry pitched his little (albeit overbored) 280cc Bultaco just for a bit of fun. Even so, he managed to work his way into second place in the race before the Bultaco seized, putting an end to his efforts. Barry's first ride on a real 500cc bike came at Snetterton that same year when he raced a crash-damaged Suzuki 500 his father had pieced back together. For once, though, Barry didn't have superior machinery, and it showed as he failed to set the world on fire and eventually retired from the race, but it was a start, and it marked the first time he'd ridden the kind of bike that would make him world famous.

With 1970 delivering the 125cc British Championship, a third place in the 250cc British series and a podium finish in his first Grand Prix, it was decided that nothing less than a full-on assault on the World Championship would suffice in 1971. The amount of travel and mechanical preparation required for such an effort necessitated Barry quitting all his little odd-jobs. From that point on, for better or worse, he would have to survive on whatever start money he could negotiate and whatever prize money he could win. He would be racing for survival.

Motorcycle Grand Prix racing today is a world of glamour and big money: multi-million-pound transporters and hospitality suites, worldwide television coverage, hosts of glamour girls pouting and posing their way through the paddock, luxury motorhomes for the riders to relax in and even more luxurious pay cheques with which to buy them. But in 1971 it couldn't have been more different, especially for a newcomer like the 20-year-old Barry Sheene. Sheene himself would later play a leading role in adding such glamour to international paddocks, but his first full season was, as for most racers, a rough and ready, hand-to-mouth experience. There were no first-class flights to the far-off rounds; instead, Sheene and his mechanic Don Mackay took turns to drive Sheene's newly acquired Ford Transit around Europe. Luxury hotels and restaurants were still some way off too, so the van doubled up as accommodation and kitchen – at least it did when there was something to cook, which for most of the time there wasn't. Don was paid a wage as and when Sheene won any prize money, and a meal in a restaurant was a rare treat if the team had done particularly well. Sheene might have been the source of some envy in UK paddocks when he turned up with ultra-competitive bikes, but when it came to Grand Prix racing he was no more privileged than any other privateer.

Money was so tight at times that desperate and innovative measures were called for just to keep the show on the road. Sheene recalled a time when he had to 'borrow' some red diesel from a cement mixer in West Germany so that he could make it to Austria. When he got there, he asked the race organizer to up his starting fee from £30 a race because he needed money for food for the coming weeks. When the organizer refused on the grounds that no one

knew who Barry Sheene was, Sheene offered a unique solu-
tion: if he could qualify in the top three in each of his three
classes, he would be paid £50 each time; if he couldn't, he
would be paid only £20. The organizer, thinking he could
save some cash, agreed, but he'd seriously underestimated
Barry's talents. Sheene got his £150.

Financial hardship aside, the year went remarkably well,
Barry scoring a third place on the 125cc Suzuki at the first
Grand Prix in Austria. He was also on the pace in the 250
and 350cc classes, but mechanical gremlins robbed him of
any more finishes, as they did in West Germany, too. A look
at the results sheets of Sheene or any other rider from that era
will show just how many mechanical breakdowns a rider
typically suffered in a season. To a modern-day GP enthusiast
this will seem inexcusable; after all, aren't top Grand Prix
mechanics paid handsomely to prevent just such occurrences?
Breakdowns are now so rare as to be a real talking point
among paddock pundits and the press, but in the seventies
they were still commonplace. Reliability has improved massively in the three decades since Sheene first hit the Grand
Prix trail, and the money now being thrown at teams allows
them to replace parts much more regularly, further lessening
the chances of any technological mishaps. While Sheene
might have suffered an apparently high number of mechanical hiccups, other riders did so too, so it all balanced out over
the course of a season. The old points system, where riders
could drop an allocated number of their worst results, further
helped to create an even playing field.

The potential dangers of mechanical problems increased
considerably when the GP circus travelled to the unforgiving

public-roads course that was the Isle of Man TT, Britain's round of the World Championship at the time, and a place Sheene learned very quickly to hate. The TT had started in 1907, and Barry had enjoyed the meet as a young spectator and paddock helper. Riding it, though, was a different matter altogether. The course is unique in that it is 37.74 miles long and lined with walls, houses, lamp-posts and every other hazard you'd expect to find on normal rural and urban public roads. Grand Prix circuits in the seventies were still nowhere near as safe as they are now, but they were a lot safer than the TT course, if only because they were shorter and easier to learn. In 1971, Sheene decided to race on the Isle of Man to try to score some valuable points for his world title campaign. It was a move that would define Sheene's views on the event and make him many enemies among traditionalists who continued to support the TT despite its perils.

Those traditionalists have always scoffed at the fact that Sheene crashed out of his first race there, but he'd actually been on the leaderboard before the incident. He posted the third fastest time in practice on his 125cc Suzuki and was leading the race at one point on the opening lap until he hit thick fog and eased off the throttle. When his overworked clutch bit too hard just after the start of the second lap, Sheene was tossed from his bike at the slow, first-gear Quarterbridge corner and his race was run – much to Barry's relief, as he'd been hating every minute of it. But that wasn't quite the end of Sheene's TT career: he still had an outing in the production event on a 250cc Suzuki. Again, he posted respectable times in practice, but after suffering a massive tankslapper (or 'speed wobble', as it was more quaintly referred to at the time), during which the front end of the bike shakes viciously from side to side, parts of his machine started to work themselves loose and Barry pulled in after just one lap. He never raced on the island again.

A rider's decision not to race at the TT would never normally cause any kind of commotion; it is a free world after all, and no one forces racers to take part in the TT. But Sheene wasn't content just to stay away from the island. Over the next few years he embarked upon a sustained one-man attack on the event and played a major role in the TT eventually being stripped of its World Championship status – a crime for which some have never forgiven him.

Racing fanatics fall into one of two camps over the whole Sheene/TT issue: if you love the TT, you hate Barry Sheene, and if you hate the TT, you tend to agree with Sheene's actions. Barry's major bone of contention was that riders shouldn't be asked to race on such a dangerous track just to gain championship points. He never wanted the TT to be banned as such, he just wanted riders to have the choice of whether or not to race there, his thinking being that when valuable points are at stake riders may be tempted to push their luck to earn a few. TT supporters claimed that the throttle works both ways and riders can take things as easy as they want to, thereby reducing the dangers. Many supporters of the event have said that Barry was just too scared to race there, or that he couldn't be bothered to spend the usual three years to learn the course well enough to win on it. The second argument falls down when you consider that Sheene was leading his first race there before he crashed, and Barry himself responded to the first accusation: 'The Mountain [TT] circuit did not frighten me in any way. No circuit frightens me. I just couldn't see the sense of riding around in the pissing rain completely on your own against a clock. It wasn't racing to my mind.'

Don Morley, a professional photographer and journalist since 1955 and one of the most respected photographers in the business, has a different take on Sheene's aversion to the TT. Morley has probably taken more pictures of Sheene than anyone else and was always privy to the gossip and chatter in the paddocks of the racing world. 'Barry made a bit of a name for himself slagging off the TT, but it was more to do with money than the dangers of the place,' he said. 'A normal Grand Prix lasted three days whereas the TT was a two-week event and it cost the riders an awful lot of money to compete there. There was very little prize money and it was awkward for the GP riders to get to the Isle of Man from the Continent. They had to drive to a port, get a ferry to England, drive again and then get another ferry to the Isle of Man which was a lot more difficult than just driving from the Spanish GP to the French GP, for example. Then they had to pay for a hotel for two weeks instead of just three days as well as all the other expenses. It was good for the organizers, but not the riders. This was in the days before lots of long-haul Grands Prix, and it just didn't make financial sense.'

In 1972 Giacomo Agostini, who won 10 TTs and 15 World Championship titles, joined Barry's protest after his close friend Gilberto Parlotti was killed on his TT debut. Ago said he would never race there again, and he kept his word. He was joined by Phil Read, though five years later he changed his mind and did race there again. The event was finally struck from the Grand Prix calendar after 1976, much to Sheene's approval.

Sheene's name was dragged up in the press for more than a decade whenever there were calls for the TT to be banned outright, and to this day there is still a lot of resentment among TT fans towards him. But it's worth remembering that while Sheene hated riding at the TT ('Why bother when it's so much easier just to shoot yourself and get it all over with?'), it didn't stop him racing on other pure road cricuits, most notably Oliver's Mount in Scarborough, a treacherous, narrow and bumpy parkland circuit. And many Grand Prix circuits such as Spa-Francorchamps in Belgium and Imatra in Finland were armco-lined pure road circuits too.

Certainly Sheene's criticism of the TT circuit ran somewhat in contradiction to his view on these other dangerous circuits, a fact he attempted to explain in *Leader of the Pack*. In justifying his decision to continue racing at the Oliver's Mount track, he said, 'As with any other circuit, if there are sections which you can't tackle with confidence, it's up to you to ride through those sections at the pace best suited to you. You can make up for lost time in other stretches, where there is less likelihood of hurting yourself.' Surely that same theory could apply to the TT circuit as well as any other?

Mick Grant, himself a seven-times TT winner and a staunch supporter of the event, was one of Barry's fiercest rivals in the seventies. He testified to Sheene's abilities on road circuits despite his aversion to the TT. 'Although Barry knocked the TT, we never actually spoke about it together. My regret with Barry was that he didn't continue with the TT. Certainly the way he rode on pure road circuits like Scarborough and Imatra, there was no way that he couldn't have done the TT. I mean, bloomin' hell, Scarborough requires all the road racing skills you'd ever need, and he could do it. He certainly wasn't slow round there.'

Still, from 1971 the Isle of Man was out of his hair for good and Barry was free to concentrate on the next round of the World Championship, to which he travelled in a bit more style – in his newly purchased caravan. To the modern GP follower this will sound more like a club racer's accommodation, but in 1971 it was the last word in luxury. For some, this was the start of Sheene the poser. Upstart relative newcomers to the GP scene were expected to sleep on the floors of their oily vans rather than tow a caravan around like a wealthy American tourist, but to Sheene it just made practical sense. With a more comfortable bed and an area for cooking some decent food, he would be in better shape for the racing. And if it added to his glamour-boy image and helped to improve standards in the paddock, then so much the better. One thing Sheene certainly wasn't slow to notice was that having a caravan greatly increased his pulling power with the ladies, and for Barry that fact alone was worth the extra expenditure.

Motorcycle racing on the Continent was huge in the seventies despite the utter dearth of professionalism involved in its organization and the lack of money available to its star performers. More than 150,000 people turned up to watch Sheene being narrowly beaten by Angel Nieto at the Dutch TT in Assen, one of the best-attended rounds on the GP calendar. The next meeting in Belgium got off to a bad start when Sheene was fined for spilling fuel on the track. He had been returning from a night out and was driving down the circuit to get to the paddock when his van ran out of diesel. He managed to bleed the fuel system and top the van back up, but not before sloshing some diesel onto the course. A vigilant Belgian policeman witnessed the incident and Barry was fined the now comedic-sounding sum of £6.60. He also incurred the wrath of his fellow riders who had to negotiate the slippery section of the track. But if the weekend got off to a bad start, it ended in the best possible way with Sheene taking his first-ever Grand Prix victory in the 125cc race. It was made a little hollow by the fact that Nieto had retired on the third lap, but Barry didn't care; a first win is always a watershed, and he couldn't have been more delighted. As he recalled, 'Once I had crossed the finishing line, I could hardly contain myself. I wanted to get drunk, kiss as many girls as I could lay my hands on and just dance with joy. That was the proudest moment of my life up to then.'

A second in the 125 and a sixth place in the 250 race on his Yamaha in the East German Grand Prix were followed by a second GP win, this time in the 50cc class in Czechoslovakia. Kreidler had approached Sheene at the Belgian GP about riding one of their factory bikes to help out their full-time rider, Jan de Vries. For Sheene it was a chance to add to his start and prize money with minimum hassle as the factory team would take care of the bike. Race day didn't start too well: Barry overslept and was 'peacefully dreaming about two blondes' when he was rudely awakened by members of the Kreidler team hammering on his caravan door. Pulling on his leathers and wandering bleary-eyed to the starting grid, Sheene was in no mood to go racing. He'd much rather have been left with his imaginary girlfriends. 'When [I] set off,' he recalled, 'I think I gave a huge yawn; I was still half asleep. But I buzzed round as quick as I could in the wet with my head thumping and my teeth chattering with cold.' In fact he buzzed round quickly enough to win the race from Nieto, who was by now firmly established as his arch rival no matter what class he seemed to race in.

He was certainly the man Sheene needed to beat in the 125cc class if he was to become the youngest ever Grand Prix world champion, and when Nieto's bike expired during the Swedish round it began to look likely that Barry might just pull off a shock title win from the Spaniard. When Nieto also retired from the Finnish Grand Prix, Sheene held a 19-point lead with just two rounds to go and was being touted as the champion elect. Unfortunately for Sheene, a non-championship event in Hengello, Holland, then all but ruined his chances: he crashed, breaking his wrist and chipping an ankle. It was Barry's first bad accident, the first time he had broken a bone while racing, and it's easy to see now why top Grand Prix riders no longer take part in non-championship events, with the exception of the Suzuka 8-Hour race in Japan which remains massively important to the Japanese manufacturers who call all the shots.

Strapped up and in considerable discomfort, Sheene rode to a highly creditable third place in Italy behind Gilberto Parlotti and Angel Nieto and refused to blame his injuries for his failure to win, saying instead that his bike was simply not fast enough on the day. He remained in the hunt for the title, but it was to be yet another non-title event, the prestigious Mallory Park Race of the Year, that really did put an end to his hopes. It seems incredible that Sheene, having had a warning with his crash in Holland, would contest another race and risk further injury so near to the final round of the World Championship, but it was the norm for the time as well as being the only way riders could make enough money to survive a season. This time Sheene was thrown into a banking when his rear tyre lost traction. He was taken to Leicester Royal Infirmary for a check-up but, despite being in great pain, was discharged after being told he hadn't broken anything. It was an extremely poor diagnosis: Sheene had in fact broken five ribs and suffered compression fractures to three vertebrae.

Oblivious to the fact, he travelled to Spain to take on Nieto for the final showdown in the world title chase. After again racing the 50cc Kreidler, which broke down on the last lap, Barry stooped over a fountain in the paddock to have a drink of water. That's when he heard the disconcerting and agonizing 'ping' as one of his broken ribs popped out of place and threatened to burst through his skin. Never one to shirk from pain, Barry forced the rib back into place and taped up his torso to hold the offending bone in place long enough to last the race. Just making it to the Jarama start grid was the first of many superhuman efforts shown by Barry Sheene in his pursuit of racing glory. He and Nieto had a fantastic scrap all race long and were heading into the final stages when Barry hit some oil and slid off the Suzuki, his race and World Championship hopes over. After all his painful efforts, he had lost his grip on a title which had been so close because of a patch of oil that should have been cleaned up anyway. The only consolation for Sheene was that he didn't further aggravate his injuries in the crash.

It might have been a disappointing way to end what had been a great year, one that had delivered 38 race wins, but Sheene didn't dwell on it for long. Having so nearly taken a world crown at his first attempt, he was confident he could definitely lift one the following year. For the 1972 season, he signed for Yamaha to ride its 250cc and 350cc machines in what was his first season with a factory team. At last he was being paid to go racing. The year started off well, and Sheene picked up his first-ever 500cc class win at the King of Brands meeting over Easter. But that only fuelled his confidence and added to the complacency with which he faced the Grands Prix. Things went wrong from the very first round when both Yamahas suffered mechanical breakdowns. The bikes were both slow and unreliable, and Barry didn't help matters when he badly broke a collarbone during the Italian Grand Prix. The only highlights of the GP season were a third place in Spain and a fourth place in Austria, both in the 250cc class, and that was hardly a step up from the year before when he'd won four Grand Prix races. Sheene was acutely aware of the fact, too.

such a disastrous season led to bad feelings between Sheene and his Yamaha team and he was desperate to leave by the end of the year to prove that it had been the bikes and not his riding at fault. These bad feelings would come back to haunt Barry years later when he once again rode a Yamaha. Those same lowly mechanics from the 1972 season had risen up the ranks to become senior personnel by 1980, and whenever he asked for a favour Sheene discovered that they had long memories. Had he kept his views on the 250 Yamaha to himself, or at least confined his criticism of the bike to behind closed doors, there would have been no problem. As it was, he made no secret of what he thought of the bike, and there is no surer way to offend the Japanese corporate psyche. Still, Sheene was prepared to shoulder some of the blame for his worst year to date: 'That poor year in 1972 taught me a salutary lesson about the dangers of becoming big-headed. Over-confidence was the root of my problems.'

With Sheene's reputation having taken a bit of a battering, he was really out to prove himself in 1973. He had a new contract with Suzuki and a new championship challenge beckoned: the FIM Formula 750 European Championship, in many ways the predecessor of the current World Superbike Championship. The Formula 750 Championship was, to all intents and purposes, a world championship even though it didn't enjoy the prestige of being conferred with official world-class status. The calendar of dates was just as gruelling as the Grands Prix, and the calibre of riders almost as impressive.

The new breed of 750cc superbike racing had taken off

in America in the early seventies and reports had reached Sheene that Suzuki's new three-cylinder 750 had been clocked at 183mph in testing – allegedly the fastest speed ever attained by a race bike at that time. Sheene couldn't wait to get his hands on one. Despite the fact that he had cut his teeth in 125 and 50cc racing, he now referred to the smaller-capacity bikes as being very 'Mickey Mouse' and was determined to prove he could win in the world's largest-capacity racing class on what he considered 'real men's bikes'. Sheene duly got a Suzuki triple from the US where his brother-in-law, Paul Smart, would be racing one. Smart had been an arch rival of Sheene's over the past few years but the pair had continued to have a friendly relationship. Barry had been as pleased as anyone when Paul tied the knot with his sister Maggie at the end of 1971, a marriage that still stands today and which produced current racer Scott Smart, Sheene's nephew.

When Barry eventually took delivery of his new Suzuki it was immediately apparent to him that it was not the exotic piece of machinery he had been expecting. Much midnight oil was burned as he slotted the engine into a Seeley chassis and rebuilt the bike to a more competitive spec. In the end, his hard work paid off. Despite winning only one round of the eight-round championship, Sheene's two second places, a third and a fourth meant he accumulated enough points to win the title ahead of Australian Jack Findlay, John Dodds and his own team-mate Stan Woods. Of the remaining rounds, he had two non-finishes and was disqualified from the British round at Silverstone for switching bikes between the two race legs. It was Sheene's most prestigious championship win to date, and he proved that he really had mastered larger-capacity machines by adding the *Motor Cycle News* Superbike title, Shellsport 500 title and King of Brands crown to his collection.

Sheene was now really starting to make a name for himself, not only as a racer but as a great PR man and a bit of a grafter, as John Cooper explained: 'Barry was always a very determined chap. He worked on his bikes a lot and they were always nicely prepared and presented. He used to try hard and he was very professional. Preparation is the thing with bikes, and he was always keen, fiddling about, changing the sprockets, altering the forks and the springs – not like today when riders just come in the paddock and dump their bikes on their mechanics. He wasn't shy of grafting. Years later I used to go down to his house when he lived at Charlwood and all his spanners were laid out neatly in his workshop and his helicopter sat there all nice and clean. He was very organized.' Cooper, like Chas Mortimer, had known Sheene long before he started racing and was happy to help Frank's boy in any way he could. 'We used to help each other out, lending each other bikes and stuff; you know, we were just friends really. But he didn't need much steering because he always had the makings of being the right man for the job, and that was apparent even in the early days.'

After such a disappointing year in 1972, Sheene was most definitely back. Readers of *MCN* recognized his achievements by voting him their Man of the Year for the first of five times in his career – a record that stood for almost two decades until Carl Fogarty accepted the award for a sixth time in 1999. Moreover, Sheene's F750 victory was enough to convince Suzuki that he deserved a ride on their all-new RG500. The four-cylinder, 500cc Grand Prix weapon was to become a racing legend in its own right, winning four world titles between 1976 and 1982, but in those early days it was an absolute beast to ride, all power and no handling. When Sheene first tested the bike in Japan at the end of 1973, he found, like everyone else who had ridden it, that the bike had a nasty habit of weaving viciously at speed and pulling wheelies under power, but it was still the fastest bike he'd ever ridden and he proved it by knocking one and a half seconds off the Ryuyo track record in tests.

The plan for 1974 was not only to defend his Formula 750 title but, more importantly, to contest every round of the ultimate motorcycle series – the 500cc Grand Prix World Championship. It would be Sheene's first ever year in the premier class and he knew the RG500 was up to winning races once the handling was sorted out. But that was easier said than done, and 1974 was to prove a tough baptism for Sheene. The gremlins in the RG's handling were never truly rooted out that season, and the bike was further plagued by mechanical faults, as most new machines are. Gearboxes and drive shafts were particularly prone to breaking, and Barry had his fair share of crashes, which only added to his problems.

The first outing for the bike was in March at the Daytona 200 race in Florida. It was Barry's first time there as well as the Suzuki's, and that meeting inadvertently led to Sheene adopting the now famous number seven. As he told me during an interview for *Two Wheels Only* magazine, 'Seven was always my favourite number even as a kid. I'd want seven this or seven that. Then, when I went to Daytona in 1974, I asked what numbers were available. The Americans usually give new riders really high numbers, but Mert Lawill had retired so seven was available. I was well chuffed.' The lucky number seven wasn't the only thing Sheene took away from the States. He also latched on to the American habit of displaying the number for all to see while brightening up his racing attire, too. 'The Americans made you wear your number on your helmet and leathers too, which was even better, and I kept the look when I got back to Europe afterwards.'

It was just as well that Barry brought *something* away from Daytona because ignition trouble ruined his chances of getting a result in the race. After that, a fine second place in the first Grand Prix of the year proved to be a false indicator of what to expect. Along with most of the other riders, Sheene sat out the German race in protest at the lack of straw bales surrounding the course, then finished third in Austria after suffering the humiliation of being lapped by Giacomo Agostini and Gianfranco Bonera.Four consecutive non-finishes followed for the fast but fickle Suzuki, and a fourth place in the final Czech round was little consolation for a bitterly disappointing 500cc GP debut season in which Sheene had managed to finish only sixth overall. The defence of his Formula 750 title had been a bit of a wash-out too; Barry hadn't really had time to concentrate on that series as well as the Grands Prix and had had to give second best to the new, super-fast Yamahas.

There were brighter moments, though, like scoring the RG500's debut win at the British Grand Prix, even though it was a non-championship event and as such shouldn't really have been called a Grand Prix at all. Barry also won the Mallory Park Race of the Year as well as the *Motor Cycle News* Superbike Championship and the Shell Oils 500 title, salvaging some home pride after a difficult year.

Suzuki were extremely disheartened, though, and ready to throw in the towel with the RG500 project until Sheene insisted on spending five gruelling weeks in Japan working on the bike to turn it into a winner. By the time he was through, Sheene was convinced he could challenge for the 1975 World Championship. But first there was the Daytona 200 to think about, and this time it would make him an international superstar – for all the wrong reasons.

CHAPTER 3

PLAYBOY

'Two women sharing my bed was old hat as far as I was concerned.'

It's fair to say that there is no long-standing tradition of motorcycle racers being pin-ups, heart-throbs, playboys or style gurus, but Barry Sheene was all of these things and a whole lot more, besides being a phenomenally successful racer. Ever since his first sexual dalliance over a pool table in the crypt of a London church, Barry never left anyone in any doubt about his sexual orientations. Certainly wealth, fame and the perceived glamour of his chosen profession helped considerably in his conquests of the opposite sex, but his boyish good looks and easy charm were already in place long before any material success.

Sheene was born with a natural blond streak in his otherwise brown hair which, he claimed, was a result of his mother having received a nasty shock during pregnancy when a child walked out in front of her car. According to Sheene, who presumably got the story from his mother, the incident was enough to leave a birthmark on his head which in turn caused the blond streak to grow from it; he related this story many times to prove he was not dyeing it and hence 'not turning into a pouffo'. It seems Sheene was destined to stand out from the crowd even before he was born. Blond streak aside, the long, flowing locks were all his own doing, together with overgrown sideburns a fashion 'must' in the seventies. 'Having your hair cut in the seventies,' he observed, 'was like having your legs amputated. It just wasn't on.'

Sheene was not built like an athlete, but his frame seemed to serve him well enough when it came to the fairer sex, and what he lacked in the Adonis physique stakes he more than made up for with his ready wit and devil-may-care attitude. In 1973, his looks were deemed worthy of an appearance in *Vogue* magazine, an accolade of which no bike racer before or since can boast. The man behind the lens was none other than David Bailey, one of England's most celebrated photographers, more used to working with Mick Jagger, the Beatles, Salvador Dali and Jack Nicholson than with motorcycle racers. The *Vogue* job wasn't Sheene's only modelling stint, either; his other assignments included posing in a pair of underpants along-side a semi-naked woman in the *Sun* – again, not the most traditional extra-curricular activity for a bike racer, a point that was not lost on Sheene. 'I reckon I finally destroyed the popular concept of a biker when I was pictured in the *Sun*. This wasn't quite what traditional bike enthusiasts had come to expect, but I'm sure it helped to undermine the myth that all those who rode motorcycles are dumb, dirty and definitely undesirable.' Sheene even went on to have his own weekly column in the *Sun* in the seventies, which gave him a much coveted mouthpiece in the country's biggest-selling newspaper.

Image was always important for Sheene, and his greatest role model was Bill Ivy, whom he had known and admired since childhood, as he admitted in an interview for Duke Video in 1993. 'I suppose one of the biggest influences when I'd just started racing was Bill Ivy because [he] used to race for my dad and was a good mate of mine and I loved his lifestyle. I mean, he was always surrounded by crumpet, all young ladies. I suppose I sort of modelled myself on Bill in that he always used to dress the way he pleased and his lifestyle was a lot of fun, and the woman side of it was the bit I envied the most.' Sheene's former rival Mick Grant witnessed Barry's dealings with the media first-hand and reckoned he played up this playboy image. 'He was just very good with the media. He was probably better with the media than he was at riding, and he was okay at riding.'

Anything Barry did to improve his own personal standing and image usually seemed to have a positive effect on motorcycle racing in general. He might have had to get rid of the saucy patches he wore on his leathers ('Happiness is a tight pussy'; 'I'll make you an offer you can't refuse') once he became famous, but he was still capable of attracting attention to himself as a rider. White leathers when most others wore black, the colourful Donald Duck motif on the helmet, the gimmick of making a victory V sign whenever he won a race (which signified victory to the spectators while appearing as something very different to the riders behind him), a caravan to take girls back to rather than an oil-stained van – all these things helped Barry's personal pulling power as well as the overall image of the sport.

The caravan was introduced during the 1971 season, and while Sheene himself claimed to have bought it on hire purchase, his brother-in-law Paul Smart said that Barry 'blew half his money on it'. However it was paid for, it was money well spent, as Smart explained: 'The only thing he was world champion at was sex. In every country, there used to be a hell of a competition for the girls in the paddock. Barry won, of course. The thing is, he'd never give up. He could have three blow-outs but he'd just keep going until he scored. The caravan body eventually fell off the chassis.' Years later, Sheene admitted this to me, and the caravan falling apart led to another problem, as he explained. 'As I was welding [the chassis] I lost the St Christopher my mum and dad had given me for luck. At the very next race [the 1972 Imola GP], my bike seized, threw me up the road and punctured my stomach, so my mum and dad bought me another St Christopher.'

The more polished Barry's image became, the more 'crumpet' he could pull. Sheene's first serious girlfriend was Lesley Shepherd, whom he met in 1967 when he was just 17. They dated for the next seven years but split in 1974 after a relationship which, by Barry's own admission, was not quite monogamous. He openly confessed to seeing other girls during his foreign travels of the period, some of whom he'd met on the dancefloor. Like most youngsters who lived through the seventies, Barry Sheene loved his disco dancing. It wasn't so much for the physical benefits that could be gained from all that strutting under a sparkling glitter ball as the fact that it was an easy way to meet girls – and when it came to that Sheene never missed a trick. When he was recuperating from injuries sustained at Mallory Park and aggravated later at Cadwell Park in 1975, the biggest frustration for Sheene wasn't his inability to ride a bike, it was not being able to dance: '[My] inability to get on that dancefloor made me even more determined to get back to peak fitness as quickly as was humanly possible.'

As usual, Sheene only wanted the best and most exclusive when it came to nightclubs, and his annual membership of Tramp near Trafalgar Square was, as far as he was concerned, £30 well spent. There he could mix with fellow celebrities and, naturally, a bevy of gorgeous models. Barry was never shy about boasting of his female conquests, once professing to be every bit George Best's equal when it came to hitting it off with top models – and in the seventies when he was at his peak, keeping up with Best was no mean feat. The evidence would certainly seem to support Barry's claim when one considers that it wasn't unusual for him to have three women on the go at any one time; he often had to juggle them around to avoid potentially embarrassing double-bookings on the same night. 'As far as women went,' he said, 'I was the man for all seasons. A different girl each night was my regular pattern. There were even weeks when I would be saying goodbye to one young lady, immediately chatting another up on the phone and eyeing the clock to see how soon the third would be

arriving.' Of course, sometimes the double-bookings were
intentional. 'I had tried everything that I had read about
and a whole lot more besides. Two women sharing my bed
was old hat as far as I was concerned.' Even when he was
fit enough to be at a race track rather than recuperating
from injury, Sheene, unlike many other top sportsmen,
refused to observe the energy-saving, no-sex rule on the
evening or morning before an event. If Barry felt like 'getting his leg over', an inconvenience like a motorcycle race
wasn't going to stop him.

During his recovery period in 1975, Sheene found that
he had a lot of spare time on his hands, and the most natural way he could think of to fill it was to chase girls. The
fact that at the time he was sharing the London home of
his great friend and aristocratic socialite Piers Weld
Forrester, who was probably most famous for his association with Princess Anne before her marriage to Captain
Mark Phillips, made for rich pickings on the female front.
Forrester and Sheene received countless invitations to high-
society parties and Sheene confessed that the women he
met were major contributors to his recuperation process.
'My favourite part of the rehabilitation process was trying
to bed as many women as possible,' he said. Chas
Mortimer, himself the product of a public-school education, admired the way Sheene was able to break down
social barriers and become accepted by the aristocracy.
'There were quite a few people from the aristocracy in
those days who used to be associated with racing. Barry
would always be up at the Piers Forrester parties in
London and he was a great one for hob-nobbing with the

landed gentry, and you know what the landed gentry are like when they meet a cockney who appeals to them. All of a sudden, like Michael Caine in the film world, you become socially acceptable, whereas in other spheres of life cockney-ism might not be acceptable for them. Motorcycling tended to be a working-man's sport and car racing tended to be the landed gentry's kind of sport. Barry was able to transcend the social barriers, which are very strong in the UK, stronger than anywhere else in the world probably.'

Forrester's death during a minor bike race at Brands Hatch in 1977 devastated Barry; it was yet another reminder of how dangerous motorcycle racing was in the seventies. According to Mortimer, the dangers of the sport even affected how close some riders got to one another. 'Barry and I have always got on quite well together, but we were never the best of buddies. We were from the same generation and it was difficult in those days because a lot of people were getting killed and you didn't want to make too much of a mate of someone in case they got wiped out.'

During the same recovery period, Barry also treated himself to the ultimate status symbol: a Rolls Royce Silver Shadow complete with personalized registration plate, 4 BSR. Racing rival Phil Read already had one, which might have been reason enough for Sheene to follow suit, but he always claimed he was swayed by Rolls Royce's reputation for reliability than by the status-symbol trip. The only probable reason Barry didn't buy a Roller any earlier than he did was because he'd lost his driving licence for 18 months for drink driving. By his own admission he'd had 'a few rounds of drinks' in King's Lynn, Norfolk, with a friend before being involved in an accident while driving home. Barry claimed he got slivers of glass in his eyes from the collision and went straight home to rinse them out, only to find a police car awaiting him. Barry later appeared at King's Lynn Crown Court protesting that he had fully intended to call the police to report the incident as soon as he had washed the glass out of his eyes, but his licence was suspended for a year with another six months added on as part of the points totting-up system (he already had various other minor offences on his licence). Sheene was also required to take another driving test in order to regain his licence, which he eventually did, but for one and a half years he needed to be driven everywhere he went, except on the Continent, where he drove himself.

The King's Lynn incident wasn't the only occasion when Barry found himself with a spot of car trouble. He very nearly drowned after some hire-car antics in Italy in 1974 went overboard – quite literally. Sheene was fooling around in the Fiat with fellow racers Kenny Roberts and Gene Romero, experimenting with a somewhat unorthodox driving method: Roberts took the wheel, Romero operated the foot pedals and Sheene applied liberal and erratic doses of handbrake at his leisure. The result was predictable, even if the location was a little unusual: the trio ended up in a canal, the Fiat turned upside down and sinking fast. Romero got out relatively easily but Barry was temporarily snagged up in the very handbrake he had so recently been abusing. He, too, eventually got out, but he still had to rescue Roberts who was calling for help, trapped in the quickly submerging vehicle.

On another occasion, again in Imola, Sheene parked his hire car in the town square unaware that the market was due to take place the following morning. When he returned to the car he found stalls all around it, one in particular utilizing the bonnet. Oblivious to the jeers of the traders who were convinced that Sheene was going nowhere until the market was over, Barry simply climbed into the car, floored the accelerator and smashed through the stalls. Dumbfounded pedestrians could well have been forgiven for thinking a James Bond movie was being filmed in their home town. After all, the two did have a certain number in common.

Sheene's laddish behaviour might have continued unchecked, but his womanizing days came to an abrupt end in late 1975 when he met Stephanie McLean, a 22-year-old glamour model, former *Playboy* bunny girl and star of the classic Old Spice surfing advert. Stephanie was at the time married to top glamour photographer Clive McLean, with whom she had a five-year-old son, Roman. Such was Sheene's standing as a national celebrity in early 1976 that a picture of him stepping out on town with Stephanie made the front page of the *Sun* – a somewhat dubious honour reserved for 'class A' celebrities and a sure sign that Barry was now a household name, in Britain at least.

Barry first met Stephanie at Tramp while he was still on crutches. She had seen the Thames Television documentary surrounding his Daytona crash and asked to borrow his leathers for an October modelling assignment which

Sheene himself attended. He was instantly smitten with Stephanie and appeared to give up his womanizing almost overnight, even if such a drastic change of lifestyle threatened his image. 'I couldn't give a monkeys about the bachelor playboy image being ruined,' he said. 'The image was only there because that's what I was like.' Sheene later admitted that settling down to a one-woman relationship wasn't as difficult as he thought, although his very words seemed tinted with an air of nostalgia for good times past. 'With a massive list of conquests behind me, I knew I had completed all the running around I had ever wanted,' he said. 'Since settling down to a steady relationship with Steph, I have never once yearned for those wild times: the days of the paddock groupies; the passionate notes waiting for me when I returned to hotels after a race; the women who simply wanted to experience sex with a celebrity. All that is behind me now.'

Meeting Steph might have marked the end of Sheene's direct involvement with other women, but it certainly didn't stop other girls swooning over him, or even rowing over him. At Cadwell Park in 1976, two girls had a stand-up fight outside Barry's caravan as they fought to get near him for his autograph, and on another occasion a girl approached Barry wielding a pair of scissors in a desperate attempt to snatch a lock of his hair. It was the kind of behaviour previously reserved for rock stars, and it prompted the media to refer to Sheene as a rock star on a bike.

Barry certainly lived up to the tag in 1979 while staying in a five-star hotel before that year's French Grand Prix. Trying to get a good night's sleep before the race, Barry became increasingly annoyed with the band playing at full volume downstairs. When a phone call to the manager had no effect, in protest Barry emptied the contents of his mini-bar over the balcony near where the band was playing, but again to no avail. When another call to the manager failed to subdue the noise, Sheene performed the classic rock star attention-grabber: the 26-inch colour television was lobbed out of the window and it shattered into a million pieces, loudly enough to be heard over and above the offending band. They stopped playing straight away and Barry got his peaceful night's sleep. In fact, he got more than that. Upon returning to the hotel after the race, he found that a new television had been placed in the room along with an ice bucket and two bottles of champagne by way of apology on the management's behalf for permitting so much noise at the dance.

Despite his attachment to Stephanie, Barry's eye for the ladies did not go unnoticed by the organizers of the 1977 Miss World competition. In an era when the contest was a worldwide must-see television event, Barry was asked to cast his expert eye over the contestants. After Mary Stavin (who would later date the aforementioned George Best) won the event, the press asked Barry to dance with her while they took some pictures. Stephanie at that point promptly left the building, leading observers to believe she was in a jealous rage and had stormed out on Barry. According to Sheene, however, Steph was just tired of all the media attention and had decided to leave for a bit of peace and quiet. The press didn't buy it, but either way it meant more mainstream publicity for Barry as most major newspapers ran a story on the incident the following day.

As infatuated as Sheene was with Steph, and as much as he claimed to have 'retired' from his sexually rapacious lifestyle, he still found it impossible to let go of his bachelor status when push came to shove in 1976. Speaking to Thames Video in 1990 for *The Barry Sheene Story*, he explained, 'We were due to get married in 1976 and everything was planned. We were living in Putney, and three days before we were due to get married I was lying in bed that night and I thought, "I can't get married. I'm scared to death of getting married, I really can't." I said to Steph, "Look, I can't get married. I can't do it. I love you, I adore you, you're the best thing since sliced bread, but I don't want to get married." Obviously for Steph it was quite upsetting, you know, because she thought, "Oh, Christ, what's going to happen now? I've split up with my husband, got a divorce, and now he doesn't want to marry me." You know, why wouldn't I want to marry her? Obviously [it looked like I] didn't want to be with her but that wasn't the truth, I was just scared to death of getting married. So it was a bit of an uneasy period for the next couple of months.'

Sheene did remarkably well to keep this story from the press at the time; it would have been the celebrity marriage of the year had he been able to go through with it. But he still had Steph to deal with in what must have been an uncomfortable situation. 'Steph took it really fantastically well,' Sheene continued, 'there's no two ways about that, and so after a few years it was all forgotten and we agreed to get married when we wanted children. At the end of

1983 we were talking, and I always intended to give up racing at the end of 1985, so I said, "What we should do is, we could get married now, start to try and have children, that'd be really nice." So we organized to get married on 16 February 1984 and then we started [trying to have children]. Steph had gone off the pill sort of three months beforehand, and we thought, "Right, we'll start trying for kids now," and the very first time we did it without protection she fell pregnant and Sidonie was born nine months and three days after we got married.'

After Sheene fell for Stephanie, a new passion for flying helicopters filled the women-chasing void. He might not have been any good at school, but Barry displayed his potential for learning by sitting and passing his helicopter pilot's licence with ease and in record time – just three weeks. The instructors at the flying school said it couldn't be done in that timeframe, but Sheene insisted it had to be because that was all the time his hectic schedule would allow. Barry passed his final exam on the very last day of his three-week course in the winter of 1980–81.

Today, many motorcycle racers – Mick Doohan, Steve Hislop and Jim Moodie, to name just a few – fly helicopters, but back in 1981 Sheene was, as usual, the first. For anyone used to handling a motorcycle at 180mph, learning the physical aspects of flying helicopters appears to be relatively easy, but what was outstanding about Sheene getting his licence was that he managed to apply himself to studying for and passing all the written examinations. Just as he had demonstrated with languages, Sheene proved once again that it wasn't a lack of aptitude for learning that had kept him back at school, it was simply because he didn't want to be there. Eleven times TT winner and twice British Superbike champion Steve Hislop cast some light on the scale of Sheene's achievement. 'You have to be very committed with your studying if you want to fly a helicopter as you have to sit exams in air law, navigation, meteorology and all sorts of technical stuff like flight performance, planning and human performance. And you also have to type-rate for different kinds of helicopters [like passing another driving test every time you change car]. I know that Barry has flown Enstroms, Jet Rangers, Agustas and Hughes 500s, so he would have needed to type-rate for each one.'

Sheene had previously owned a Piper Aztec aeroplane, a light, twin-engined six-seater which he often hired out for charter work to earn some extra cash, but he sold it in 1982. Having found light aeroplanes unpractical for flying to race tracks where there is not always enough room to land, Sheene bought himself an Enstrom 280 Turbo three-seater helicopter capable of almost 120mph. He single-handedly set the trend for turning up at bike meetings from the air, thus avoiding the queues, cutting down on travel time and further enhancing his image while he was at it. There was another practical side to buying a helicopter, as Sheene explained to Thames Video. 'I spent money on cars, which was a total waste of bloody time. At one time I had a bloody Rolls Royce, a 500 Mercedes, a 928 Porsche. I walked outside one day and thought, "What on earth do I want this for?" So by the next day I'd got rid of two of them and I bought a helicopter. The helicopter was something that enabled me to do five or six things in a day, and it was productive because in a week I'd be doing 30 things that I got paid for so it was something that earned itself a living.'

For Barry Sheene, flying helicopters was at least the equal of sex and racing bikes when it came to the ultimate in pleasure. He once admitted that he was much prouder of being able to fly a helicopter than he was of being able to win bike races, and when asked what he missed most while in hospital in 1982 recovering from his huge Silverstone crash, he didn't hesitate with his reply: sex and his helicopter. But after being incapacitated for three and a half weeks following that crash, Sheene was horrified to read on his helicopter pilot's licence that he would need a medical to be passed fit to fly again. Accordingly, he went straight off to see a civil aviation doctor at Gatwick airport just a few miles from his Charlwood mansion – while still in his wheelchair. Only Sheene could have had the audacity to expect the doctor to pass him off in such a condition as fit enough to fly again. Barry did, however, wring a guarantee from the doctor that he could pass his medical if he proved he could function well on crutches. Sheene procured a set and headed straight back to Gatwick where he employed an enviable stroke of cunning to fool the doctor into thinking he was fitter than he actually was. Still unable to stand and sit unaided, Sheene instructed his father to help him in and out of the doctor's chair while Barry shouted at Frank for interfering and fussing. The ploy worked perfectly, and his licence was reinstated.

When he moved to Australia in 1987, Sheene refrained

from buying a helicopter, claiming it would be a waste of money. He told *Bike* magazine, 'I have no real need for one out here and I've never been a waster of money. I never have something unless I need it and can use it.' Only in August 2002, after being diagnosed with cancer, did Sheene finally indulge himself and buy a helicopter beyond his needs: a 1995-vintage 180mph, twin-engined Agusta 109C eight-seater with only 600 hours on the clock. It cost him $3 million. Sheene had type-rated for the Agusta in England in early summer 2001 so he was already qualified to fly it when he bought it. He had originally intended to buy an Agusta in Europe and fly it to Australia but had been forced into a rethink in the aftermath of the terrorist attacks on New York in September 2001, when security regarding flightpaths was stepped up. As a helicopter fanatic, the purchase of the air-conditioned, autopilot- and radar-equipped Agusta represented the fulfilment of a lifetime's ambition for Sheene, yet he was still at pains to point out the practicalities of owning such a luxury: 'I've got my own property development business and it's a way for me to go around and look at potential sites and ferry clients about.'

But for all his sophistication in other walks of life, Sheene was always a grassroots man when it came to dress sense. He went out of his way to avoid wearing suits, shirts and ties in preference of his beloved blue jeans and T-shirt. Barry became so synonymous with jeans that he was even paid to wear them by French firm Mashe, whose name he often splashed across the chin bar of his helmet. But he was wearing jeans 'every day of the year' long before that, as most kids in the seventies did. By Sheene's own admission his dress sense 'isn't particularly sharp', but by wearing jeans he was actually portraying an image that endeared him to the younger generation, as well as making the statement that he was just like everyone else, not a pompous, stuck-up businessman in a suit. Extremely rich he might have been, but Barry Sheene was still a guy who dressed like the man on the street and risked his life racing motorbikes for a living. He was no spoiled, pampered prima donna and didn't want to be seen as one. He hated any restaurant or club that insisted on a suit or tie and more than once walked out of such establishments in disgust. He said of such proprietors, 'It doesn't matter to them if [my] jeans and jumper have just been cleaned and pressed and are as fresh as a daisy. A guy will happily be welcomed wearing a dirty old suit that hasn't been to the cleaners for six months and a smelly, filthy shirt. To me, those double standards are total bullshit, sheer hypocrisy.'

And woe betide any party who objected to the Sheene jeans; they were likely to suffer swift retribution for their indignation. In 1971, Barry was booked to stay at a hotel in South Africa which happened to have a jacket, shirt and tie policy for diners. After a row with the management during which Sheene failed to gain any concession, he emptied a can of oil into the hotel's swimming pool before setting out to seek more accommodating quarters. On another occasion ten years later when Sheene was infinitely more famous, he was refused entry to another dining room in a South African hotel. This time there was no need for drastic measures, only for Sheene to exercise the considerable clout fame had bestowed upon him. The hotel's rules were relaxed during GP week to meet Sheene's requirements.

Sheene's casual dress standards were bettered only by one of his best mates, racing driver James Hunt. In Gerald Donaldson's biography of the late Formula One star, Sheene explained, 'I got on really well with James because we had the same daft kind of mentality then, before I was married. We were both sportsmen and we drank and smoke and chased women, went to places you shouldn't go and did things you shouldn't do. We had a lot of laughs. It was hilarious in Tokyo [when Hunt was racing at the 1976 Japanese Grand Prix where he secured the World Championship and Sheene was staying in the same hotel on a business trip] when James would make the Japanese embarrassed at all his press conferences by showing up in his jeans and T-shirt. I hated wearing formal clothes too, but I loved going somewhere with James because he always made me look well dressed!'

One of the few occasions when Barry Sheene did agree to wear a suit and tie was when he visited Buckingham Palace in 1978 to accept his MBE from the Queen in what Iris Sheene recalled as her proudest moment. Never one to be overawed by any given situation, Sheene was as comfortable in royal company as he was in any other. He even managed to raise a giggle from the Queen when she told him to be careful on his race bike; Sheene famously retorted that it was a lot safer racing a bike than it was riding one of her horses.

In that same year, member of the British Empire Barry Sheene moved into the Manor House in Charlwood on the

Surrey and Essex border, just four miles from Gatwick. It wasn't his first flirtation with country mansions. Back in 1972, he had moved out of his single-bedroom, self-contained flat in Holborn and into Ashwood Hall in Walton Highway near Wisbech, Cambridgeshire, which he had spotted while pheasant shooting in the Fens. It was a big, six-bedroom building standing in four acres of land; it had been empty for eight years and it needed a lot of renovation but it was large enough for Barry and his mum and dad to live in and offered some privacy and space for the family away from the throngs of fans and the press. Sheene was reluctant to cut all ties with his native London so he also purchased a four-bedroom terraced house in Putney. In April 1978, a year after buying the Putney house, Sheene sold both properties and bought Charlwood, whose 34 rooms cost him in excess of £100,000. Charlwood offered Sheene everything he required, from workshop space for his bikes to a completely self-contained annexe for his parents to live in. There was ample room to land his helicopter, too, and fields aplenty to graze the local farmers' animals and keep the grass short. Sheene bought the manor outright having been horrified at the interest rates charged on a mortgage. In 1983, he estimated the house to be worth £400,000, a figure that would be well into the millions in today's money.

Financially, Sheene was always a very shrewd mover. Like any good businessman, he consistently refused to talk specifics about earnings – for one thing, it would have started a war among his underpaid team-mates during his racing days – but he certainly didn't argue with the commonly held assumption that he was a millionaire by the time he won his first world title in 1976. And in the pre-Lotto era of 1976, being a millionaire really meant something – especially if you were a long-haired cockney biker. There were others before him, like Mike Hailwood, who were born to serious money, but Barry was the sport's first self-made millionaire. Every year after 1974 he managed to increase his income right up until his peak in 1981, at which time Sheene himself reckoned he was the highest-paid sportsman in Britain. Ironically, Barry was to make much more money from his business interests when he left the sport, but in an age when Grand Prix racing actually *cost* the rider money (Sheene estimated that he lost up to £600 on most GPs), it is testament to his financial acumen that he earned as much as he did, mostly from appearance money. This was partly due to sound advice from the various agents and consultants Sheene was connected with, who advised him to compete as a limited company – Barry Sheene Racing Limited – making him the first racer in history to 'trade' under his own name.

One of Sheene's greatest achievements was gaining mass recognition outside his chosen sport, especially as it was a sport that had been almost completely ignored by the general public until he came along. Television appearances, advertising campaigns, radio slots and tabloid column inches contributed to making Barry the best-known bike racer in history.

To this day, the BBC's *Parkinson* is regarded as the most prestigious of the talk shows, the one slot all the world's top actors, singers and celebrities are keen to do; Sheene remains the only bike racer ever to have appeared on the

---

show, which he did in November 1978 alongside veteran actor Sir Ralph Richardson. Soon afterwards, on 25 January 1979, Barry received further public acclaim when he was chosen as the subject of the hugely popular TV show *This Is Your Life*, which was then being hosted by Eamonn Andrews. Sheene, who had always thought the subjects of the show knew about it in advance, was genuinely surprised when Andrews, the famous big red book in hand, walked into an interview Sheene was doing at a bike show in London. The show was watched by a massive TV audience of 19.35 million. It might have run out of steam in recent years, but in the seventies *This Is Your Life* was generally the domain of major household names. It was indisputably another unique coup for a motorcycle racer. Sheene also appeared on Russell Harty's chat show, telling the host that he was 'no madder than him' when Harty questioned his sanity when it came to racing motorcycles, and he was voted sportsman of the year by viewers of Noel Edmonds' *Multi Coloured Swap Shop* on 26 March 1978. Other winners in various categories included pop superstars Abba, *Starsky and Hutch* star David Soul and comedian Ronnie Barker of *The Two Ronnies* fame. Sheene's proud mother Iris collected the award from presenter Frank Bough on Barry's behalf. Confirming his popularity with the younger generation, Barry also appeared on Jimmy Savile's *Jim'll Fix It* when 13-year-old bike-racing fan Craig Bramley wrote to the programme and asked to spend the day with his hero.

Even radio stations were clamouring to land Sheene, and he agreed to star on one of the biggest when he guested on the prime-time show *Desert Island Discs*. Sheene's must-have records (for the record) were 'Crackerbox Palace' by his friend George Harrison, 'In the Mood' by Glenn Miller, 'If You Leave Me Now' by Chicago, 'San José' by Dionne Warwick, 'New Kid in Town' by the Eagles, 'Don't Let the Sun Catch You Crying' by José Feliciano, 'Sunshine after the Rain' by Elkie Brooks and 'Nights on Broadway' by Candi Staton.

Barry's TV career continued after 1987, when he made the move to Australia. He became a household name on the other side of the world after starring in Shell Helix adverts with Australia's most famous car racer, Dick Johnson. He also signed a deal with Aussie TV station Channel 9 before moving on to Network 10 in 1996 to commentate on motorsports. And Sheene still featured on British television years after he retired from racing, even if it was more likely to be on nostalgic programmes such as the BBC's *I Love 1975*. Barry's infamous Daytona crash was among the topics up for recollection, along with the movie *Jaws*, the television show *The Sweeney* and pop stars including David Essex and the Bay City Rollers. To be remembered amid such mainstream popular culture is proof of Sheene's bona fide celebrity.

It was the public persona that did it, and Chip Hennen, brother and one-time manager of Sheene's former rival and team-mate Pat Hennen, believed it was not entirely of Sheene's making. 'If you talked to Barry away from the race track he was a fairly ordinary guy. He was really easy to talk to and you didn't hear all the witticisms that you would in his interviews. He was truly a very nice guy, but he seemed like a very different guy from when the camera was turned on. We found out that Andrew Marriot [who edited Barry's book *The Sheene Machine*] and Barry Gill, Barry's PR men who also looked after James Hunt, created Sheene's public persona. I think they prepared answers for him for the 100 questions he was most likely to be asked. I started listening to Barry in interviews and noticed that he *did* keep getting asked the same questions and he *did* always give the same answers. Midway through the 1977 season I approached Marriot and Gill and asked if they would take on Pat as well. They agreed, but then they told Barry about it and he said, "Absolutely not, no way. If you take Pat on you're fired." That was the end of the story, but we knew that if people like that were willing to take Pat on then so would others. Those guys created the Barry Sheene persona and they promoted it; they did an absolutely fabulous job and Barry was the perfect person for that. He followed their instructions explicitly.'

Naturally, Sheene the celebrity had his share of big-name friends, most notably the late George Harrison who was often to be found in Barry's garage at race meetings during the seventies. Sheene first met Harrison at a race in Long Beach, California, in 1977. The former Beatle and car-racing fan was strolling around the garages so, never backwards in coming forwards, Barry introduced himself and started a friendship that was to last until Harrison passed away. Sheene was distraught when Harrison died of cancer in November 2001 but said in his *Bike* magazine column, 'If anybody could make a laugh of it, it's George, so I'm sure he's having fun wherever he is.' Harrison had appeared on *This Is Your Life* as a surprise guest for Sheene, and according to Marriot, Harrison even wrote a song about Barry which was never recorded. George did, however, include a dedication to Barry on his self-titled 1979 solo album, one of many Harrison LPs Barry proudly owned.

What Harrison would have made of Sheene's rock buddies Prodigy, can only be guessed at. Lead man Keith Flint, a massive bike-racing fan who has raced in some club events himself, was known to visit Sheene's house when he was in Australia.

It wasn't, of course, only popular radio and TV shows Barry Sheene was appearing on in the seventies; viewers were just as likely to spot him during commercial breaks. He is probably still as well remembered for his Fabergé Brut 33 adverts as he is for his racing. Fragranced splash-on lotions for men were virtually unheard of in 1974, but Fabergé were determined to educate the masses with their TV advertising campaign. Their first effort with a semi-nude male model was rejected by the Independent Broadcasting Authority as indecent, so the idea was hatched of using family-friendly boxer Henry Cooper and the dashing young Sheene to urge viewers to 'splash it all over'. The ads were an instant and sensational success. Fabergé's other sports stars included boxer Muhammad Ali and Sheene's F1 friend James Hunt, and the firm spent £1 million in 1978 promoting Brut 33, a quarter of that sum being splashed on Sheene's campaign. Rival Grand Prix racer Randy Mamola, who had just arrived from America to race in Europe when the adverts were being shown, recalled being amazed at the level of exposure Sheene

enjoyed. 'Being at one with the press is very, very important throughout your career. If you're not kind to people in
any manner you can be written about in a very different
manner. I remember the Brut 33 adverts Barry did and I
thought, "Man, this is cool, this stuff's on TV." Back then
Barry set a benchmark with the British and world press in
terms of how to present yourself to the media, and it's
something I learned very well. I'm very well known with
the press and with the fans, and that was part of my lesson
from Barry.'

Barry also starred alongside Michael Crawford (then of
Frank Spencer fame and later to become the star of the hit
musical *Phantom of the Opera*) in adverts for oil firm
Texaco. There seemed no way he couldn't become a household name, even if he wasn't always the man in the
pictures. Don Morley, one of the most respected sports
photographers in the business, explained: 'Barry at that
time could be quite difficult to work with and he sometimes wouldn't show up for photoshoots I was doing for
Suzuki, Fabergé or Shell. There was a Suzuki mechanic
who had a similar build to Sheene so I used to photograph
him dressed in Barry's leathers when Barry didn't show up.
Sometimes we would superimpose Barry's head onto the
shot, but other times I just shot the mechanic with Barry's
helmet on and the visor down.'

Sheene even carved out a niche for himself in the lucrative
toy market with the release in 1978 of the Barry Sheene
'Steponit' toy, a gyro-powered miniature motorcycle similar
to the hugely popular Evel Knievel models of the same
period. Such was the pulling power of Sheene among

youngsters that the *Tiger* comic ran a full-page front cover competition to win a Steponit. In the seventies, it seemed that everyone, from grannies to toddlers and bikers to glamour models, was caught up in the Sheene phenomenon, and Barry was quite happy to play along for as long as it lasted.

CHAPTER 4

NO FEAR

'There must be somebody up there who loves me.'

Daytona Beach Raceway, Florida, March 1975. Barry Sheene has every inch of his gangly frame tucked into the blue and white Suzuki's bodywork to minimize wind drag. As he winds on the throttle to the maximum, he kicks up another gear, and another, until he is travelling as fast as his 750cc three-cylinder machine and the laws of physics will allow. There is no speedometer on his bike, but the gearing has been set up to allow it to reach almost 180mph, and Sheene has the throttle pinned to the stop. His every move is being followed by a documentary team from Thames Television in London, headed up by award-winning film-maker Frank Cvitanovich, a man eager to feed the British public's appetite for the dashing young cockney who's gunning for world glory in the 500cc Grand Prix World Championship.

Sheene is hot favourite to take the honours in the prestigious Daytona 200 race being held in Florida in a few days' time, ahead of the upcoming Grand Prix season. This is the very last private practice session before the race proper, and Sheene is out to run a full race distance to make sure his Suzuki will last the event.

Now on his fifth lap, Sheene howls down the main straight in front of the huge grandstand with his rev counter reading 8,500 as he nudges 180mph. Daytona is unique among bike-racing circuits in that it features a steep banking; Sheene, like all the other top racers, is aiming to get a sling-shot effect off it to increase his speed as he rockets down the asphalt slope.

Then, almost quicker than the human eye can detect, it all goes wrong and Sheene's worst nightmare comes true: shards of rubber splinter off his back wheel just milliseconds before it locks solid at around 178mph. Instinctively, Sheene whips in the clutch lever, hoping he can persuade the machine to coast to a halt, but it's too little too late. With a huge puff of blue smoke from the rear tyre, the Suzuki slews violently sideways and Sheene is thrown along the tarmac at sickening speed. His body is flipped and tossed, battered and broken with every turn, his leathers quickly wearing through as a result of the intense abrasion. The noise of metal on tarmac as the bike screeches along the track amid a shower of sparks is all that can be heard by the documentary team as the cameraman tries to remain professional and capture the horrific moment. His efforts will soon be seen throughout the world.

Sheene's severely battered body finally comes to a standstill some 300 yards down the track. The whole terrible incident lasts just eight seconds. Every eyewitness presumes he is dead as they run to his assistance. They know motor-cycle racing; they know that no man can survive being thrown from a bike at 178mph when all there is to land on is solid, unforgiving. It seems that the huge potential Barry Sheene has shown over the last few racing seasons will never be realized. It looks like the dream is over.

But Barry Sheene was not dead. Somehow, against all the odds, he had survived one of the fastest, if not the fastest, crashes in the history of motorcycle sport. Whether he would ever be able to walk again, never mind race a motor-cycle, was another matter, but Sheene was alive, albeit in a highly distressed condition. He had broken his left femur, his right wrist, his right forearm and collarbone, and six ribs; he'd also suffered compression fractures to several vertebrae as well as losing enough skin to 'upholster a settee', as he later remarked. On top of that one of his kidneys had split open. But he was alive.

Barry's future team-mate Pat Hennen saw the whole thing. 'All the Suzuki factory bikes and riders went to Daytona for a couple of days for tyre testing a week or so prior to the Daytona 200 race. We were all riding Suzuki's old Waterbuffalo triples. That was when Barry crashed at close to 175mph on the front straight. He was already on the track when I arrived. I joined everyone sitting on the pit wall when it happened, right in front of us. Those were the days before mufflers, when the bike's pipes still had straight stingers. I can still remember the sound his bike made coming down the straight. The engine was howling, and just like that it went woomp! The bike went down and started cartwheeling down the track, and it sounded like an automobile crashing, it made that much noise. It was frightening. The tread on the rear tyre had actually come away from the tyre's casing, and it jammed between the swingarm and the tyre casing, full stop. Barry was taken away to the hospital.'

Sheene had retained consciousness throughout the horrifying experience. He explained what it was like to live through every bike racer's worst nightmare in *The Story So Far*: 'The sensation of the machine swinging sideways in a sudden jerking movement was terrifying. As I skated down the road on my right-hand side, I was still moving incredibly quickly and I could painfully feel the skin being brutally scraped off my back. I was also aware of my limbs being battered about and I deliberately tucked my head into my shoulder to try to minimize the possibility of serious neck injuries.'

When any rider comes to his senses after a crash, his first instinct is to appraise any possible damage to his body by checking that all limbs are present and that he can move his legs to rule out the possibility of paralysis. When Sheene finally came to a halt, he ran through the by now familiar routine and was horrified when he couldn't see his left leg. Numbed by the shock and pain of the crash and unable to feel the leg, he was convinced he'd lost it. In fact, the leg had been twisted so grotesquely behind his back that Barry simply couldn't see it. What he could see was a lot of blood, caused by losing so much skin, and he could also tell by the sheer agony he was experiencing that he'd broken the leg, an arm and some ribs. But the fact was that he was alive, and he really shouldn't have been.

It was by far the worst crash of Barry's career to that point, and about as bad as a crash gets without being fatal or resulting in paralysis – one of Sheene's, and most other bike racers', biggest fears. When I interviewed Barry in 2001, I asked why he had kept his 'lucky' number seven on the bike after having such a bad accident while sporting it. His answer spoke volumes about his attitude to racing: 'It was only good luck that saved me from death in Daytona that day.' For Sheene, the glass was always half full. He didn't stop short at wearing just a lucky number, either; there was a famous lucky T-shirt and some not-so-famous lucky underpants, too. Having looked at a picture of himself on a winner's rostrum (he couldn't remember where), Sheene noticed that he'd been wearing a T-shirt emblazoned with the name of his close friend, American racer Gary Nixon, as well as a pair of blue underpants. It struck him that he'd won quite a few races while wearing the same garments, so he decided to stick with them from then on. 'Gary was a great rider and a great friend of mine,' Sheene explained, 'and when he came over to Europe from the States in 1970 he gave me some of his T-shirts [which are still available on Nixon's website for $17.95]. I always wore them, and even when bad shit happened I realized I had been lucky to get away with it, so the T-shirts stayed.' When I asked Sheene if he had ever forgotten any of his lucky clothing, he was quick to remind me of how organized he was and how important they were to him. 'Don't be daft, I'm not a bloody idiot. I never forget things.'

After the briefest trackside treatment at Daytona, Barry was taken straight to Halifax Hospital just one mile from the circuit and the surgeons set to work rebuilding his shattered bones. As he lay on the operating table, Sheene could have had no idea that the crash he had just survived would do more to make him famous than any amount of World Championship victories. His fame was set to rocket practically overnight. The Thames Television crew was at that moment syndicating their footage around the world; on top of that, every daily national newspaper was preparing to run a story on the crash the following day. Everyone, it seemed, was marvelling at Britain's answer to Evel Knievel, the only other motorcyclist capable of making global head-lines by breaking ludicrous numbers of bones. By the time he got back home, Sheene, like Knievel, would be a house-hold name.

Those who knew Barry were horrified by news of the accident, and those who'd never heard of him before wanted to hear more after seeing footage of his crash. Who was this guy who quite literally risked life and limb in his bid to win a world title for Britain? Who was this modern-day gladiator who dressed in leathers and crash helmet for combat, and who muscled motorcycles around concrete wall-lined circuits at 180mph? Suddenly, Barry Sheene was on everyone's lips. He was a PR man's dream come true. Shrewd as he was, even Barry couldn't have planned it better himself.

For any bike racer, crashing is an accepted part of his job. When you're pushing a motorcycle and its tyres to the absolute limits of adhesion on a regular basis you're going to fall off from time to time, it's as simple as that. In most cases, riders will get up and walk away from a spill, especially now in an era when track safety and protective equipment is so advanced. In Sheene's era, much less thought went into protecting riders in the event of a fall, and consequently there were far more fatalities. Of course, riders do still get killed, but it is becoming rare, especially on 'safe' Grand Prix circuits which have lots of run-off areas, inflatable air fencing and first-class medical facilities. The worst today's riders can expect from a crash is a few broken bones – unless, of course, they happen to be extremely unlucky. Sheene's career broken-bones list makes for gruesome reading: left-side femur, tibia and fibula once, right tibia and fibula twice; right ankle four times, left ankle once, along with three left toes and two right toes; 12 vertebrae, four left ribs and five right ribs; right collarbone four times, left collarbone three times; right forearm once, left wrist four times, right wrist once; four left metacarpals (the bones in the back of the hand), four left knuckles and four left fingers.

No amount of run-off space or safety equipment could have saved Barry at Daytona; after all, he didn't actually hit anything, he just slid down the road. The actual cause of the crash is still a matter of some conjecture; naturally, no one wanted readily to accept the blame for such a public near-fatal accident. Sheene himself was initially adamant that the rear Dunlop tyre had exploded, but he wasn't regarded too highly by Dunlop for saying so in public. In *A Will to Win*, Michael Scott maintained that the tyre was still inflated after the crash, meaning it couldn't possibly have been a blow-out. Scott also pointed to evidence provided by the mechanic who stripped the wrecked bike afterwards; he said that a chain tensioner had collapsed onto the tyre causing the wheel to seize momentarily. Sheene insisted he'd had his chain tensioner removed from the bike before he rode it and continued to believe that the tyre had simply blown out.

Component failure is always embarrassing for any company, whether it be Suzuki, Dunlop or anyone else, and it's doubtful if the truth about the cause of the accident will ever be known. Certainly Sheene was quick to point out at the time that a Dunlop of the same compound blew up in the Daytona race itself, a fact which lent some weight to the argument that the tyres couldn't cope with the unusually high speeds permitted by Daytona's unique banking. Speaking to Thames Video in 1990, Suzuki team manager Rex White, in Barry's presence, offered the most likely explanation, one which Sheene did not contradict. 'The Dunlop people hadn't imagined how much the tyre could grow [with the intense heat generated at Daytona]; the tyre was growing about 12mm in diameter and it was rubbing on the side of the swing arm depositing a load of rubber on it, and it just destroyed itself with getting too hot.'

Whatever the cause of the accident – and it is now purely academic – the result for Sheene was the same: he had been poised on the verge of a brilliant career in motorcycle racing and was now confined to a hospital bed, trying to persuade nurses to wheel him outside for a cigarette at every given opportunity. But it was during this period that the world first saw what Barry Sheene was made of, and it was impressive stuff: within seven weeks of his crash he was back racing a motorcycle again. Sheene openly admitted that his Daytona accident was the most frightening thing that had ever happened to him, but he was determined not to let it have any kind of psychological effect on him. All his thoughts were set on getting back on his bike, even if he did have an 18-inch pin inserted in his left leg to strengthen his femur.

His fight back to fitness was a routine that would become all too familiar over the following years: gruelling rounds of strenuous exercises, swimming and cycling punctuated by regular painkilling injections to allow him to continue. But Barry's greatest ally on the road to recovery wasn't anything a doctor could prescribe, it was his willpower, and he had stacks of it. Every single day he would claw his way through the pain barrier, trying to lift that extra weight, trying to stretch his battered body that bit further, trying to do more repetitions on his home-made wrist-exerciser – a bar with a weight attached to it by a cord which he would endlessly wind in and out. His refusal to acknowledge the pain was steadfast. 'When I tried out a bicycle I had just bought to help regain full knee movement,' he recalled, 'the sheer effort of pedalling at first made tears stream from my eyes.' But it wasn't enough to stop him. Barry remained mentally upbeat throughout the recuperation period, always insisting he'd soon be back on his bike despite the state of his battered body. With a gust of bravado not unlike the one he would employ 27 years later when he developed cancer, he told the *Guardian*, 'It's a fight between me and my body, and I'm going to win.'

It was testament to Sheene's increasing popularity that he received around 2,000 get-well cards after Daytona, all of which cheered him up and encouraged him to carry on. In fact, the psychological after-effects of his crash seem to have been more positive than negative. 'If the crash changed me in some way,' Sheene reflected, 'it perhaps made me a little more carefree, if anything. I had been through the worst, or just about the worst, that racing could be so any other mishap would have been mild in comparison.'

Eleven times Isle of Man TT winner and twice British Superbike champion Steve Hislop is no stranger to injury, having broken his back, his neck and many other major bones. He was full of admiration for Sheene's ability to overcome injury. 'Barry must heal really well to have come back from those injuries. I've known guys who still suffer from a broken leg two years later. You really need to *want* to come back from injury. After my big Rockingham crash [in 2001, when he smashed his ankle, leg and collarbone], I was lying there thinking "I don't need this shit", but then I got messages from people and spoke to people who encouraged me and I got charged up again, and Barry must have gone through the same sort of process.' Sheene's contemporary Ron Haslam agreed. 'It must take a lot of push to come back from injuries like Sheene had. He had his arms, legs, everything damaged at the same time. To have your health set back so much and to find the push to come back again is amazing.'

Believing the worst to be behind him, Barry set off for Cadwell Park in April 1975 to make his much-anticipated

comeback to racing. The fans turned out in their thousands
to see if their hero still had what it took to be competitive,
but unknown to them Sheene had already held a secret test
session around the circuit just to see for himself if he could
still ride properly. Within an hour he was up to speed and
convinced that he could take on the field and win. And he
very nearly did. Sheene was leading the race and looked set
to take an emotional victory had he not made one small
error during his recovery period: he hadn't exercised his
hands and had consequently lost all feeling in them. They
turned blue from the effort of hanging onto the big Suzuki
around Cadwell's undulating turns, and Barry was forced
to retire from the race. It was a small matter, easily recti-
fied with some exercise; the main point was that he was
back, and just three months later he won his first ever
500cc Grand Prix. The first mountain in Sheene's life had
been successfully climbed.

Daytona might have been Barry's biggest and certainly
most publicized crash – the full Thames documentary was
broadcast a month after the incident and turned Sheene into
an even bigger star – but it was by no means his first. He had
famously tumbled off in his very first race without major
injury, and there had been many more accidents between that
1968 debut and his bone-crunching Daytona disaster. Sheene
first broke a bone racing in Holland in 1971, and shortly
afterwards crashed at Mallory Park in England, breaking five
ribs and suffering compression fractures to three vertebrae. As
he moved up to the fearsome and not-so-well-behaved 500
and 750cc machines, the number of incidents increased. In
1974, the first year of the four-cylinder Suzuki RG500,

Sheene had a particularly nasty crash at Imola in Italy: he haemorrhaged in one eye, broke a bone in his heel, lost a considerable amount of skin and knocked himself out. 'I awoke to find what appeared to be a covey of nuns in starched white uniforms scrubbing iodine into me where I had lost large areas of flesh,' Sheene recalled. A further crash in 1974, this time at the Swedish Grand Prix at Anderstorp, saw Sheene slice the top off a fence post with his shoulder, but he managed to escape without major injury.

Strangely, none of Barry's horrendous accidents ever made him consider retirement from the sport, but he did come very close to quitting when his best friend Gary Nixon was badly injured in a crash in 1974. On Sheene's recommendation, Nixon was testing a Suzuki RG500 when he collided with Japanese test rider Ken Araoka and very nearly lost his life. Sheene felt partly responsible because he had arranged the test session, but he eventually accepted, as he'd done after Bill Ivy's death, that it was just one of those things that happen in bike racing. Nixon recovered.

After Sheene made his remarkable comeback from the Daytona crash, further injuries were just around the corner. While contesting the Race of the Year at Mallory Park in England in late 1975, Barry cracked his right knee on a kerb going through the Esses at around 100mph. It was excruciatingly painful, but Sheene still managed to win the race before having a medical check-up afterwards. Again, doctors failed to notice any structural damage and sent Barry about his business with a relatively clean bill of health.

Because of the damage done to his left leg at Daytona, Sheene had been putting all his weight on his right leg. But with that now hurting too, he didn't have a good leg to stand on, so to speak. This still didn't stop him from turning up at Cadwell Park to race soon afterwards. In true Sheene style, he had blocks fitted to the foot rests of his bike to enable him to ride it more comfortably. All looked well for the race until a fan saw Barry messing around on a trials bike in the paddock and asked him to pull one of his famous wheelies. Always one to oblige his fans, Barry hoisted the bike up onto its back wheel but was forced to step off the machine as it threatened to topple over backwards. It was a big mistake. The weakened right leg buckled under the strain and Barry was left lying in an ungainly heap, unaware of the serious mess his knee was now in. According to a London doctor (Sheene refused to undergo surgery anywhere else in the country, believing that any doctor worth his salt would practise in the capital) who performed a five-hour operation to rebuild it, the knee was 'just like a hamburger, just crushed up completely'. Before the surgery, Sheene had been told there was only a 50-50 chance of the knee ever being fully operational again; as he famously said at the time, had he been a racehorse he would surely have been shot. But the operation went well and Barry was once again in high spirits, despite the fact that he now faced a second massive convalescence period to rival anything he had undergone after Daytona.

From October 1975 to January 1976, Sheene followed another intense training programme in a bid to restore some strength to his shattered knee. To get around he needed to use two crutches, but the extra pressure he was forced to put on his left leg eventually made the 18-inch

Daytona pin move around, causing his thigh to swell up. The pin was eventually removed from Sheene's left leg after the Venezuelan Grand Prix in 1977 when the bone was considered strong enough. As ever, television cameras were present. The footage makes uneasy viewing for the squeamish as doctors use a heavyweight hammer to knock out the pin. The two screws in Barry's right knee from the Cadwell incident were left in place. Sheene later got a painful reminder – not that he needed one – that they were still there in 1979 when the bike he was following in the Yugoslavian Grand Prix threw up a stone which smacked straight into one of the screws, pushing it half an inch deeper into the bone. Sheene said the pain was terrible, and he openly admitted to crying in agony as he rode back to the pits.

In 2000, Sheene still couldn't squat down on his haunches for any length of time because of his shattered knees and legs. When I tried to encourage him to crouch down beside his Cagiva Raptor and MV Agusta F4 for a photograph for *Motor Cycle News*, he fell over in the attempt and another pose had to be worked out. But that was not half as embarrassing as Barry's trip to the toilet during a visit to Interlagos in Brazil. Discovering it was a stand-up-only loo where the patron is expected to squat over a hole in the ground, Barry realized that his injured legs would never take the strain. He attempted to use the women's toilet instead, where he would at least have the luxury of being able to sit down, but Sheene's plans were foiled by a 'huge mama' of a toilet attendant. As a puzzled crowd began to gather, he had no option but to 'hang on' until he got back to his hotel.

The Mallory/Cadwell injuries were another major blow for Sheene, but as ever he saw the funny side to his problems. In this case it was his newly discovered ability to pivot his right knee by two inches either side. Barry claimed this was a great party piece, though he wasn't so enamoured of the fact that his disco dancing days were as good as over. 'A 10-minute shuffle on the dance floor and I have to sit down,' he moaned. 'Three or four days later, the pain would still be with me.'

Sheene's biggest fear when it came to crashing was amputation. Right from the beginning of his racing career he had repeatedly told his family and team members not to let doctors cut anything off him if he happened to be unconscious and couldn't speak for himself. He simply couldn't stand the thought of losing a part of his body, so it's no wonder that Sheene rated his 1980 French Grand Prix crash as the worst of his career, despite the fact that his tally of injuries wasn't as high as at Daytona. Barry had been riding out of his skin to make up for the inferior speed of his privately entered Yamaha when he lost the front end of the bike as it started to patter through a corner. The little finger of his left hand was still wrapped around the handlebar when he went down and Sheene tumbled end over end several times before rolling to a halt in intense pain. 'I could feel blinding pain coming from my left hand,' he said, 'and I looked at it to see the finger hanging down through the disintegrated leather of my glove, amid pieces of smashed knuckle bone.' The finger was in such a mess that doctors at the local French hospital wanted to amputate immediately, but Sheene flatly refused and had what was left of his finger patched up and packed in ice before flying back to London in a bid to have it saved. Surgeons at the University College Hospital tried their best to save the digit, but the knuckle was so badly smashed that the finger wouldn't move, and Sheene finally, grudgingly, accepted that amputation was the only answer. The removal of the top half of the finger didn't cause him any problems while on a bike, but he did admit that he couldn't cup water in his hands any more because it ran out through the gap where his finger used to be.

There was more pain in store during 1980 when Barry crashed out of an invitation race at Sugo in Japan. He broke his wrist in such a way that doctors had to re-set it, a routine so painful that patients usually require an anaesthetic. Sheene, who desperately wanted to catch an early flight back home, refused to be sedated and decided to accept whatever pain the re-setting would cause. It was intense. So intense, in fact, that Barry rated it as the worst he'd ever experienced. The doctors had to hold him down and muffle his cries while the wrist was snapped back into shape. Steve Hislop has undergone a very similar procedure, and despite inhaling gas to lessen the pain he, too, rates the pain as the worst he's ever endured. 'A couple of people held me down and a doctor wrenched the wrist back into place,' he recalled. 'Christ, but the pain was unbelievable – I think without the gas I would have passed out. Just take a minute to imagine your entire hand being torn from your wrist and then some bugger stretching it to snap it back into place. Then hope you never have to go through that. It's not funny, believe me.' Showing his determination yet again, Sheene visited his

English doctor when he got back home and took with him a set of handlebars from his bike. The reason? He asked the doctor to mould a plastercast round his wrist while he was gripping the bars so that his hands would be set in a position that enabled him to race.

Any bike racer would consider himself extremely lucky to have lived through so many nasty crashes and would probably have quit the sport grateful to be alive. But all these tumbles paled into insignificance compared to Sheene's biggest and most horrific crash, which happened at Silverstone in 1982. Sheene had already suffered a 120mph spill at Abbey Curve while testing in 1973, a crash he blamed on hitting a worm on the track while his bike was banked over. The story sounds incredible, and has been laughed at on occasion – Sheene himself said 'it all sounds too ridiculous for words but the tyre mark over the worm was there for all to see' – but it's one that triple British Superbike champion Niall Mackenzie believes plausible. 'There's so little contact between the tyre and the road when a bike is leaned over, especially with the slimmer-profiled tyres back then, that the slightest reduction in grip could cause you to crash,' he said. Again Sheene was extremely lucky to walk away after such a high-speed incident. In 1982, he wouldn't be so lucky.

Silverstone, Northamptonshire, July 1982. As Barry Sheene pulls out of the pit lane, a trackside offical indicates that there are only two laps left of this crucial Wednesday afternoon session. It's the last chance for Sheene to test the unfamiliar (to him) V4 Yamaha before official qualifying begins for the British Grand Prix on Friday. Barry has modified the Yamaha's chassis and needs every minute he can get on the machine to become accustomed to its power and handling characteristics. And the only way to really test both is at racing speed. The track is literally swarming with bikes, from little 125cc machines right up to the big 1000cc superbikes, about 80 of them. Sheene has complained that it's dangerous, but he has no choice but to go out there if he wants to have his bike ready for the biggest race of his year, and a race he has never won.

The difference in speeds between the bikes is as much as 40mph in some cases, so Sheene has to treat the smaller bikes (and some of the slower big bikes) like mobile chicanes as he tries to string together a fast lap. Weather conditions are good: it's dry and there's only a slight breeze blowing as Sheene circulates at around 117mph, just short of his own lap record. Things are looking good. Sheene overtakes last year's British GP winner Jack Middelburg at the end of the Hangar straight, looks over his shoulder to see how the Dutchman's Suzuki compares on acceleration out of the corner, and is satisfied to notice that he's already pulled 20 yards on him. The Yamaha is flying.

Tucked back into the Perspex bubble, Sheene lines himself up for Abbey Curve. It's more of a kink than a corner, but it's blind so Barry can't see the exit; more importantly, he can't see what has just taken place over the blind rise leading to the *Daily Express* bridge. In front of him, as he ups his speed to 165mph, lies the fallen bike of 250cc rider Patrick Igoa. The Frenchman had been trying to pass a slower 125cc rider, German racer Alfred Waibel, when he was forced wide, touched the grass and slid off. Both rider and bike had bounced back into the middle of the road, and both now lie there on the racing line like a death trap, waiting to catch out the next rider through the corner. In the absence of a full complement of trackside marshals there's no one to wave a flag to warn the oncoming riders. Barry Sheene is just a few hundred yards away with his chin on the fuel tank of his bike, pinning the throttle to the stop and going as fast as it is possible to go.

Amazingly, some bikes manage to negotiate the wreckage and ride through safely, but not everyone is trying as hard as Sheene is – after all, it's only a practice day. But this looks like being Sheene's best chance ever of winning his home Grand Prix and he's trying everything he knows to break the lap record, if only for the psychological advantage it would give him over his rivals. The scene is set for one of the most talked-about accidents in motorcycle sport.

As he crests the blind rise, Sheene smashes into Igoa's fallen bike with incredible force (Igoa himself escapes with just a broken collarbone), causing its fuel tank to explode. Sheene's Yamaha tank explodes too. Clouds of flame and smoke obscure the wreckage, and the scene is immediately reminiscent of a terrorist bombing or an airline crash. Chunks of metal and debris from the bikes fly through the air just as Middelburg becomes a third casualty (although he, too, gets off lightly with abrasions and a jarred vertebrae). The result is total carnage on a scale rarely seen in motorsport.

In the space of milliseconds, the ball of flame from the fuel tank explosion blasts up through Sheene's helmet and singes his eyebrows off. As he is launched forward with the impact of the collision, his knees crush his hands, which are still holding the handlebars, snapping his left wrist, smashing his knuckles and ripping off one of his fingernails (Sheene would find the nail in his glove some weeks later). His crotch is slammed against the exploding fuel tank. The force also completely shatters both Sheene's legs from the knee joints down; the damage is so severe that the only thing holding his lower legs onto his upper legs are the arteries. All this happens in the blink of an eye before he's even been thrown from the bike. When he is catapulted from his machine, Barry is launched some 30 feet into the air, hits the track 100 yards further down the road and slides for another 300 yards before grinding to a halt, unmoving and unconscious. Every eyewitness fears he is dead. It is just like Daytona all over again, but this time it's even worse.

Unsurprisingly, those witnesses later described the crash as absolutely horrific. Former 350cc world champion Jon Ekerold was returning from a shopping trip and had stopped to watch some practice on his way back to the paddock. When he saw Patrick Igoa's crash and realized his fellow rider was lying unmoving on the racing line, he dropped his shopping bags and rushed to his aid. Then Sheene's bike hit. He told the now defunct *Motor Cycle Weekly*, 'There was a hell of a bang and I jumped back as the front end of Igoa's bike shot at me. It brushed my leg, and I was lucky it didn't take it off.' Ekerold was convinced there must be fatalities, and probably dismemberment as well. It was not a pretty sight.

Randy Mamola, Sheene's replacement in the factory Suzuki team in 1980, was soon on the scene. He is still uncomfortable talking about what he saw. 'It was like an airplane crash, you know, two bikes, two riders and shrapnel everywhere. It was like "Oh, Jesus, what happened here?" because it was on a straight. If you can imagine doing about 160mph then hitting something, then things are going to travel a long way. That was the start of the end of [Sheene's] career. I hate to speak about such things because, being a rider, nobody likes to see anything like that happen. It was much like what happened to Mick Doohan in 1999 at Jerez [his leg was broken so badly that it cut short his career].'

Sheene's arch rival Kenny Roberts stopped at the crash scene and carefully removed Barry's helmet, mindful of the need for caution because of the possibility of spinal injuries. A trained nurse, who was present only in her capacity as the wife of a circuit official, put a plastic tube down Barry's throat to ease his breathing, but official medical help seemed to take an agonizingly long time to reach the scene. Roberts was reported as having tears streaming down his face; he genuinely thought Sheene was fatally wounded.

Simon Tonge had started working as a mechanic for Sheene in 1981, having worked for Steve Parrish before Parrish broke his wrist. He, too, feared the worst. 'I was the first of our lot to get to the crash site. The session had stopped and Barry hadn't come into the pits so I set off on a scooter to look for him, and that's when I came across the carnage. I remember putting my head on Kenny Roberts' shoulder and thinking, "That's it." He was in a bad way. It was the first time I'd been confronted with such a sight. I'd never run across someone as badly injured as that before. There was just wreckage for 200 metres; you could even see the gearbox of Igoa's bike because it had been ripped open. I worked in Grands Prix for another 11 years but I never saw anything like that again.'

British racer (and latterly Sky Sports TV commentator) Keith Huewen was far enough behind Sheene and Middelburg to avoid the wreckage, but he too was convinced that Sheene was dead. 'I was just cruising back round to the pits when the two explosions went off and I had to ride through the huge black cloud of smoke that came off them. When I came through the smoke there was complete carnage with bodies and bits of shattered bikes lying around everywhere among all the flames and smoke. It looked like there had been a plane crash. I slowed down and noticed Barry lying there; his body was actually smoking. In my mind there was no question that he was dead. I had seen hundreds of crashes but never anything as bad as that. I was actually shaking as I rode back to the pits.'

Sheene's father Frank and his girlfriend Stephanie McLean were, as always, in the paddock when the accident happened. As word filtered through that it had been a very bad accident, both made for the crash site as quickly as they could despite Ekerold's protestations to Frank not to go because 'you don't want to see'. Stephanie later told the *Mail on Sunday* that she had genuinely feared for her man's life. 'I went rushing up to the track and saw him lying unconscious. I thought he was dead.' Incredibly,

Barry managed to mutter something to his father, the first real indication that he was actually alive, if only just.

Initially, Barry was taken to the circuit medical centre which was obviously unequipped to deal with such serious injuries. He was therefore put on a drip and taken to Northampton General Hospital by ambulance, gibbering in Spanish en route and at one point shouting out (in English), 'For fuck's sake, someone give me a cigarette!' There was obviously still life, and cravings, left in Barry Sheene. Sheene's distrust of provincial doctors had rubbed off on his father, who was less than keen to allow anyone in the Northampton hospital to work on Barry. He only gave his consent to a consultant orthopaedic surgeon called Nigel Cobb after receiving word from Barry's regular doctor in London that Cobb was the right man to put his son back together again.

Nigel Cobb would soon become almost as famous as Barry for the work he carried out on his celebrity patient. In the course of an eight-hour operation – he'd originally estimated that it would take two or three hours – Cobb completely reconstructed Barry's legs, wrist and fingers in what he claimed was one of the most intricate operations he had ever carried out. 'The leg injuries are very severe, probably among the most serious fractures that one can have,' he told the *Daily Mail*'s Sarah Boseley. 'It is almost as if the upper quarter of each tibia [lower leg bone] had simply exploded.' Cobb added that when the legs were opened up at the beginning of the operation 'the muscles and bones just fell apart and we were left with this jigsaw puzzle to sort out'. Two seven-inch buttresses of pliable stainless steel and two five-inch plates were inserted into Sheene's legs as a form of scaffolding to hold the shattered bones together, secured with a total of 27 alloy screws. Two more metal plates and five more screws were used to piece together Sheene's shattered wrist. His two crushed fingers presented another challenge for the gifted Cobb.

Working in a hospital so close to the M1 motorway, Cobb was well versed in dealing with severe injuries resulting from road accidents, but what he wasn't used to was national fame and teams of reporters wanting to talk to the man who had rebuilt Barry Sheene into some sort of bionic being. Images of Sheene's X-rays clearly displaying Cobb's metalwork were shown on every news channel and printed in every daily paper to the astonishment of the general public, most of whom were unaware that limbs could be patched together using metal.

Sheene was given regular doses of pethedine to numb the pain, and he drifted in and out of consciousness for the first few days after the operation. Had he been allowed to regain full consciousness during that period, he would have been in absolute agony. At least he was spared from his ultimate nightmare of amputation. There was some initial concern that he might lose his legs simply because they were so badly crushed, but thanks to the protection his racing leathers offered against abrasion, his skin had remained largely unbroken so there was no risk of infection.

As usual, it was sex that Barry missed most in hospital (his helicopter notwithstanding), even though it wouldn't have been physically possible in the first days after the crash, as he explained. 'I did whack what I term my lusting tackle on the tank extremely hard. That really hurt! That part of my anatomy soon got better, but I have to say that one enjoyment in life I did miss lying in a hospital bed was sex. Steph was with me nearly all the time but a hospital's not the easiest place in the world to get your leg over!'

What astonished everyone, especially Nigel Cobb, was the speed of Barry's recovery. After an accident of such severity, Cobb normally kept his patients hospitalized for three months; Sheene was discharged in three and a half weeks. His pain threshold proved to be extremely high and his Daytona experience had taught him all he needed to know about self-physiotherapy; he was already exercising his ankles when Cobb came round to check him after the operation, and he stayed awake every night to practise bending his knees just a little further each time, despite the agony it caused him. After those three and a half weeks Sheene threw back his bed covers and performed two full knee bends to a baffled Cobb. He sent him home the very next day. Barry has always been quick to express his gratitude to Cobb for the sterling work he carried out on his legs, even if his tongue was quite often lodged firmly in his cheek. 'I think a lot of the credit has to go to Nigel Cobb,' he said. 'Without him I'd have been totally legless.'

Barry knew he was in for another long, painful and laborious route back to race fitness, but his spirits remained high (at least in public) throughout his ordeal, helped on by the 25,000 get-well messages he received from friends and fans around the world. But every day was filled with hurt and tedium as well as the frustration and anxiety of not knowing how he would perform on a bike again, or if he would even be supplied with one by any of the top manufacturers. Still, the only time he cried had nothing to do with the pain, nor was it anything to do with self-pity; it was simply because he had missed his chance of winning the British Grand Prix on one of the new V4 Yamahas he had acquired especially for the event. Until the British round Barry had been forced to run the previous year's bike, an across-the-frame four-cylinder machine as opposed to the new and faster V4, and the Silverstone round had been his best chance of beating arch rival Kenny Roberts who had so narrowly defeated him in the same race in 1979 in what is one of the all-time classic motorcycle races. Sheene was gutted for his fans more than anything else. He knew what a home win would have meant to them.

Mercifully, Sheene remembered nothing of his Silverstone crash. 'I came over the crest of the rise on my usual line,' he said, 'and there was a bike lying in the road and I hit it. Then all I can recall seeing was a big ball of flame. Nothing else.' As a result, and to his credit, he was quick to play down the fuss made of his bravery by the national newspapers. As he said some time after the accident, 'I didn't consider myself as brave. All I had to do was to get the legs mended as quickly as possible and get back on a bike. What's brave about that?' But whether Sheene liked it or not, there was no denying the bravery with which he set about his recuperation, fighting the pain and pushing that little bit further every day to get his legs and wrist working again. After leaving hospital, he spent six weeks in a wheelchair, then progressed to crutches, then to walking sticks; by November he was walking unaided. He told the *Daily Express* the secret to his rapid recovery: 'If you start relying on aids, you never improve. I was told I could do myself no damage, only suffer a bit of pain, so I threw the sticks as far away as I could.'

Sheene in fact often played down his injuries to deny his rivals any psychological advantage. Chip Hennen related one particular tale which sheds some light on Sheene's determination not to let his physical shortcomings dominate his life. '[Suzuki GB racing director] Maurice Knight had arranged to meet Barry and Stephanie for breakfast on the morning of a race, I believe some time during the 1978 season. Maurice arrived early at Barry's hotel and Barry told him to go on up to his room. Barry was just getting out of bed and he rolled his legs over the side of the bed. According to Maurice, Barry sat on the side of the bed for nearly 30 minutes massaging his legs to get the circulation going well enough for him to stand up. He had busted his legs up so badly over the years that he had trouble getting the circulation going in them in the morning. Given the myriad physical problems Barry had then from his many racing injuries, it's truly incredible to believe he was able to go as fast as he did. I think it speaks volumes about his strength of character and incredible determination.'

Sheene always remained level-headed about the risks of his profession. 'Whatever is going to happen is going to happen,' he said. 'No one can decide fate. I know I have had lots of misfortunes in previous years so that should be even more reason not to be nervous.' And contrary to what most people must think, he was no masochist; in fact, he had a very healthy fear of pain. 'The prospect of having my body, no matter which part, racked with pain scares me,' he admitted. 'I've endured enough in my racing career and the thought of more physical punishment coming my way sends shivers of fear through my body. My toes curl with terror when I even contemplate a visit to the dentist: the injection, the drill . . .'

But Sheene certainly showed no signs of being nervous about riding bikes again. Fewer than 10 weeks after the crash that so nearly killed him, he was back on a bike again in front of 20,000 cheering fans at Donington Park. He rode two laps round the track on a road-going Yamaha RD350 with fellow racer and best buddy Steve Parrish riding pillion, just to act as a stabilizer should anything go wrong. Five months after that, he was back on a race bike for the South African Grand Prix at Kyalami where he received the biggest cheer of the day for finishing tenth. It seemed no punishment short of death itself could stop him.

CHAPTER 5

THE RACER: PART TWO

'Out of sight . . . I had done it. I had bloody
well done it!'

Giacomo Agostini is the most successful motorcycle racer
of all time with 15 world titles and 10 TT wins to his
credit. In 1975, he won the last of those world titles from
another all-time great, Phil Read. But in June, at the Dutch
round of the World Championship, Ago, for all his years of
experience, was outfoxed and outridden by a 24-year-old
Barry Sheene, who chalked up his maiden 500cc Grand
Prix victory.

The young Londoner had already eclipsed the old master
in practice by claiming pole position, despite the fact that
he had had to plug the hole left by an extracted wisdom
tooth with cotton wool before heading out for practice. It
was his first 500cc pole position from an eventual tally of
19 – the same number of 500cc class victories Barry would
accumulate in his career. In the event itself, Sheene
displayed all the racecraft of a seasoned veteran. He
repeatedly made a point of showing his front wheel on the

right-hand side of Ago's bike as the pair negotiated the final right-hand corner before the start/finish line. This was merely a ruse to fool Ago into thinking Sheene was going to overtake him on that side towards the end of the race. As a consequence, Agostini began to take a tight line into the chicane to protect his right-hand side from attack. Sheene, however, waited until the very last lap before passing Agostini on his left-hand side, which the Italian rider had unwittingly left open. Sheene's faster exit speed from the corner allowed him to win the drag race to the line, and he crossed it first in front of 150,000 screaming fans, many of whom had made the ferry trip across from the UK to cheer on their homegrown hero.

It was an emotional moment when Sheene pulled in at the end of the pit lane, removed his famous Donald Duck helmet and hugged his father in the sweltering Dutch sunshine. They had come a long way, the father and son team, from a quick test run at Brands Hatch seven years earlier. Now they had reached the very pinnacle of the sport they both loved, the 500cc World Championship, and Barry had broken his cherry in the premier class, the only class that really mattered. He had already won four Grand Prix races in the 50cc and 125cc classes, but this was the big time and there was to be no turning back.

Winning a 500cc GP is always an achievement whatever the circumstances, simply because the winner has to beat the very best motorcycle racers in the world, but for Sheene it was even more special as three months earlier he had been facing an uphill battle just to be able to walk again after his huge Daytona smash. Now, not only was he walking, he had beaten the most successful bike racer of all time and had accomplished the feat by using his head rather than by riding beyond his limits. It was the perfect comeback from the worst of crashes.

Sheene's first race after Daytona had been at Cadwell Park in a national event, but his first time back at a Grand Prix, in Austria, had ended in disappointment. Concerned that Sheene's legs might not be strong enough to push-start his bike off the grid as the rules dictated, race officials asked him to demonstrate that he could do so without causing any danger to himself or other riders. Sheene obliged and managed to start his bike without incident, but for reasons known only to themselves the race organizers decided on race morning that Sheene would not be allowed to start after all. It was a totally wasted trip, and Barry did not hide his feelings from the offending officials, sticking two fingers up at them as he stormed out of the meeting. He was allowed to start in the German and Italian rounds, but he needn't have bothered as both resulted in non-finishes thanks to mechanical gremlins.

Despite the glorious victory in Holland, Sheene had dropped too many points in the early part of the season to present a serious challenge for the world title, and despite another win at the Swedish round in Anderstorp he finished sixth overall in the standings. His European F750 challenge had also suffered. He was leading the series with one round to go before his unfortunate tumble from a trials bike at Cadwell Park which ruled him out for the rest of the season and saw his F750 title going to Jack Findlay. Mick Grant scooped the British Superbike title from

Sheene during his absence, leaving Barry without a title to his name for the first time since 1972. But the signs were good: if his bike was reliable in 1976 and he didn't suffer any more major injuries, Barry Sheene looked every bit the world champion elect.

Winning the world title had become more crucial than ever for Sheene's credibility. He was receiving way more media attention than any motorcyclist can rightly expect, yet he had never won the sport's top prize. Other riders such as Phil Read had won several world titles yet were still largely ignored by the mainstream press. Barry knew he simply had to deliver the goods in 1976.

For a few lucky and gifted sportsmen, there are years when they can do no wrong, when everything goes their way and their confidence increases with every victory, leaving their rivals with only the hope of finishing second at best. For Barry Sheene, 1976 was one of those years. He won the 500cc World Championship, regained the *MCN* Superbike championship and the Shellsport 500 championship, and was voted *MCN*'s Man of the Year for a third time. On top of that, he was reported to have earned his first million, he started to date his future wife, and he consolidated his position as the most famous motorcycle racer in history. Britain went Sheene mad.

It is much easier to identify the greats in any given sport with the benefit of hindsight, and Sheene had his share of critics over the years who were all too keen to point out that there were no established 'greats' around during his two championship-winning years, 1976 and 1977. One of those critics is a rider from the modern era, four-times

Born to ride. An eight-year-old Barry helps his dad Frank before a race at the now defunct Crystal Palace track in 1958.

After crashing out of the 125cc TT at Quarterbridge in 1971, Barry refused to race there ever again.

Chain smoker. Barry smoked since he was nine and developed a 60-a-day habit for most of his life.

King of Brands. Barry rounding Brands Hatch on his 750 Suzuki in 1973. The Kent track had been the scene of his racing debut five years earlier.

'Just one more lap son, I'm not even tired yet.' Franco acts trainer to his boy – Rocky style.

'Keep that bloody thing away from my washing!' Barry not being too helpful with the domestic chores at his Wisbech home.

'Told you I'd do it, love.' Barry with future wife Stephanie after winning his second world title at Imatra in 1977.

With the first of his three Rolls Royce Silver Shadows in 1975. Note the personalised number plate.

A rare picture of Sheene wearing a suit. Showing off his MBE in 1978 alongside his parents. He told the Queen that riding bikes was safer than riding horses!

The race of his life. Even though he was beaten by 0.03s, the 1979 British Grand Prix battle with Kenny Roberts was one of Sheene's greatest moments.

Receiving The Segrave Trophy in 1977 – awarded for outstanding performances on land, sea or in the air.

No pain. Despite having a broken left wrist, Barry lines up for a race at Brands Hatch on his private Yamaha in 1980.

King Kenny. Roberts takes the mickey out of the King of Spain, Juan Carlos after the 1982 Spanish Grand Prix. Sheene is third from left while '82 world champ Franco Uncini is second from right.

Happy families. Barry with wife Stephanie, and her son Roman (left) and a friend.

Rebel alliance. The leading figures of the proposed breakaway World Series. (L-R): Sheene, Graeme Crosby, Takazumi Katayama, Marc Fontan, Jack Middelburg, Kenny Roberts and Kork Ballington.

The scant and burnt remains of Sheene's OW61 Yamaha after his 165mph Silverstone crash in 1982. The rider was in an equally bad state.

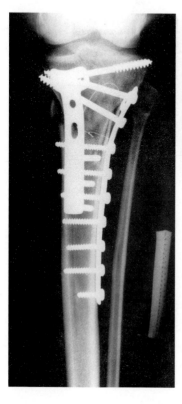

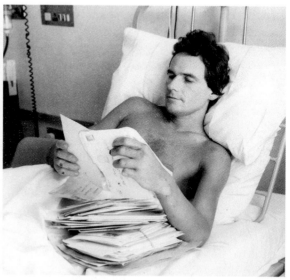

Above Sifting through the thousands of get-well cards he received after the smash.

Left Bionic man. After Silverstone it took two plates and 27 screws to piece his legs back together.

A dejected Sheene contemplates his underpowered Suzuki RG500 at the Italian Grand Prix. He knew the best he could hope for was a top ten finish.

Blasting off mid-pack in the 1984 Austrian Grand Prix. Barry finished a credible tenth.

With arch rival Kenny Roberts at the 1984 Transatlantic Match races. Note the lucky Gary Nixon T-shirt.

The Dutch TT at Assen in 1984. Barry was running as high as second at one point before his bike blew up. Haslam (9) and Mamola (3) lead the way. Barry is fourth.

Up yours. Sheene at the 1982 Spanish Grand Prix. He was particularly fond of the V-sign.

World Superbike champion Carl Fogarty. In his autobiography *Foggy*, Carl reflected that 'some of the better riders, such as Phil Read and Giacomo Agostini, were past their best. And the up-and-coming riders, like Virginio Ferrari, were still a bit too young to mount a proper challenge.' Ago and Read were indeed in the twilights of their careers at the time, and Sheene's future nemesis Kenny Roberts had yet to make the trip across the Atlantic to join the European GP circus. But it would be unfair to tarnish Sheene's achievements by pointing to an apparent lack of quality competition. In any race in any discipline – in any sport, moreover – all one can do is beat the opposition. It cannot be denied that the best riders in the world at that time were still in the 500cc class, and Sheene beat them all convincingly.

As far as rivals were concerned in 1976, Sheene rated Venezuelan Johnny Cecotto, the reigning 350cc title holder and the youngest-ever world champion at the time, and Italian Marco Lucchinelli as the men to fear at the beginning of the season, although in the end neither produced a strong challenge for the world crown. In fact, Cecotto's mentor, Andrew Ippolito, withdrew him from the championship mid-season, bizarrely claiming that he was 'too much at risk' because of all the crashing he had done. But Cecotto was there in April for the opening round of the season in France, and as Barry had predicted, it was he who gave him the most serious run for his money after Sheene, armed with a new engine and lightweight frame for his Heron Suzuki GB RG500, made a bad start. Despite the fact that he had qualified on pole, Sheene had asked the race organizers if he could start from the back of the grid with someone to help him push his machine as his legs were aching in the unusually cold French air. Barry's request was denied and he was forced to start from pole position, pushing the bike himself. It took some time and a considerable amount of effort to get the Suzuki fired up, and he found himself down in ninth place after the first lap. Undeterred, Sheene worked his way through the field, and by half distance he was in the lead, a position he still held when the finish line hove into view. *Motocourse* reported that 'Sheene's reception from the crowd was astonishing. The cheers could hardly have been greater if he had been a Frenchman.' Given the state of Anglo-French relations, then as now, it was quite an achievement and a sure indicator of Sheene's international popularity.

Sheene's one-time friend but by now sworn enemy Phil Read led for the first eight laps of the Austrian Grand Prix at the Salzburgring in May before Barry swooped past on the ninth lap, no doubt muttering a few obscenities under his helmet as he did so. Read, no less determined to beat his former friend, managed to sweep back past, but a run of record-breaking laps finally allowed Sheene to regain the lead and hold it through to the chequered flag, which he passed 13.4 seconds ahead of the young Italian rider he had earmarked as a classy rider at the start of the season, Marco Lucchinelli. Sheene had taken maximum points from the first two rounds of the series but was still only eight in front of Lucchinelli as the GP circus moved to the Italian's home track at Mugello in what was the first GP ever to be held on the new circuit.

The meeting was overshadowed by the death of two riders in the smaller-capacity races, but the 500cc event was a classic, the old guard of Agostini and Read showing all their combined years of experience and giving Sheene a hard time. Read caught Ago and Sheene on the sixth lap and the trio swapped positions repeatedly until Ago's Suzuki broke down on lap 14 to leave a straight dogfight (and grudge match) between Sheene and Read. The two fought furiously right to the last corner, where a back-marker very nearly decided the race in Read's favour. Sheene gave it everything he had through that last corner. He allowed Read through on his inside while taking a wider approach, and as a result he got a much faster exit and beat Read over the line by one-tenth of a second. He'd stolen the race by inches and increased his championship lead over Read and Lucchinelli to 23 points. It was a fantastic result for Sheene considering that he'd hated the Mugello circuit from the moment he arrived due to its bumpy surface. But if there was one incentive guaranteed to raise Sheene's game it was the sight of Phil Read in front of him. Still, he paid tribute to the man he had become 'unfriends' with: 'Of all the riders in all the classes I have faced, he [Read] has always been the most difficult one to beat.' Read himself wasn't quite as complimentary in return, believing himself to have been cheated out of his rightful status: 'I was the hero of the meeting and he [Sheene] didn't like it.' Read went on to complain that his wife and Sheene's girlfriend Stephanie 'had a bit of a fight in the hotel afterwards. Stephanie was so bloody rude because I'd taken the limelight from Barry.'

With three wins in a row under his belt, Sheene left the Isle of Man TT to the diehard road race fans and those hoping to earn a few championship points in the absence of most of the top GP riders – riders such as Tom Herron. Herron, who was a fine GP racer before his tragic death in 1979, won the Senior (500cc) TT and hoisted himself up into fifth place in the World Championship standings from a position outside the top 10.

Normal service was resumed in June in Holland where Sheene maintained his unbeaten run of wins despite setting off in 22nd place from a field of 27 riders thanks to his bike not firing up. In fact, it was becoming a rather embarrassing display of dominance: Sheene eventually crossed the finish line a full 45 seconds ahead of his nearest challenger, American Pat Hennen – another rider Barry was to become 'un-friends' with in due course. Once again, Sheene had proved his stamina in extremely hot conditions, a talent that won him many a race in coming years as his rivals wilted; one rider in this particular race ran onto the grass and collapsed from heat exhaustion. The temperature in Holland hovered around the mid-thirties Celsius, and *Motocourse* reported that 'by the end of the day there was not a single bottle of drink available at any point on the circuit, and shrewd farmers in the vicinity were selling glasses of water to parched and weary spectators'.

Sheene could quite easily have had a 100 per cent win ratio during the 1976 GP season had his RG500 Suzuki not suffered fuel starvation problems in the Belgian round, forcing him to splutter across the line in second place. His team-mate John Williams – no lover of Sheene, whom he accused of hogging all the best factory parts, not to mention pay cheques – was set to obey team orders by slowing up to let Barry through, but when he saw that Sheene was nowhere in sight he wisely decided to cross the line before any non-Suzuki rivals got there first. Sheene followed some seven seconds later. Still, by this point the World Championship trophy already had Barry Sheene's name at least half etched onto it, despite the fact that there were still five rounds to go in the 12-round series – a measure of just how dominant Sheene was at his peak. In 1976, riders took points from their six best finishes of the season with 15 points for a win down to one point for 10th place. By July, when the riders assembled in Sweden, all Sheene needed was a decent finish to wrap up the title. Instead, he was hell bent on taking the championship with a win to force home his mastery.

Just before that decisive race of the 1976 season, Sheene effectively saved the life of his team-mate John Williams, even though Williams was to begrudge the fact for the remainder of his tragically short life. During a practice session, Barry was following Williams when the latter crashed. Sheene managed to avoid both bike and rider as they tumbled, and stopped his own bike to assist. He carefully undid Williams' chin strap, cleaned the dirt out of his mouth and freed his tongue to prevent him choking. It was a good job for Williams' sake that he did so as two other bystanders were looking on in ignorance before Sheene took decisive action. Williams, while being grateful for the life-saving assistance, found it galling that he owed his survival to a team-mate he couldn't stand. At the end of the season he stated that he would never ride in the same team as Sheene again, complaining that 'when I signed with Suzuki the deal was for equal opportunities that never came my way'. And he never was a team-mate of Sheene's again.

The Swedish GP was initially led by Scotsman Alex George before New Zealander Stu Avant picked up the gauntlet; he carried it well into the eighth lap when Teuvo (or 'Tepi') Lansivouri, Sheene's closest challenger in the championship at this stage, took over the reins. Then Sheene, who had made a slow start, decided to attack. Barry's plan had been to pounce three laps from the end of the 28-lap race, but when he'd tried a pass earlier just to test Tepi out he realized the Finn was having serious problems with his bike. Sportingly, and with concern for his rival's safety, Sheene checked Tepi's tyres for oil as he rode alongside him and, seeing they were clear, gave him the thumbs up. It was a nice gesture, but unfortunately for Lansivouri the problem was actually a swinging arm fixing bolt which had worked its way out, causing the bike to handle very badly and ruining his charge. With Tepi no longer a threat, Barry romped home a massive 34.18 seconds ahead of second-place man Jack Findlay, who had cashed in on Sheene's 1975 injuries to scoop the European F750 title. Revenge was Sheene's, and Findlay didn't begrudge it a bit. He approached Barry afterwards and told him, 'I'm glad you got it, son. You missed out on the Formula 750 championship last year and gave that to me. Now you've got your reward.'

Sheene was ecstatic. It had taken eight years of hard work and travel, of injury and pain and risk, but he was finally the champion of the world and no one could deny the fact. He had finally acquired the professional credibility to justify the column inches he commanded, which were now set to increase. Playboy he might have been for many a year, envied and adored in equal measure, but he had taken on the best riders in the world and not only beaten them but annihilated them. In his own, very seventies words, Sheene said of his win, 'Out of sight. I stood up on the foot-rests as I went under the flag. I had done it. I had bloody well done it!' Until that point, Sheene had always regarded his first Grand Prix win in Belgium in 1971 as the high point of his career, but his world title easily overshadowed that achievement. To mark it, Sheene's entourage got through 30 bottles of champagne at their evening reception – and at £14 a bottle in 1976, it wasn't just any old plonk.

With the world title in the bag, Sheene could afford to sit out the remaining four rounds of the championship. He offered to attend, but only if his start money was greatly improved. It wasn't, so he stayed away. The absence of the world's biggest biking star at four Grands Prix prompted race officials to make all rounds count in 1977, as opposed to just six, partly as a way of forcing Sheene to attend them. In the meantime, Sheene was kept busy. With the 500cc crown secured, he'd never been so inundated with media requests and well-wishers. Britain had a new world cham-pion, and Barry Sheene was quite happy to talk about it.

When you've won the 500cc Grand Prix World Championship no other title matters, so Sheene wasn't too disappointed to lose out in the Formula 750 series again. But it was through no fault of his own that he didn't wrap up that title, too. The rival Yamahas had somehow found more speed than his Suzuki, and in a bid to make his bike more competitive it was tuned to the point of being unreliable. Sheene had been running in third place during the first round of the series at Daytona when his chain came off. Interestingly, that was the last time he ever raced there, or anywhere else in America, not because of bad memories but because of the (now all too common) American pastime of suing under the most bizarre circumstances. Sheene cited one example he'd heard about: 'A guy came out of a bar, got in his car, and knocked down a motorcyclist who lost both his legs. The bloke who was driving the car was drunk, didn't have a licence, no insurance. So the lawyer sued the bar he'd just been drinking in and got a million dollars.' Another case concerned a woman, a poodle and a microwave. 'She was throwing a dinner party and she washed her poodle. It wasn't dry so she stuck it in the microwave. The thing exploded and she sued the microwave company – and she won the case because it didn't say in the instructions that you mustn't put wet poodles in the microwave. When it gets to that stage, it's bloody ridiculous.' Urban myths aside, albeit ones genuinely indicating a worrying trend, Barry's F750 season went from bad to worse. He had a non-finish in Venezuela, finished third at Imola and retired twice more in Belgium and France before giving up on the series. It was a lost cause, but that didn't really matter. With the *MCN* Superbike and Shellsport 500 crowns on his head as well, it was by far the most successful season of his career.

Sheene being Sheene, he naturally sought to maximize the bargaining potential his new position as world champion conferred. Despite having won the world title on a Suzuki, it was by no means certain that he would sign up with the firm again to defend it, or at least that's what he wanted Suzuki to think. His Japanese employers saw Sheene as the number one rider at Suzuki, with John Williams and John Newbold acting only as a kind of support act, but Sheene was sick of the bitter in-team fighting and back-stabbing. He eventually came up with an ultimatum: either team manager Merv Wright (a supporter of the two Johns) left or he would go. Unsurprisingly, it was Wright who got his marching orders. His parting shot, as reported by *Motor Cycle Weekly*, was that results might have been 'very different' in 1976 had Williams and Newbold been given machinery equal to Sheene's.

But however good Williams and Newbold were as riders, they certainly couldn't touch Sheene for marketability and popularity, and that just happened to be another bee in Barry's bonnet: he didn't feel that Suzuki were willing enough to cash in on his promotional value, as proved by the fact that the Japanese company wanted to deduct the cost of 100 T-shirts (a total of £100) Barry had given away as promotional items to spread his (and Suzuki's) name. In an age of endless promotional materials it now appears an absurdly mean and short-sighted gesture, and it certainly proves how far ahead of his time Sheene was when it came to marketing.

In the midst of the negotiations with Suzuki, there was even talk of Sheene setting up his own private Suzuki team with backing from his close friend Lord Hesketh. There also existed the possibility of running Yamahas in his own set-up, but in the end Barry agreed to ride Suzuki's new RGA500 machine for an undisclosed, though no doubt very healthy, fee. He was ready to defend his title.

Well, nearly ready. First, the 18-inch pin from his Daytona smash had to be removed, then he had to star in another major documentary to appease his adoring public, then there were TV ads with Henry Cooper to film, and there was also a three-week holiday to be enjoyed on Treasure Cay in the Abaco Islands. Only after that was it time to go racing again.

Barry Sheene declined to exercise the world champion's right to wear the number one plate on his bike in 1977, preferring instead to stick with his lucky number seven. As a measure of how rare it is to decline the honour that is every bike racer's dream, no one else did so until 2002 when reigning 500cc world champion Valentino Rossi opted to keep his favoured 46.

Sheene kicked off the Queen's Silver Jubilee year in March by celebrating a first-round victory in the sweltering 90-degree heat of Venezuela, and in true Sheene style too: he came from the back of the grid to storm to victory by 1.3 seconds over new American hotshot Steve Baker and his new team-mate, soon to become team-hate, Pat Hennen, who in 1976 had become the first American rider to win a 500cc Grand Prix. Both were extremely promising riders, but Hennen's potential was never to be realized. Unlike Sheene, he did choose to compete in the Isle of Man TT, and suffered severe head injuries there in 1978 after a

170mph crash which put an end to his career and very nearly his life.

The second round of the championship was scheduled to take place at the Salzburgring in Austria, but the meeting ended in chaos and sadness with all the top riders refusing to race over safety concerns. A multiple pile-up during the 350cc race had resulted in the death of Swiss rider Hans Stadelmann and left three other riders seriously injured. Of the top 10 finishers in 1977, only Australian Jack Findlay raced in the 500cc event, and in the absence of any worthy competition he won the race. Sheene was issued with a fine for being a 'ringleader' of the walkout, but it was never paid. After all, he was only trying to ensure that no one else got killed.

The next three rounds of the championship were happier for Sheene as he cleaned up in West Germany, Italy and France. Barry might not have been happy with Pat Hennen as a team-mate, but he was jubilant over the choice of a third Texaco Suzuki team member – his old mate Steve 'Stavros' Parrish. With these two buddies and renowned pranksters travelling the world together as team-mates, 1977 looked like being a non-stop giggle. Stavros justified his position in the team at Hockenheim by giving Sheene a hard time in the early stages of the race before eventually finishing fourth.

Sheene and Parrish's antics over the years became the stuff of legend. According to an article in *MCN*, Parrish once donned Barry's leathers and helmet and went out to qualify for Sheene on his behalf because Sheene himself was too hung over to ride. The same article described how

Parrish once bedded a girl by telling her that he was Barry Sheene, and it went on to detail the time when the duo squirted some mayonnaise into a condom and placed it inside team manager Rex White's sandwich, with predictable results. The hapless White again fell victim to the comedy duo when they became bored on a ferry crossing. They tied a rope to White's door and attached the other end to the door on the opposite side of the corridor. After knocking on both doors, Parrish and Sheene withdrew to watch the mayhem from a safe distance. Every time one man tried to open his door, he pulled the opposite door shut just as the occupant of that room was trying to open it. Even when things got dangerous the two found reasons to laugh. In his *Bike* magazine column, Sheene related the story of how a tyre blew out on his Rolls Royce at 120mph while Parrish was a passenger. 'This thing was on the verge of flipping end over end and Stavros had his feet on the roof screaming, "For fuck's sake, we're gonna die!" It came back down and went from one side of the autobahn to the other. Basically, I pulled it up and we broke out into hysterical laughter, then sat on the side of the autobahn and had a cigarette before we got out to put a new tyre on.'

Barry's dominance of the 1977 GP season continued in May in Italy where he won again, despite being hampered by another bad start which saw him languishing down in 14th place on the first lap. For the French Grand Prix at Paul Ricard a few weeks later, Sheene was equipped with the ultimate paddock pose: his very own Beatle. George Harrison joined the Sheene camp as a friend of both Sheene and Parrish, whom he actually sponsored the following season. For once, Sheene made a good start in front of the 100,000-strong crowd, but finding a way past Steve Baker proved difficult until the American's bike started to slide badly because of fuel leaking on to his rear tyre. When he was forced to ease the pace, Sheene accepted his invitation to lead and eventually finished three seconds clear of a hard-charging Agostini, who had ridden magnificently after being last off the grid. With his expected main challenger for the title, Cecotto, still sidelined as a result of injuries sustained in Austria, Sheene's championship defence was looking good.

Barry was beaten for the first time that GP season in June at Assen by local hero Wil Hartog, who rode the tricky damp-but-drying conditions superbly and kicked off a Dutch party that lasted for days. Sheene claimed his Suzuki's wheels were out of line, a set-up error that caused his bike to handle badly, but he was happy enough with a second place which increased his championship lead to 26 points. Sheene was plagued by another stroke of ill fortune during the following race in Belgium when a hornet got inside his leathers during practice and decided to unleash its sting. The antibiotics prescribed by the track doctor made Barry's throttle hand swell up badly, but despite this difficulty he won his fifth Grand Prix of the season by some 11 seconds from Steve Baker. To this day there has never been a faster lap on any circuit anywhere in the world than Sheene's final lap in Belgium that year, clocked at an average of 135.067mph. The record is likely to stand for ever, as Grand Prix circuits are increasingly made 'slower' by the strategic placing of chicanes. Indeed, the

Spa-Francorchamps circuit where Sheene set his record lap was modified just two years later. The only average lap speed that even approaches Sheene's figure was recorded during the Isle of Man TT at just over 127mph. For Sheene, however, at least at the time, it was all academic: 'I didn't care I was going faster than anyone had ever gone,' he claimed, 'I was just glad to be winning,' although he admitted in *Bike* magazine in 2002 that he was quite proud of the achievement and that it was 'nice to go down in the record books for it'.

In July, Barry once again displayed his concern for the well-being of his fellow riders during practice for the Swedish GP. When Czechoslovakian racer Philippe Coulon crashed out of the session, Sheene and another two riders stopped their bikes to rush to his aid. For a time Coulon's life hung in the balance, but he eventually made a full recovery. Sheene's compassion lost him a lot of practice time, but his priority had always been safety. He finally posted a lap quick enough to put him on pole position anyway – a just result after his selfless action. Victory in the race by a newly fit Johnny Cecotto left Sheene needing just a sixth place in the Finnish GP to retain his world title.

At Imatra, Barry could now smugly enjoy the luxury afforded by the modern toilet and shower facilities, as well as being able to take full credit for their existence. The Imatra toilet-block story is one of the most enduring Sheene legends and is worth relating here. By all accounts the toilets there were extremely primitive and unhygienic in 1976 so Sheene and some fellow riders hatched a plot to blow them up, thereby forcing the circuit owners to build a new block. After pouring 10 gallons of high-octane fuel down the offending U-bends, Sheene's co-conspirators lost their bottle and refused to finish the job. 'It was left to me to strike the match,' Sheene confessed. 'The bogs went up with a deafening bang and the whole lot went skyways, finishing in the adjoining lake. We had previously put a car and caravan across the entrance gates to the paddock to stop the fire engine from getting through to put out the flames. It wasn't necessary – there was nothing left to save.' Suzuki GB team manager Rex White later pointed out the seriousness of the offence in the eyes of the Finnish authorities. 'There was a bit of a hue and cry about it because they're very susceptible to forest fires up there [and] they were seriously after the person who had caused the explosion.' Sheene added that 'it was a federal offence punishable by 30 years in jail', though as the GP circus was leaving the country immediately after the race there seemed little point in pursuing the matter.

So Barry had a double reason to celebrate at the 1977 Finnish GP: he had his clean and modern toilets to enjoy and another world title for good measure. Sixth place was exactly where he finished after his Suzuki overheated and used up every last drop of water in the radiator. One place further down the field and the battle would have moved on to Brno in Czechoslovakia, but as it was, Barry had done enough to retain his title with 107 points to Steve Baker's 80. Although he didn't need to race in the remaining two rounds, he couldn't resist competing at Silverstone that August in the first British Grand Prix to be held away from the dangers of the Isle of Man TT course.

Sheene turned up at the super-fast airfield circuit as the new world champion, ready to show his adoring home public what he could do on a motorcycle. But both he and his public were to be gravely disappointed. His factory Suzuki blew so many head gaskets in practice that Sheene decided on a drastic course of action: he borrowed Steve Parrish's standard-production machine in a bid to post a decent qualifying lap. Demonstrating not only how skilful he was on any bike he rode, but also how good the production Suzukis were by that time, Sheene set pole position on Parrish's bike but made the mistake of starting the race on his factory machine. Somewhat predictably, it blew its head gasket again. Sheene, in a moment of fury, blew his own gasket and rode the bike straight into his garage wall, bending the forks so badly that Suzuki was forced to give him a new bike – yet another example of unorthodox but ultimately successful tactics.

The Silverstone race did have a lighter side, although Parrish probably didn't find it all that funny at the time. After his bike packed up, Sheene took it upon himself to signal for Parrish, who was leading the race going into the last lap. 'As I came past the pit wall,' Parrish recalled, 'I saw Barry holding up a board which said "Gas it, wanker". So I did, and I crashed a few corners later.'

It had been another good year on the home front for Sheene as he once again scooped the *MCN* Superbike and Shellsport 500 titles as well as the *MCN* Man of the Year award for a fourth time. His second world title made him more popular than ever with the mainstream public, but to counterbalance this there was a growing army of Sheenehaters. Not everyone, it seemed, liked their racers to be rich and famous with model girlfriends and rock-star buddies. Double world champion or not, Sheene was about to experience an altogether more unpleasant side to his adoring British public.

CHAPTER 6

THE GREAT DIVIDE

*'They wanted me to kill myself. One person said
it was a pity I didn't crash.'*

The British are particularly good at, and seemingly fond of,
building up heroes only to become quickly bored with their
success and to start knocking them down again. Actors,
singers, sportsmen, TV presenters – no one in the public
eye is immune from this peculiar phenomenon, and Barry
Sheene was no exception. As he explained to Michael
Parkinson, 'It's a funny thing, but there seems to be a tradition in England that they build up the underdog. They did
it with me. They said Sheene was going to win the World
Championship one day, and then I did, and then I won it
again. I won a lot of other races too, then people started to
say, "It's a bit boring this bloke Barry Sheene winning all
the races."'

There were always those involved in racing who were
jealous of the fact that Barry had had factory Bultacos and
one of the best two-stroke tuners in the business (his dad)
working for him from the outset, but generally speaking he

was popular with race-goers and most fellow racers, particularly for the guts he showed in bouncing back from his massive Daytona crash. But after two world titles and years of blanket media coverage, there was a growing faction who had become thoroughly sick of the Sheene publicity machine.

Before Barry Sheene came along, motorcycle racing in Britain had a pretty grubby image, all black leathers, oil and grease, and it has to be said the image was fairly well justified: it *was* all black leathers, oil and grease. 'The whole image of motorcycling is out of date,' Sheene told the *Daily Mail* in 1973. 'The public still associate it with a man with dirty fingernails and shapeless black leathers tearing away from the Busy Bee café to beat up an old widow in Southend. It isn't like that – we're quite civilized really.' The more forward-thinking supporters of the sport agreed with Sheene and appreciated the need for a change of image, but not everyone felt the same way, especially those who resented Sheene's playboy image and wanton display of riches, and therefore his views. As far as members of the old regime were concerned, bikers were supposed to arrive at race meetings on bikes, not in helicopters, and they certainly weren't interested in wearing Brut 33 or looking at half-naked pictures of him in the *Sun*.

Nowhere was this anti-Sheene feeling demonstrated more openly than at Oliver's Mount in Scarborough where tough northern bikers felt unable to abide the 'southern softie' Sheene perhaps more than at any other track in the UK. The chosen champion of those race fans was down-to-earth Yorkshireman Mick Grant, who by 1977 had already won two Grands Prix in the 250cc class and racked up three TT wins out of an eventual career total of seven. Sporting a moustache and speaking with a thick Yorkshire accent, Grant was the complete antithesis of Sheene, and his fans loved him for it. There was nothing they liked to see more than one of their own beating the (to them) over-paid and overrated Londoner.

Given his hatred of the Isle of Man TT course, it has always been a matter of some conjecture why Sheene continued to race on a circuit like Oliver's Mount. At 2.41 miles long, the track is set on a hillside overlooking the seaside town. It has absolutely no run-off areas and is lined with trees along its entire length. Worse still, the bottom section of the course is extremely undulating with trees and bankings on one side and a virtually sheer drop of several hundred feet on the other. It is not a place for the faint-hearted, yet Sheene competed there until the end of his career in 1984. Part of the reason might have been the fact that the Oliver's Mount course is considerably shorter than the TT, and therefore Sheene knew it well enough to be able to avoid most of its dangers. Mick Grant explained the incentive to race at Scarborough and also revealed how he and Sheene managed to keep the risks to a minimum. 'Scarborough always paid very well in appearance money, and although we never fixed or threw a race, we used to make a deal to put on a good show then go for it three laps from the end. It just made sense on the more dangerous circuits to do that. The good thing about Barry was that he was very trustworthy, so if we did a deal, we did a deal.' The other motivating factor that Sheene did not hide was his friendship with circuit owner Peter Hillaby, which ensured repeated returns to the track to participate in demonstration laps long after his retirement.

Sheene brought up the subject of racing at Scarborough in his regular column for *Motorcycle Racing* in 1981. 'I will ride where I want to ride,' he wrote, 'so I go to Scarborough but I don't race at the TT. After 12 years as a regular there I reckon I ought to know whether I like it or not.' He might well have enjoyed the track, but Sheene was surprised by the extreme ill will held by some of the spectators. On one occasion when his bike broke down at Scarborough, he was booed and taunted with obscenities from behind the fences. Sheene told the *Northern Daily Mail*, 'They wanted me to kill myself. One person said it was a pity I didn't crash.' Verbal taunts are one thing, and unpleasant enough, but physical and potentially lethal abuse is another. At an Oliver's Mount meeting in 1977, some spectators started to jab sticks through the picket fencing that lines most of the circuit as Sheene rode past; others threw beer cans at him. Mick Grant was not proud of the fact and tried his best to calm things down, even going so far as to act as a bodyguard for his rival. 'At that time in Britain you were either a Sheene fan or a Grant fan. I remember one year when Barry won at Scarborough I actually went round in the car with him on his victory lap so that the spectators wouldn't throw things at him.' Sheene responded to his detractors in *Leader of the Pack*: 'People like this would seem more at home at a football match. Not only were their antics offensive, dangerous and clearly designed to slow me down or to frighten me, but they attracted the type of publicity racing could well do without.' He added, 'Maybe because I didn't sport a tattoo, wear an ear-ring in my left lobe or drink brown ale, I did not qualify, in some bikers' estimation, as a suitable standard-bearer for the motorcycling fraternity. But I don't conform to a pattern. I'm Barry Sheene – an individual who likes to do things in his own special way.' Surely even Sheene's most enthusiastic knockers couldn't deny that last fact.

The subject was brought up by Michael Parkinson during his interview with Sheene. 'Aren't there traditionalists within the sport who see you appearing in advertisements and gossip columns and don't approve?' he asked. Sheene's reply was philosophical: 'Whatever you do, you can't please everyone. As long as you please the majority then I am happy.' In truth, Sheene usually did have the majority on his side as far as sheer numbers went across the world, but it wasn't always the case at race meetings where only diehard race fanatics attended rather than the hordes who had a passing interest in Sheene the pin-up. Things only got worse when he raced 'up north' against more down-to-earth local heroes. Grant believed a lot of the anti-Sheene feeling could be put down to Barry's outspokenness. 'Barry was a bit like Carl Fogarty in that he said what he thought, and sometimes, you know, he opened his mouth before engaging his brain, but that's the way the guy was, although I think Barry was a bit more subtle than that. But he was outspoken, and I didn't tend to be. But the thing is, if you've got a fairly strong verbal side a lot of people accuse you of being big-headed, and obviously you could never accuse Barry of being short of confidence. But that was the guy, and it certainly never did the sport any harm, that's for sure.'

Without question, Sheene was always supremely confident, but as he matured he lost much of the arrogant big-headedness that had been an irritating feature of his make-up as a younger rider – thanks, perhaps, in part to a dressing-down he received from his mechanic Don Mackay in 1970. During a long trip back from Finland, Mackay confronted Sheene on the issue. 'When he realized he was good, he started to get big-headed,' Mackay explained. 'He used to tell everybody how good he was, and how many birds he'd had.' The argument got so heated in the confines of the van that when the pair got back to London Mackay walked away and didn't return for a year.

Another issue that rankled with some fans was the size of Sheene's appearance fees. Spectators at Oulton Park in Cheshire once presented Sheene with a rather sinister image when they hung an effigy of him from a hangman's noose by the side of the track. Incensed by the amount of money Sheene was being paid to ride, certain members of the crowd also painted 'Sheene – rip-off' slogans around the track. It's difficult to say how much these incidents affected Sheene, but as usual he put a brave face on it, even going to the extent of framing a picture of a spectator wearing a T-shirt proclaiming 'Sheene is a Wanker' and hanging it on his office wall at the Manor House in Charlwood. 'If he knew I had the picture specially framed and had given it pride of place in my home, I'm sure he would be devastated,' Barry said. 'The greatest satisfaction for someone trying to break you down mentally comes from letting him know he has pierced your defences. That bloke didn't affect me, and nor will anyone else intending to hurt me because of his jealousy.' Even so, it is hard to imagine Sheene, who went to such meticulous lengths to cultivate his public image, not being worried in some way by such public signs of disapproval.

After 1977, the British bike press began to receive and print more and more anti-Sheene letters as readers wrote in to voice their opinions on the double world champion. Some accused him of demanding too much money, others complained that he wasn't prepared to sign autographs, yet others disapproved of his outspokenness. All this dissatisfaction registered with Sheene. 'Some of the spectators were beginning to resent my continuing run of success,' he said, 'and it was never a surprise to find the occasional letter from a race fan in *Motor Cycle News* and *Motor Cycle Weekly* complaining about a selection of deficits in my character, from asking too much money to not wanting to devote time to the followers – something which was emphatically untrue.'

Ron Haslam, not through choice, became another of the chosen champions for the anti-Sheene brigade because of his down-to-earth style and less polished appearance. 'The anti-Sheene crowd got behind me or Mick Grant or Joey Dunlop because I think they could relate to us more. They could look at us and think, "That could be me, that could." But they couldn't imagine being Sheene because they didn't have all the money and glamour that he had. There was also the normal thing of people wanting to support the underdog because Sheene had been winning so much. But I never saw any violent anti-Sheene stuff like throwing beer cans or anything.' Haslam recalled Sheene's 'other-worldly' quality compared to everyone else in the paddock, a feeling he suspected others shared. 'Ever since I've known Barry he's had the flash cars and lots of girls lifestyle. He loved being a superstar and going to night-clubs and stuff whereas I just stayed in the paddock or went home after a race. I never approached him because he always seemed so different to me. It was like, "That's Sheene from down in London. He's different from us." I think a lot of other riders felt like that. They always felt he had plenty of money behind him and that he had an advantage over them. But I never thought it was an unfair advantage; I would gladly have accepted any advantage I could have got, and so would the others. I never got jeal-ous. I didn't spend any time socially with Sheene. We were at the rough end of the paddock sleeping in a transit van so we didn't see much of him. I think we were a bit too down-market. He was never a snob, though; whenever I did speak to him in the paddock he was marvellous. We just led different lives, and he definitely had a bit of an aura about him. He was a superstar.'

Despite the fact that he was so different from Sheene, Haslam never had any personal run-ins with Barry, and neither did Mick Grant, but there were plenty of other riders who did. His most famous rival was undoubtedly American racer Kenny Roberts, of whom more later, but plenty of others were prepared to go on the record about their dislike of the most famous bike racer on earth and his annoying habit of securing all the best deals, in terms of both money and specialized motorcycle parts. Unsurprisingly, most of the complaints came from team-mates who felt Sheene was receiving preferential treatment. Sadly, many of his partners from the halcyon Suzuki days are no longer with us and cannot tell their side of the story. John Williams, Tom Herron and John Newbold, for example, lost their lives racing at the North West 200 in Northern Ireland in 1978, 1979 and 1982 respectively. Pat Hennen sustained career-ending head injuries at the TT in 1978. It is a grim toll, one which justifies Sheene's measured decision not to race on pure road circuits, Oliver's Mount notwithstanding. Barry was, of course, still popular with a large number of riders. Even close rivals over the years such as Angel Nieto, Paul Smart, Johnny Cecotto, Steve Parrish, Gary Nixon and Marco Lucchinelli were great friends. But Barry being Barry, you either loved him or you hated him, and there was no shortage of riders on the other side of the fence.

Eight-times world champion (if you include his one-round Formula One TT title from 1977, as he does) Phil Read had known Sheene since he was a child, having raced some of Frank Sheene's bikes in the sixties. The two were chummy enough for many years until, as Sheene so delicately put it in Michael Scott's book *Barry Sheene: A Will to Win*, they became 'un-friends' in 1975 over a disagreement during a 500cc world championship race. According to Scott, Sheene says Read asked him if during the race he would let Read through, should such a position arise, in order that he could take the world championship ahead of Giacomo Agostini. Sheene was deeply offended and went out determined to win the race, which he did. Not only does Read dispute the race in question – claiming it was the Finnish Grand Prix as opposed to the earlier Swedish Grand Prix from Sheene's account – he maintains that he simply asked Barry 'as a mate' if he would help him out and was gravely offended when Sheene refused his request.

The animosity between Sheene and Read can be traced back at least as far as 1971 when Read agreed to take Barry's bike to the Spanish Grand Prix in his van while Barry flew out there, only to find that Barry hadn't bothered to reserve a place in his workshop for him. Instead, Sheene had allowed another 250cc rider to share his space. Read was furious. 'He managed to get himself a workshop while I was left with the choice of the dust of the paddock or a hacienda some way from the track. I told him to get someone else to take his bike back to Britain.'

The two did, however, patch things up, and by the time the 1974 season came round they were good friends again. Read even used his influence at MV Agusta to try to get Barry signed up as a rider, though Sheene declined the offer. Then Read began to suspect that Sheene had had an affair with his wife Madeleine. Sheene eventually admitted to it in the *News of the World*, adding, as a final insult, that Madeleine hadn't been very good 'at it'. Sadly, Madeleine Read later took her own life, as Don Morley remembered only too well. 'She rang me up and said she was going to kill herself, so my wife and I rushed over to her house straight away, but we were too late.'

Pat Hennen was another rival who didn't quite fall for Sheene's cheeky cockney charms. Pat's first crime, as far as

Sheene saw it, was to accept the Suzuki GB ride for very little money – a move Sheene thought undermined the professionalism of the sport. In his *Motorcycle Racing* column, Barry famously said of Hennen, 'If you pay peanuts, you get a monkey.' Another grudge match had begun.

Hennen was anything but a monkey. He was the first American rider to come to Europe with a dirt-bike background and was therefore the first exponent of the wild-sliding riding style that was to become the norm over the next two decades. Sheene claimed Hennen was dangerous, but he must have recognized him as the genuine threat he was to his own fast-becoming-outdated European riding style, which put more emphasis on corner entry and mid-corner speed than on corner exit speed. The Americans would soon head for Europe in their hordes and would concentrate on riding off the edges of their tyres as they slid and spun their way out of corners before the Europeans had even opened the throttle. It was a devastatingly effective technique that would net American riders 13 world titles between 1978 and 1993.

Sheene's psychological battle with Hennen went beyond snide remarks in the press; he would also leave misleading set-up information about his bike lying around for Hennen to find, hoping he would try to copy it and therefore set off at a disadvantage. There's no evidence as to whether or not Pat fell for this, and by all accounts he was too smart to be taken in in such a way, but it is an indication of how much of a threat Sheene thought the American was. Relations between the two sometimes got so bad that Steve Parrish had to act as a buffer between his feuding team-mates, trying to keep up a respectable team appearance. 'There was quite a bit of aggro between Pat and Barry,' Parrish admitted. 'I'd be the one to park my van between their motorhomes to make it look like a team.'

Hennen's brother Chip was also his manager during Pat's GP years from 1976 through to 1978. He recalled how the in-team rivalry started. 'Off the track Barry and Pat got on pretty well, but Pat was a threat to Barry almost from the get-go, and because he was an American with a background in dirt track I think Barry saw Pat as potentially another Kenny Roberts. I think the 1976 Mallory Park Race of the Year was the first time Barry really started seeing Pat as a serious threat. Pat was still a privateer, so Barry had superior everything, but the following year he became Barry's team-mate although we pretty much kept things separate that year. Barry's bikes and mechanics went in his own truck and we used the factory truck which carried all the spare parts and stuff.

'Our relations with Barry started to deteriorate pretty badly [after] an incident which happened during qualifying at the 1977 Austrian Grand Prix. Barry leaned on Pat very hard and nearly took him down. Afterwards, Barry came over to Pat and apologized, and Pat took him into the motorhome and talked privately. Their attitude towards each other changed from that point on. We used to keep a blacklist of riders that we knew we had to look out for so if Pat found himself out on track with those guys he'd know to be extra careful. After that incident Barry was on the blacklist.'

How serious a rival Hennen might have eventually

become we will never know. He was certainly beating Sheene regularly at the end of 1977 and during the first half of 1978, but his tragic accident in the middle of that year, which put him in a coma for three months, brought everything to a premature end. Hennen, now 49, lives in San Mateo, California, and has almost completely recovered from his injuries.

Ron Haslam recalled that Sheene wasn't always charitable when it came to homegrown riders he considered a threat either. 'Barry was a bit jealous of other Brits getting into Grands Prix. Heron Suzuki offered me a ride on one of Sheene's 500cc Grand Prix bikes at Oulton Park – I think it was in 1975 – but when Sheene found out he said he wouldn't race if I was given a bike. Suzuki didn't like that attitude and gave me the bike anyway, but I crashed after three laps and broke my wrist so it was never a problem. It was actually a brake problem that caused me to crash, but I never said that because I wanted to keep in with Suzuki. When I started riding for Honda in GPs in 1983, the tables were turned because I had the factory bike and Sheene had a lesser bike. He was struggling to get into the top 10 at that point and wasn't really a threat to me any more.' Chip Hennen also noted the more ruthless side to Barry when it came to racing. 'When Barry got on a race track a switch would throw and it became an extremely serious sport for him. He became a businessman. His attitude changed, everything about him seemed to change. A lot of the Europeans were the same, and we weren't used to that, coming from the US. It was more about fun over there.'

Even away from the track Sheene could bare his teeth at anyone he sensed was getting in his way, as Don Morley recollected. 'Barry did actually become very difficult to deal with. I wrote an article about the rising American riders like Kenny Roberts and Pat Hennen and said that Barry would have to watch out because these guys were good. Barry took great exception to that piece and he instantly tried to get Suzuki to sack me from my PR job. He even got on to Richard Poulter of *Motocourse* and said he wouldn't have his picture in *Motocourse* unless I was sacked as chief photographer. That really surprised me. I was definitely *persona non grata* in Barry's eyes, despite the fact that I lived just five minutes from his mansion in Charlwood. His public persona always remained the same, but Barry became a very changed person with fame and there were all sorts of behind-the-scenes tantrums. We never really smoothed things over until the late nineties when Sheene phoned me at five o'clock in the morning. I asked if he was in Australia and he said no, he'd just flown into Gatwick and was now on my front lawn. And he meant it quite literally. Instead of driving round my drive-way he had driven his hired Mercedes straight onto my front lawn. We had a coffee and a good old chat and Barry asked for some pictures for a poster Shell was making in Australia. He was adamant the shots had to be on a Yamaha though, because he never forgave Suzuki for not giving him better bikes. Anyway, at one point he said, "When I look back, all the good pictures are yours." That was his way of burying the hatchet, which I thought was rather nice.'

But of all the rivalries Sheene had, there was one that stood head and shoulders above the rest, and it involved a certain young American rider called Kenny Roberts. Roberts was born in Modesto, California, in 1951 and he proved to be Barry Sheene's undoing. Not as far as his popularity was concerned – Barry proved to be more than adept at maintaining, and in fact increasing, his public profile no matter what he chose to do – but certainly as far as his racing career went. Once Roberts appeared on the GP scene in 1978, Sheene never won another World Championship.

Roberts was a well-established dirt-track racer in the USA having already won two AMA Grand National titles (held on dirt and tarmac) in 1973 and 1974 for Yamaha, but when the Japanese firm decided it could no longer match the pace of the all-conquering Harley-Davidsons on the US ovals, they offered their man a chance at Grand Prix racing. He would have one bike, one truck, a two-man team, and that was it. The mission? To dethrone Barry Sheene as the greatest motorcycle racer in the world. As Roberts told journalist John Brown in 1979, 'One thing is for certain, if it wasn't for Barry Sheene I would still be racing in America. There's no other reason why I should want to win the 500cc world title except to beat Barry Sheene, because he's made it what it is.' In a final statement which speaks volumes about the rivalry between the pair, Roberts added, 'I made a little money in 1978 but it didn't compensate for what I put out in effort. Yeah, the only reason I did the World Championship was Barry Sheene.'

Roberts might not have made much money in 1978 and

he might not have had much of a glitzy team set-up, but he did have one secret weapon that was to prove both invaluable and invincible: his riding style. Having muscled torquey, heavy, twin-cylinder, four-stroke machines around shale and shingle tracks back home in the States, Kenny lost no time in transferring that dirt-track style to road-racing machines. His ability to get on the power early as he exited corners, regardless of how much his bike bucked and weaved in the process, became legendary. It also brought him three consecutive world titles.

Roberts had made his British road-racing debut as far back as 1974 in the Transatlantic Match Races, an annual series that, as its name suggests, pitted the best American riders against the best Britain had to offer. Over the next few years he beat Sheene on many occasions in the UK, but as long as he stayed away from the World Championship Sheene wasn't overly concerned. Even when he did sign up for a full season of GPs in 1978, no one really thought Kenny would be able to sustain a season-long challenge. After all, he was a foreigner in strange lands, and Americans had traditionally needed time to readjust to European ways. His team was minimal and he was the only rider running on unproven Goodyear tyres. On top of that, Kenny was unfamiliar with most of the circuits he'd be racing on. So, on the surface at least, Kenny Roberts didn't appear to be much of a threat to Barry's campaign for a third straight title.

But as soon as Roberts began to prove that he was a serious threat, the off-track rivalry with Sheene snowballed. This time round Sheene had met his match when it came to one-liners and put-downs: Roberts was every bit as sharp with off-the-cuff remarks and every bit as cocky with them, although his delivery was much more deadpan than Barry's. The press had a field day, and who could blame them when Sheene came out with such jewels as 'Kenny Roberts couldn't develop a cold, let alone a motorcycle' while Roberts' comeback was 'If I'm so bad and I'm beating him, what does that make him?' It was all part of the psychological warfare that accounts for so much of a motorcycle racer's make-up. Don Morley recalled a specific example of Roberts' cunning. 'Kenny was a master at out-psyching his rivals. I remember once at a riders' meeting when Barry thought he was on for a surefire win at whatever track they were at and Kenny started on about a slippery patch of new tarmac at a particular corner. I saw just a flicker of doubt in Barry's eye as he pretended he had noted it too. But it was just Kenny trying to unsettle his rivals.'

Sheene took every opportunity to unsettle the American, too. In *Leader of the Pack* he repeatedly attempted to undermine Roberts' technical knowledge while acknowledging that he was a very good rider. 'Although he may be an absolutely brilliant rider, Kenny's knowledge of how to set up a racing bike is limited to say the least. Like hundreds of other riders today, he can detect something alarmingly wrong with a bike after a few laps. But to pinpoint the problem accurately, and to suggest possible remedies to his mechanics, is beyond him.' Short of hanging around Roberts' garage or working for him as a mechanic, it is difficult to imagine how Sheene could have formed these opinions. How could he possibly have known what Kenny was telling his team after every test session? The most likely answer is that he didn't; he simply based his views on how the Yamahas Roberts had developed felt to him when he finally got to ride them. But what works for one rider rarely works for another, so it wasn't the most accurate way to make a judgement. Still, no one could dispute that Sheene was on strong ground when it came to discussing the technical aspects of motor racing, as his former mechanic Simon Tonge testified: 'He had a good understanding of engineering and would really think about setting a bike up. He had a really good feel for it, and I think that showed in his wet-weather riding. He was, first and foremost, a very good rider. I mean, some people say riders back then weren't as good as riders now, but for his time he was a fantastic rider. Even in 1984 on an uncompetitive bike he showed he was a really good rider.'

Most people remember the Sheene/Roberts battles as Suzuki/Yamaha battles, which indeed they were in the seventies, but the duo were effectively team-mates for three years from 1980 to 1982 as they both rode Yamahas, albeit very different ones for the most part. Roberts was Yamaha's favoured son and was always supplied with the very latest factory tackle, whereas the Yamahas Sheene initially rode were standard-production bikes; only later was he given upgraded equipment.

But while their rivalry was so intense that it led Roberts to proclaim that the only reason he got out of bed each day was to beat Barry Sheene, the two had immense respect for each other as riders, and in actual fact they didn't hate each other at all, as both admitted in later years. In an interview for *Motor Cycle News* in the year 2000, Sheene told me that he'd actually got on with Kenny quite well and that the whole hatred thing was just hype. It was good for racing, good for the press and great fun for the fans. He also confessed, despite his many quips to the contrary, that as a rider he'd thought Roberts 'brilliant, no two ways about it. You know, a really good, fair rider who would never ever cut me up and would always give me plenty of room, and I'd always give him plenty of room.' For his part, Roberts stated in a 1993 TV interview that he'd enjoyed his battles with Sheene, on and off the track. 'A lot of the hype in the press was with Barry because of a few reasons. One of them was that Barry was English, and I could read the English press so I think that made him more of a rival for a lot of different reasons other than his [riding] ability, which was good. And I think his style, his flamboyancy, the way he used to shoot his mouth off was all a part of it, and I enjoyed racing with Sheene, obviously. I even enjoyed the off-race-track routine. Sometimes it wasn't fun at the time, but now I look back on it, it's like, hey, that's racing.'

Randy Mamola was perfectly placed to observe the relative skills of both riders, as he was usually mixed up between the two of them on the factory Suzuki Sheene had vacated in 1979. When asked recently whom he thought the better rider, Mamola replied that he slightly favoured Kenny. 'I think in terms of diversity Kenny had more of an uphill battle than Barry, in terms of having to learn race tracks, machinery and so on. Kenny did that very quickly and was a very determined racer. Being an American I might have taken Kenny Roberts' side more than Barry's, but looking back I realize Barry wasn't the bad guy he was made out to be in the press. I knew Kenny's side and he wasn't a bad guy either. The press were just playing up to all that rivalry stuff.' Unsurprisingly, as Sheene's best friend, Steve Parrish plumped for Barry when I asked him the same question, 'not just because of his riding but because of his ability to blag parts and get the right bikes because of his contacts. And he's a mate!'

Mamola, now a pit-lane reporter for Eurosport, has fond memories of the years when he raced against Sheene and Roberts. 'Looking at the era back then, it was one of the best rivalries and one of the best eras to come through. I came over to Europe in 1979 and was running in the 250cc and 350cc classes, then I got the chance to ride an RG500 Suzuki, a private bike for a Belgian team, and I rode the last eight races. One of my fondest memories is of a race between Kenny, Barry and myself at Le Mans for the French Grand Prix. Barry won the race, I was second and Kenny was third. I have a wonderful picture of me going down the main straight pinching Barry's backside!'

Sheene's on-track rivalries were over by the mid-eighties – he did not make any enemies during his classic racing career – but even after retirement from the sport he retained an uncanny knack of courting controversy with other riders, as he proved with his much-publicized bust-up with four times World Superbike champion Carl Fogarty, often referred to as Britain's most popular motor-cyclist since Sheene himself. In typically straight-talking fashion, Carl undermined Sheene's achievements in his autobiography *Foggy*, which was released in the year 2000. His opening shot was a claim to be 'a far better rider than Sheene ever was', but he went on to say that Sheene 'was only famous because he had set out to make himself famous' and that 'one of the main reasons he had the success he did was because his bikes were better than the rest'.

It was exactly the sort of bait guaranteed to provoke a response from Sheene, who if anything had been even more outspoken than Fogarty over the years (and Fogarty is no amateur when it comes to expressing opinions). Barry used his own soapbox, his column in *Bike* magazine, to hit back at Carl, accusing him of being as 'thick as pigshit' and saying he was a 'complete embarrassment' to motorcycle racing who suffered from an 'eye disease' in that 'every other word is I, I, I'.

Naturally, the motorcycling press were quick to pick up on this verbal feud between two of Britain's biggest biking names. Sheene insisted he would stand by his words even when Foggy announced he was consulting his lawyers, but nobody really believed it would come to a legal action; after all, both riders were as guilty as each other when it came to expressing their relative views. Still, it was only when news of Sheene's cancer broke in July 2002 that Carl backed down and realized how petty the whole thing had been. He, like everyone else in the sport, paid tribute to Barry and wished him well.

Fellow riders aside, Sheene also displayed a habit of falling out with Japanese manufacturers over the years, and things never worked in his favour. As early as 1972, long before Barry was a major star, he publicly criticized

Yamaha's 250cc bike. To the non-Japanese mind that may seem fairly unremarkable, hardly worth further comment, but in a culture whose very cornerstones are corporate pride and loyalty it was unforgivable, as Barry was to find to his cost. Years later, and years too late, Sheene realized the error of his ways. 'Perhaps I was more critical of their machines than a person of my age and experience should have been. From the word go I maintained that their new dream bike, a water-cooled twin, was useless.' He added, 'My fault in 1972 was that my comments, usually critical, on the machines should have been directed to one person such as the chief engineer instead of to the public at large.' Had Sheene complained about the performance of his machine behind closed doors to Yamaha staff, all would have been well and remedies could have been sought. But Barry, more through youthful innocence than any real malice, chose to air his disgust through the national press, a move that came back to haunt him eight years later when he switched from his factory Suzuki deal to running private Yamahas. Sheene, so accustomed to receiving preferential treatment because of his massive popularity, suddenly found himself out of favour when it came to getting special parts for his bikes, or indeed special bikes as a whole. The Japanese have long memories and once offended are not easily placated.

Yamaha wasn't the only Japanese manufacturer Sheene offended. Having decided to ride their bikes in his own team for the 1980 season, Sheene was audacious enough to wear a Yamaha T-shirt at the 1979 *MCN* Man of the Year awards while he was still contracted to Suzuki. It was another dishonourable and unacceptable crime in the eyes of the Japanese. Moreover, Sheene had been spotted by Suzuki top brass in a restaurant shortly before the *MCN* function and had been warned that he would forfeit the final £5,000 instalment of his Suzuki contract if he went ahead with the stunt. He did it anyway. After all, what's a few grand to Barry Sheene when he can have a bit of a larf? 'I wore the T-shirt for a bit of fun,' he explained, 'just to aggravate race chief Maurice Knight who, to his credit, took it in good part.' Steve Parrish, however, recalled the incident as the most embarrassing of his life.

Mick Grant believed that Sheene's numerous fall-outs with teams constituted the biggest drawback of his career. 'Barry's Achilles heel was that he burned a lot of bridges along the way. When he left Suzuki and went to Yamaha he tended to rub their noses in it a wee bit, and he did the same with various people, but again, that's Barry. It was all publicity, I suppose.'

And no one had more belief in the old adage that 'there's no such thing as bad publicity' than Barry Sheene.

CHAPTER 7

THE RACER: PART THREE

*'I'm riding like an old woman. I don't know
what's wrong with me.'*

Batman and the Joker, Spiderman and the Green Goblin,
Superman and Lex Luthor. Every hero has an arch enemy,
and for Barry Sheene it was Kenny Roberts. It was Suzuki
versus Yamaha, America versus England, the cheeky,
chirpy cockney versus the deadpan Yank, classical
European high-corner-speed riding style versus a revolutionary American dirt-bike style, the double world champ
versus the rookie. Sheene and Roberts were complete
opposites, but the one thing they did have in common was
that they were both great riders, and the 1978 season
promised to be vintage stuff. In the end it was ruined, not
by injury on Barry's part, but by a mysterious debilitating
illness that sapped Sheene's energy and robbed him of his
finest form when he needed it most. Or so he claimed.

After consulting several doctors and specialists, Sheene
came to believe that he had Bornholm's disease, a viral
infection that affects the chest and causes headaches,

lethargy and general fever. The condition has been subject to a fair amount of scepticism over the years and has been variously known as myalgic encephalomyelitis (ME), pleurodynia, chronic fatigue syndrome, devil's grip and even, most derogatorily in the eighties, yuppie flu. Whether or not Sheene was correctly diagnosed, whether or not he really did have a genuine illness, we will now never know, but it is safe to say that he was never a man to shy away from riding when he felt below par. On the contrary, and as we have seen, Barry was famous for making racing comebacks in record time despite horrific injuries, so it would seem only fair to give him the benefit of the doubt in this case, even if the press at the time, and some other parties, didn't. Don Morley was highly sceptical: 'Barry had by far the best bike at the right time in 1976 and 1977 and despite all of his riding abilities, which were undoubted, when the Yanks came over in 1978 Barry suddenly found himself outclassed on most fronts. I always believed the virus business was psychosomatic.'

Psychosomatic or not, Sheene claimed to have felt the first symptoms of his illness in March, at the airport on the way back from the Venezuelan Grand Prix, which he had won from Pat Hennen, Roberts having lasted only two laps before his Yamaha gave up the ghost. As he was waiting for his flight home to be announced, Barry started to shiver. He continued to feel generally unwell throughout the seven-hour flight to the UK. When he did get home, his temperature began to fluctuate wildly, and he fell asleep again just hours after waking up in the morning having vomited frequently through the night. Sheene left no stone unturned in his search for a diagnosis, consulting everyone from Harley Street specialists to tropical disease clinics. X-rays failed to reveal the source of the pain in Sheene's chest, and apart from being prescribed various vitamin tablets there was no other known treatment, only rest. The general consensus was that there was no consensus: the illness could clear up in two days, two weeks or two months.

Sheene soldiered on, though his results were, by his standards anyway, disappointing: fifth place in Spain in April, third in both Austria and France and fifth again in Italy; Roberts enjoyed a three-race winning streak in the latter three races. Barry was becoming ever more disheartened. 'I'm riding like an old woman,' he complained. 'I don't know what's wrong with me.' The press increasingly felt he was making excuses, that he couldn't admit he was simply being outridden by a more mature Hennen and a devastatingly talented Kenny Roberts. Roberts agreed with the press to a certain extent. 'Before I arrived in Europe,' he said, 'Sheene looked as if he had no competition. But during 1978, a few other guys, Wil Hartog of Holland and later Virginio Ferrari of Italy and Michel Rougerie of France, showed that they were good and could win too. I am not taking anything away from him [Sheene], but I showed up and I was as good as him.' Ron Haslam, though not speaking specifically about Sheene's virus, also believed his former rival was not beyond making excuses when he couldn't win races. 'He did have a lot of excuses that other riders wouldn't have even mentioned. Rather than trying to ride round any small problems he would blame them for a poor performance.' Sheene was not unaware of this reputation for making excuses, even if he vehemently denied it. When speaking about the 1979 Mallory Park Race of the Year (he was beaten by Randy Mamola), he said, 'At the garlanding ceremony afterwards when Fred Clarke, the commentator, asked me what problems, if any, I had experienced during the race, I replied that the bike was plagued with a misfire. I gave him a truthful answer, but certain sections of the crowd groaned, assuming it was another Sheene excuse.'

But Chip Hennen related a wonderful tale that seems to prove Sheene was not making excuses. 'This mysterious illness was affecting his physical stamina, and all the newspapers reported it. But several people close to Barry at that time said that they didn't think Barry really had an illness, just that he simply couldn't go fast enough to compete with Pat and Kenny. But I think there was some truth to his having a problem with stamina, and I put it down to his not being able to properly exercise his cardiovascular system because of all the injuries he had sustained over the years. After Pat won the Spanish GP, Barry invited him and the rest of his team over to Barry's father's villa, somewhere south of Madrid on the coast, for a couple of days. I told him that I thought his problem was the result of his not getting enough of the right kinds of exercise. I thought he should do some concentrated cardio exercises, especially swimming. He flat out told me that I was wrong and that he was as fit as he had ever been. Shortly after we arrived at his father's villa, Barry, Pat, myself and a couple of other people got into a discussion about fitness and he challenged everyone to compete with him doing one-armed push-ups. He got down on the floor and started doing one-armed push-ups, and after the fourth or fifth one his left knee with the plastic knee cap suddenly popped and his foot was sticking out 45 degrees in the wrong direction. It was truly a sickening sound and sight. To everyone's amazement, Barry calmly grabbed his foot and turned it so it was pointing in the right direction, causing his knee to pop back into place. Then, incredibly, he started doing one-armed push-ups again, and did quite a few. I don't remember anyone taking him up on his challenge. I don't think I've ever met anyone with that kind of mental toughness, and I've known quite a few pretty exceptional athletes through the years.'

Frustrated and upset by his lack of success in 1978, Barry decided to spend a week in June cruising the Mediterranean on a yacht belonging to Heron Corporation chief Gerald Ronson, who would later make headlines with his involvement in the Guinness affair. Much to his surprise and relief, Barry woke up on the second day feeling fine for the first time in months. 'It was as if someone had removed a shadow from me,' he claimed.

Sure enough, Sheene's form began to pick up, although sceptics point out that this was at least partly due to the fact that Pat Hennen was no longer racing, having been so badly injured in the meantime at the TT. A third place at the Dutch TT was followed by a win in Sweden – his first since the opening race of the season, before the illness had struck. The win not only proved that Barry was back to full race fitness, it also put him within three points of Roberts' title lead. All Sheene needed now was a bit of luck in the closing stages of the season to successfully defend his title.

Fastest in practice in Finland in July, Sheene was still very concerned about the amount of vibration coming from his bike and suspected that one of the Suzuki's crankshaft bearings was about to break up. He asked his Japanese mechanics to strip the bike and check the bearings, but they insisted the parts were fine and refused. It was costly. Five laps into the race, while Sheene was in the lead, a crankshaft bearing failed. Barry's anger can be imagined. Rumours quickly began to circulate that he had actually punched the offending mechanic. Barry always maintained that this crankshaft failure was what cost him the World Championship in 1978 and he never forgot the incident, claiming it was the beginning of the end of his relationship with Suzuki.

Sheene's relationship with the organizers of the British Grand Prix, too, was strained to say the least in August 1978. Slick tyres, with no tread pattern whatsoever, were still relatively new to racing in the late seventies and there weren't sufficient rules to govern their inclusion in the sport. The British GP started in dry conditions with 100,000 spectators hoping to cheer Sheene on to a win. If he beat Roberts into second place the pair would be on even points going into the last round in West Germany. It was do or die. There was everything to play for, but then the heavens opened.

The riders might as well have been on ice as their slick tyres offered absolutely no grip in the conditions. Bikes aquaplaned through the puddles, and some riders even felt they had to put a foot down to steady themselves through corners. It was a complete farce, but in the absence of any red flags they continued to tiptoe round at ridiculously low (though fully understandable) speeds, many raising their hands in query as they passed race control. Why wasn't the race being stopped? Why couldn't the riders change to wet tyres and then have a restart? It was chaos. Riders not desperate for World Championship points pulled out of the race, others pitted to change tyres before going back out, yet others continued in the hope of staying on their machines and gaining some points. Both Roberts and Sheene opted to pit to change tyres, which is unheard of in GP motorcycle racing as it takes so long: for Roberts, on this occasion, it took two and a half minutes; Sheene's crew took an agonizing seven and a half minutes. The race was therefore won in the pits. Showing he had in fact lost none of his determination, Barry unlapped himself twice in a bid to catch Roberts, but it was always going to be in vain having given away so much time to the American. He still finished an incredible third while Roberts was credited with the victory, although it took the race organizers several hours to confirm the final standings. Roberts complained bitterly when interviewed by Murray Walker. 'I don't know who won it, I [couldn't] even see where the hell I [was] going. I think the goddamned race should have been stopped and everybody put on rain tyres and go again.'

Sheene was thus eight points behind Roberts going into the last race of the season at the Nurburgring, but he still had an outside chance of taking the title: he needed to win and for Roberts to finish lower than fourth. With the way the American was riding it was a tall order, one made even taller by the lethal nature of the 14-mile, tree-lined course – a track Roberts had to learn on a road bike in the week leading up to the race. In the end, Sheene wasn't prepared to risk it on such a dangerous track and trailed in fourth, one place behind Roberts, to whom he conceded his title. Barry had been praying that Roberts would suffer a mechanical breakdown but Kenny's team had deliberately detuned his bike to minimize the chances of Sheene's prayers being answered. It worked, and Kenny Roberts in his debut Grand Prix season was the new world champion with 110 points to Sheene's 100. Barry would never manage to wrestle his title back, from Roberts or anyone else.Despite losing the world title in 1978, Sheene was still a dominant force on the home front where he won the Snetterton Race of Aces and the Mallory Park Race of the Year as well as holding on to his *MCN* Superbike and Shellsport 500 titles. He was, however, beaten into second place in the *MCN* Man of the Year poll by Mike Hailwood, who stunned the racing world by winning his comeback TT 11 years after retiring from the sport.

By the time the 1979 Suzukis were ready it was clear that Barry Sheene was no longer the favoured son of his Japanese employers. Suzuki wheeled out two versions of the new bike for testing; Barry liked one model (with the radiator in the nose of the bike, which he found improved its handling) but his new team-mates Virginio Ferrari and Wil Hartog preferred the other. Suzuki went for strength in numbers and forced Barry to ride the machine he didn't like. His team-mates later changed their minds – at least according to Sheene's version of events – and agreed with Barry that the bike they had chosen actually didn't handle well at all. Barry might have been vindicated, but it didn't do him much good. He still had to start the season on a bike he didn't like.

Despite the fact that he was unhappy with the new RGA500, Sheene still managed to win the opening Grand Prix in Venezuela for the third consecutive year while Roberts was recovering from crushing several vertebrae and breaking a foot during a crash in pre-season testing. But from that point on Sheene endured a run of bad luck that effectively put an end to any world-title aspirations he had for 1979.

In Austria, a mechanic (who remains unnamed) put too many washers on a retaining bolt in the brake disc. As a result, the brake pads were pushed out and Barry had to repeatedly pump his brakes to get any sort of response from them, a practice that was both time-consuming and distracting; he limped home in a lowly 12th place as a fresh, newly returned Roberts won the race and proved he was every bit as adept as Sheene when it came to recovering from injury. A broken crankshaft ruined the German GP for Sheene while he was lying second, and, unhappy with the unfamiliar sliding characteristics of his Dunlop tyres – it was the first time he had used Dunlops since his 1975 Daytona crash and he had only chosen to do so because he was unhappy with his Michelins – in the Italian race he could only manage fourth. In May he was languishing in fifth place in the championship, 23 points behind Roberts. Things didn't improve in Spain as Barry's machine was slow to fire into life. By the time it did, the rest of the field were halfway round the first lap. Sheene rode round for 10 laps but pulled out of the race when he realized there was no chance of scoring any points. And when Marco Lucchinelli's bike threw up a large stone in the Yugoslavian GP, it hit one of the screws in Sheene's knee, forcing him out of the race and causing him a great deal of pain.

Because Sheene's team-mate Ferrari was now Roberts' closest challenger for the championship, Barry decided, or was told, to wave the Italian past in the name of Suzuki. It wasn't something he was comfortable living with, and he made sure he never found himself in a similar position again, either with Suzuki or anyone else.

With all the top riders sitting out the Belgian round in protest at the slippery and highly dangerous new surface, it was off to Karlskoga for the Swedish GP where Sheene's luck finally turned, albeit much too late in the season. This victory was his fifth in a row in Sweden, even though the race was held at Karlskoga in 1978 and 1979 rather than at Anderstorp. A third place in Finland after rubber had started chunking from his rear tyre left Barry looking forward to his home round at Silverstone, where he finally hoped to score an elusive home win to make up, at least in part, for conceding the world title for a second year. With Sheene somewhat back on form and looking like his run of rotten luck was behind him, all the elements were in place for a great race, but no one could have imagined that it would for ever more be regarded as an all-time classic.

For bike-racing fans the world over, 12 August 1979 will always be remembered as the day on which the best British GP in history took place. It attracted the biggest sporting TV audience of the year, beating off football, F1, golf, tennis, the lot; re-runs of the race were still being shown years later on programmes such as *100 Great Sporting Moments*. It was such a popular event that it even made the main television news in the evening – an almost unheard-of honour for motorcycle sport.

Practice had gone miserably for Sheene, every change he made to his bike failing to provide the set-up he needed. Somewhat in despair, he spent the night before the race at his close friend Lord Hesketh's house wondering if the final adjustments to the frame (made after last practice) would do the trick. Come race day, Sheene pulled a massive wheelie off the start-line – it can be seen in the David Essex movie *Silver Dream Racer*, which was being filmed at the event – to begin the epic confrontation with his arch rival Roberts. The post-practice changes to his bike had worked, and Sheene knew he finally stood a realistic chance of winning his home GP.

Virginio Ferrari briefly got in on the action with Kenny and Barry, and Wil Hartog likewise put up a good performance in the early stages, but the race quickly settled down to a two-man affair as Roberts and Sheene pulled clear and made the race their own. Roberts told *Bike* magazine in 2002, 'Sheene and me were the two fastest guys on the race track. I couldn't pull away from him and he couldn't pull away from me. I had advantages in faster corners. I could get through Abbey flat in fourth and I'd never seen anyone else do it at that time. And if I could do it one time I would get 10 bike lengths on anyone I was racing. That was the only sort of plan I had.'Sheene had his own plan, of sorts, as he also told *Bike*. 'It was always going to be a last-lap job. My plan was always to get him into Woodcote on the last lap. I was going to pass him on the brakes, and I knew I was quicker going around Woodcote.'

As each rider passed and re-passed the other without actually breaking away, things quickly developed into a high-speed game of cat and mouse, the only visible advantage being the superior speed of Roberts' Yamaha down the super-fast Hangar straight. At one point, as Sheene passed Roberts, he stuck two fingers up at him behind his back, famously prompting commentator Murray Walker to shout, 'Sheene's waving at Kenny Roberts!' It wasn't exactly waving, but the gesture did exemplify the friendly rivalry between the two supposedly sworn enemies. It was an indication, too, of how much the pair were enjoying the race.

By the start of the last lap, Sheene appeared to have lost any hope of a win thanks to backmarker George Fogarty, father of four-time World Superbike champion Carl, who unwittingly got in Barry's way. A 10-yard deficit quickly became a 200-yard one. It looked like the race was over. It wasn't, but years later Sheene had still not forgiven Fogarty, who, he claimed, had had 'no business riding in the Grand Prix'. Interestingly, Carl Fogarty remembered things differently and stated in his autobiography that 'Sheene told him [George Fogarty] after the race that he wasn't to blame.' Two decades later, of course, Barry mounted his famed verbal attack on George's son, further reducing his popularity in the Fogarty household.

Showing uncanny speed and determination, Sheene made up all but 0.03 seconds of the time he'd lost on Roberts and so very nearly slipped past him on the line, as he'd planned all along. Had the finish line been a few yards further down the track, it could have been a victory for Sheene, but as it was no one felt cheated. They had witnessed one of the greatest races ever, and surely Sheene's finest, even though he didn't win. Both riders were visibly jubilant as they took their helmets off, Sheene declaring on the podium that 'It's good to race with Kenny. He always gives me lots of room and I always give him lots of room. That's the way to race.'

It truly was a monumental race, the closest Sheene ever got to winning a British Grand Prix. It had certainly gripped the entire nation: everyone was talking about the race the following day. Even the taxi driver who took Kenny Roberts to the airport asked him if he'd seen the race on TV, blissfully unaware that his passenger was the very man he had watched racing to victory. But Kenny did achieve a lingering fame, of a sort, in this country, as Sheene pointed out: 'To this day I can get in a cab in London and the driver will say, "Oh, I remember that race years ago when you gave the V-sign to that Kenny Rogers guy." They always remember him as Kenny Rogers.'

Sheene won the last round of the championship in France, while Kenny settled for third and enough points to secure his second world title. Barry finished third behind Virginio Ferrari in the overall standings which, considering his early-season run of bad luck, was commendable. Of more significance, however, is that the 1979 French Grand Prix marked Barry's last GP outing on a Suzuki after having joined the firm in 1974 as a works rider. In 1980 he would be Yamaha-mounted – and it would be his worst year ever.

British racing fans saw a lot less of Barry Sheene in 1979 than they had previously been accustomed to as his negotiations for ever greater appearance money, even without a world title to his name, fell flat. Four of Britain's biggest circuits – Brands Hatch, Mallory Park, Oulton Park and Snetterton – were at the time controlled by a company called Motor Circuit Developments, and director Chris Lowe decided enough was enough when Sheene's already hefty demands – reputedly five-figure sums for every meeting – were increased. 'If I had met his terms,' Lowe said, 'I'd have had to screw other people, which is not fair, or ethical, and in the long term is bad for business.' To compensate for his loss of earnings on MCD circuits, Sheene reached an agreement with the owners of the reopened Donington Park circuit, where he happily raced until the end of his career. He did compete at some MCD tracks for events such as the Transatlantic Match Races, for which he negotiated separate fees, but he missed out on many of the *MCN* Superbike and Shellsport 500 rounds and as a consequence relinquished both titles in 1979, though he was once again voted Man of the Year by *MCN* readers, more because of his continued popularity and his efforts in the British Grand Prix than for any notable results.

*   *   *

THE RACER: PART THREE

Sheene shocked the racing world when he announced he was to run Yamahas in a private team for the 1980 season. His principal reasons for the change were that he didn't think Suzuki had believed he had any kind of illness in 1978, he was upset that they had trusted Hartog and Ferrari's judgement of the 1979 bikes over his, and he certainly hadn't been impressed by his Suzuki mechanic's failure to change that crankshaft bearing in Finland. Despite these grievances, there is still much speculation as to whether Sheene really meant to hand in his notice with Suzuki GB or whether he was just trying to negotiate a better deal for himself. If it was the latter, he failed disastrously.

Sheene had long been keen to run his own team, primarily so he could take his bikes home and prepare them in the luxury of his own workshops. Suzuki Japan were strongly against this idea; like every other manufacturer, they jealously guarded their technical secrets and never liked their bikes to be out of their control or off their premises if they could help it. When Sheene visited Suzuki GB's racing director Maurice Knight to tell him of his decision and/or bluff that he was leaving the firm to race Yamahas, Knight explained that he was pushed for time and couldn't wait around to barter with Barry. 'I believe that Barry was bluffing,' Knight explained, 'that he really hoped to get Suzukis to run from his own home. But what he didn't know was that I had the whole board of Heron behind me. We'd agreed that if it was going to get difficult, then we weren't going to go into it any longer.' In *Leader of the Pack*, Sheene's official biography, Barry wrote that he 'could not envisage life without being part of a Team Suzuki of some description', and suggested that he was the victim who 'came out of his [Knight's] office with absolutely nothing – no bikes, no contract and no income whatsoever'.

According to Don Morley, Sheene had no intention of leaving Suzuki; he simply pushed his luck once too often. 'In my opinion, Barry was at war with Suzuki at that time. He would put a gun to their heads and say "I want this and that or I'm walking", and of course they finally told Barry to get on his bike. He was gobsmacked. He didn't really want to go to Yamaha, he really didn't. It was all a ruse to get Suzuki to up their game. There was talk at the time that Barry singlehandedly killed off Suzuki's trials efforts because he was demanding so much of Suzuki's budget. I don't mean to run Barry down, but sometimes people get so big in a set-up that they can't see the woods for the trees.'

Whatever the truth of the matter, Suzuki's immediate acceptance of Sheene's supposed 'resignation' meant there was no further room for negotiation: he was going to have to ride Yamahas. At least he had the satisfaction of taking most of Texaco's money with him when he left Suzuki, and there was no shortage of other firms lining up to pay for Barry Sheene to go racing. He was, after all, still the most famous bike racer in the world. The most telling sign that Sheene was bitter about leaving Suzuki was that Yamaha T-shirt-wearing incident at the *MCN* Man of the Year awards, but with that final act of defiance he set about the serious business of setting up a race team because there was one thing in that department he was still lacking – motorcycles.

By the time the new decade dawned, 'King' Kenny
Roberts had amply proved his loyalty to his Japanese
Yamaha employers. He had stuck with their dirt-bike team
in the States when they were being hopelessly outclassed by
Harley-Davidson and had then gone on to win two 500cc
Grand Prix World Championships. More importantly, he
had never bad-mouthed his bikes in public, even if they
were giving him a hard time. The same could not be said of
Sheene who, as we have seen already, had not been shy in
publicly criticizing his Yamaha 250 in 1972. So when
Sheene approached Yamaha for bikes in 1980 he was never
going to get the same tackle as Yamaha's favourite and
most loyal son, as Mitsui Yamaha's Robert Jackson confirmed: 'Unless your name was Kenny Roberts, the [Yamaha]
factory weren't going to let you have the works bikes.'
Morley added, 'Barry always said that Yamaha had
promised him the same machines as Roberts, but that was
a load of old bollocks. They hadn't forgotten what he said
back in 1972.'

But in an era when Honda were struggling with their ill-
fated NR500 four-stroke machine, Sheene had little choice
but to go with Yamaha and whatever they might have to
offer. And what they did offer was far from satisfactory for
a two-time world champion – bog-standard production
racers any privateer with the right cash in his pocket could
buy over the counter. Barry Sheene was a genuine privateer
again for the first time in nine years. Fortunately, however,
he had the advantage of being the richest privateer racing
was ever likely to see, and he had the potential to attract
sponsors like no other. Chief among these was Japanese hi-fi

and video manufacturer Akai, although he had additional
support from Texaco, DAF trucks and Marlboro in a
£300,000 sponsorship package. Sheene knew the value of
publicity better than anyone, and he made sure his team
launch was the most expensive in bike-racing history. Held
in January 1980 at the Royal Garden Hotel in Kensington,
it was compèred by the then BBC sports presenter Frank
Bough, who just happened to be part of the same marketing agency as Sheene (it's not what you know . . .).

With Sheene now out of the picture, Suzuki signed up
American youngster Randy Mamola as his replacement.
Mamola had seen what his hero Roberts had achieved in
Europe and he wanted some of the action. 'Basically, the
draw for me [to come over to Europe] was Kenny Roberts
because he was one of my idols. I idolized who he was and
what he did. At the time I just thought, "My God, I'm
gonna ride for Barry Sheene's former team!" But there was
probably a lot of people at the time frowning and asking,
"Why are they taking on this red-haired, freckle-faced guy
to take Barry Sheene's place?" A lot of people were saying,
"Hey, you're trying to fill Barry Sheene's shoes," but
nobody could fill Barry's shoes. Still, I finished second to
Kenny Roberts that year and proved a point.' He might
have proved a point, but Mamola is the first to admit that
he was no Sheene clone when it came to personality, at
least in those early years. 'I didn't know anybody so I kept
pretty much to myself. In fact, I was called a brat because I
didn't talk to anybody, but I didn't know anybody.
Basically, I was out of my mum's womb and onto a race
track!' Sheene, at least initially, felt Mamola's reputation

was deserved. 'I could never understand why he hardly ever smiled after winning a race,' he wrote. 'There wasn't a hint of happiness on his freckled face whenever he headed the field home.' But Barry was quick to change his mind when he got to know Mamola better. 'If ever a guy was misunderstood, it was Randy,' he claimed. 'He's easy to get on with and will offer definite views to those who are prepared to stop and listen. The commonly held notion that he lacks any kind of personality and would make the most boring champion the sport has ever experienced is simply mistaken.'

Sheene won two races at Cadwell Park first time out on his TZ750 Yamaha, but not against world-class competition, and it was on the well-proven 750 rather than the less-established TZ500. As things turned out, 1980 was to be an appalling year for Sheene, eventually resulting in his lowest-ever finish in the 500cc Grand Prix World Championship – 14th. In fact, his only two finishes of the year were a seventh in Italy and a fifth in Spain. Kenny Roberts took a third consecutive title. It was to be his last, but it beat Sheene's tally to the tune of one.

Right from the start of the season Sheene knew he was up against it, as he told *Motocourse*: 'The engine is slow, the frame handles so badly it overworks the suspension so that fails, and the tyres [Michelins] are uncompetitive.' On top of these problems Barry's worst nightmare was finally realized when he lost a part of his body to amputation: the little finger of his left hand had to be cut off following a crash at the French Grand Prix. He tried to race at the next round in Holland but retired, unable to ride properly. He had no more luck at the Belgian Grand Prix, where the flawed timing system listed Barry as down in 38th place after qualifying. Disgusted, he turned tail and headed for home, adding a did-not-start to his growing list of did-not-finish results. The Finnish GP at Imatra counted as another DNS as Sheene disliked the circuit and decided against racing there, but his morale was boosted at Silverstone when he received a factory engine from Yamaha (albeit an older one than Roberts') and a special frame built by Harris Performance Products. But after setting third-fastest time in early qualifying, the new engine refused to make full power and a puzzled and frustrated Sheene slumped to 10th place on the grid. During the race itself the Yamaha gradually lost more and more power to the point where it wouldn't even pull top gear. Sheene retired with five laps to go, jinxed by Silverstone once again. He sat out the last GP of the season at the Nurburgring, again because he deemed the track too dangerous. Besides, there hardly seemed any point in going there given his position in the championship. The only highlights of Sheene's dismal season were a couple of wins in the *MCN* Superbike series and a victory in one of the *World of Sport* Superbike rounds.

Still, Sheene proved one thing to Yamaha bosses during 1980: he had learned to be more diplomatic when things weren't going his way, and to Japanese sensibilities at least that's every bit as important as being able to win a World Championship. It had always been Sheene's intention to 'suck it and see' during his first year on a Yamaha, hoping that by being publicly loyal to the firm they might give him increased support for 1981.

His chance to really convince the top brass that he was

worth supporting came at the end of the 1980 season with an invitation to a special Yamaha race at Sugo in Japan. It was a chance he didn't waste. With all competitors, including Kenny Roberts, riding 1981 production racers, Sheene finally had an opportunity to prove that it had been inferior machinery that had been preventing him from winning Grands Prix. Barry was leading the first race before his bike seized and brought him to a premature halt, and in the second event he was holding a similar 10-second advantage on the very last lap when a front tyre puncture saw him thrown into an armco barrier, resulting in a broken wrist. To Western sensibilities that might sound like a disaster, but not so to the Japanese way of thinking. Barry-san had proven his honour by leading the race, but even better, he had physically hurt himself in the great Yamaha cause. There could be no better way to display company loyalty. As Sheene lay by the trackside, the president of Yamaha himself rushed over to check on his condition, happy to learn that Barry-san was not too badly wounded but equally happy with the job the Londoner had done in his company's name. All of a sudden, Sheene had a foot in the door at Yamaha again.

It was just one foot, however. Sheene was told that, though he would be supplied with factory bikes for the 1981 season, they would only be 1980-spec in-line four-cylinder TZ500 machines, at least initially, while Roberts would receive the new square-four OW54 bikes. It was a disappointment, but still a step in the right direction.

In the 1981 season-opener in Austria in April, Sheene finished a creditable fourth while Roberts failed to finish the race due to a faulty rear suspension unit. There'd been ample time, however, for it to be clear that Roberts' bike was much faster than Sheene's older model, and the American forced the point home by winning the next two rounds of the series, in West Germany and Italy, while Sheene finished sixth and third respectively. The latter was a good result on his 'old' bike, and one which was made possible only by the performance-levelling wet weather and Barry's undoubted skills in such conditions.

It was also Sheene's last race on the TZ500, as Yamaha at last came up with an OW54 for him. Sheene was delighted with the huge power difference between the new bike and the old, but just as one problem was solved another took its place, and this time it was tyres. Apart from upsetting bike manufacturers such as Yamaha and Suzuki over the years, Sheene had also created waves at tyre manufacturers Dunlop in 1975 by publicly blaming their tyre for his Daytona crash. Whether or not he was justified in doing so is debatable, but his actions had yet again cast a long shadow.For the French GP at Paul Ricard in May, Sheene wanted to try a 16-inch front rim as opposed to his more usual 18-inch choice in a bid to improve steering and braking. He felt that Dunlop tyres would be more suited to the ultra-fast Paul Ricard circuit than the Michelins he usually rode on, but Dunlop only had enough 16-inch front tyres for their contracted riders – or so they claimed. Had Sheene not offended Dunlop so grievously back in 1975 he might have found them a little more accommodating. In motorcycle racing, it pays to keep everyone sweet. During the race itself Sheene enjoyed a good scrap for the lead with Roberts before both were forced to slow with tyre problems, but Barry still managed to hold Kenny off for fourth place, finally proving that he was a match for the American when all other things were even.

Things were rarely even, though, as Barry and Kenny were to find out over the next few months. Both experienced a string of mechanical problems that forced them to pull out of too many races to enable them to challenge for the championship. In Sheene's case, his bike wouldn't fire up at the Dutch TT, he had clutch problems in Belgium which left him in fourth place, he crashed out of the British round when Kiwi Graeme Crosby fell in front of him, and he suffered a broken power valve in the Finnish GP. However, there were moments worth savouring, such as a fine second place at Imola in July and a long-awaited win a month later at the final round in Sweden. Sheene could well have ended the year with two GP victories had he not been so sporting on the starting grid at Imola. Seeing that eventual 1981 world champion Marco 'Lucky' Lucchinelli had selected the wrong tyre, Sheene suggested he change it as he believed it wouldn't last race distance. Lucchinelli duly changed his tyre and eventually passed early leader Sheene to take the win. It was a fine gesture from Sheene, but it ultimately worked against him. It probably didn't please his Yamaha bosses either: Lucchinelli was mounted on a Suzuki.

Barry's win in Sweden, his first GP victory since the French round in 1979, has become something of a landmark in British racing. Incredibly, it remains the last time a British rider won a 500cc Grand Prix, and there doesn't appear to be any British rider on the horizon ready to alter that fact. Sheene himself graciously said that 'Nobody would like to see that record beaten more than me.' More poignantly for Barry, it was also his last-ever Grand Prix victory, 10 years after his first GP success in the 125cc race in Belgium. But there were some notable victories in the UK in 1981: Sheene won all three ITV *World of Sport* races and bagged the usual brace of wins at Oliver's Mount parkland circuit in Scarborough. All in all, Yamaha was impressed enough with Barry's 1981 performances to offer even more help in 1982, but sadly, his massive Silverstone crash that year effectively ended his competitive career.

Results don't always tell the whole story, and it's a great irony that Barry Sheene often rode harder, faster and better in his non-championship-winning years than in 1976 and 1977, when he admitted he only had to ride at around three-quarters of his potential. It's true that Kenny Roberts had felt in 1978 that Sheene could have tried harder to defend his crown – 'Barry says he rides at 80 per cent. Well, I reckon I give a little more than 80 per cent. I think that the Dutchman Wil Hartog and perhaps a couple of other guys give more than 80 per cent too. I don't think it is possible winning at 80 per cent of the total potential any more. I think Barry also realizes that now' – but certainly in 1981 Sheene put in some terrific performances, especially when he was given an up-to-date bike. It was only bad luck and mechanical failures that prevented him from being more involved in the title chase.

In 1982, at the age of 31, Sheene was riding even better, and with his machinery proving to be ever faster and more reliable he looked very capable of reclaiming the world crown he had last won five years before. With Akai withdrawing its sponsorship money for 1982, it fell to cigarette firm John Player's to cough up the necessary cash to send Sheene off on the World Championship trail once more. He had the option of riding for Giacomo Agostini's Marlboro Yamaha team, but he turned down the opportunity when he learned that there was no possibility of keeping the bikes at Charlwood. As far as running his own team for a third successive season went, Sheene fully believed he would be given the same bikes as Kenny Roberts, but yet again the favoured son was the only Yamaha rider to be gifted a new V4 machine (from the second round of the championship onwards), much to Barry's annoyance and increasing frustration.

At first, Kenny struggled to get the V4 to steer as he wanted; an onlooking Barry was convinced he could have it handling sweetly within a matter of weeks if only he were given the chance. It was Roberts' struggles with the V4 that led Barry to say, 'It really opened my eyes when I rode with Kenny, because he knows nothing about setting a bike up. He starts with it at the beginning of the year, and it doesn't handle, and he ends up with it at the end of the year, and it still doesn't handle.' Accusing another rider of being ineffectual when it comes to setting up bikes is commonplace between rivals searching for any way in which to gain a psychological edge. In actual fact, both Roberts and Sheene were well known for their skills in developing and setting up bikes, so anything one said about the other needed to be taken with the proverbial pinch of salt. Ron Haslam, one of the world's most respected development riders, certainly thought Sheene knew his stuff in that department. 'I think Sheene was pretty good at setting bikes up and developing them. Sometimes he maybe looked too deep into stuff that was more like bike design than set-up, and maybe that held him back a bit. You've got to deal with what you've got sometimes rather than trying to re-design a bike. He knew what a bike was doing, though.' In fact, Sheene had reprimanded the young Haslam about his set-up skills the first time they ever spoke. 'I first spoke to Sheene at the Mallory Park Race of the Year, although I can't remember which year it was. Barry won the race and I was either second or third. Anyway, Sheene's bike broke down on the victory lap and he asked if he could borrow mine to complete it. I gave it to him, but he gave me a right telling off when he brought it back, saying, "What a load of shit that bike is. You can't turn the steering." I explained that I'd had two steering dampers fitted because I didn't know much about setting a bike up back then. He wasn't impressed.'

What must be borne in mind about Sheene's years at Yamaha is that Roberts was in the front line when it came to developing new bikes, and Sheene wasn't. In theory, therefore, whenever Barry was given a 'new' machine, all the early teething troubles should have been sorted out by Kenny and his team. It wasn't until the last days of July 1982, the week before the Silverstone race, that Sheene received a V4, and he immediately set about fixing it to his own requirements – but more of that later.

Sheene kicked the season off in fine style in March with a second place to Roberts in Argentina which could so easily have been a win had he not been balked by a backmarker on the final lap. The Transatlantic Match Races, held between the Argentine and Austrian GPs, were a complete triumph for Sheene: he took five wins from six races, easily his most successful performance in the annual event, and a marked contrast to the year before when he'd managed only one victory. For the Austrian Grand Prix, Roberts used his new V4 for the first time but couldn't beat a highly motivated Sheene into second place. Sheene felt particularly smug about that since his bike had suffered engine problems in the race and hadn't been performing at its best. Unhappy with the circuit and the paddock facilities, the top riders agreed to boycott the French GP, so wheels didn't turn again in anger until May and the Spanish round at Jarama where Sheene notched up another solid second, putting him just four points behind championship leader Roberts. It was shaping up to be an awesome season, Sheene's best for years.

If Sheene was angry because Roberts had a V4 and he didn't, he was positively livid when Yamaha wheeled another one out for Marlboro Yamaha rider Graeme Crosby to test during practice for the Italian Grand Prix. Yamaha insisted Crosby was acting only as a test rider to speed up development of the bike and that there was no possibility of Crosby actually racing it, but Barry must have been deeply regretting his criticism of Yamaha back in

1972. It was almost as if the firm was going out of its way to infuriate and stymie him. Crosby didn't race the V4 in Italy, and Sheene recorded his first non-finish of the year, complaining to *Motocourse* that his bike had been 'slow, and it wouldn't handle. I was riding like hell and getting nowhere.'

The problems had obviously been ironed out by June when the GP circus rolled up in Holland, for the spectators at Assen should have seen Sheene win his first GP of 1982. After the race was stopped because of heavy rain, Sheene was leading the restart and looked a sure bet in the closing stages until he suffered a monstrous slide which caused his arm to break a fairing mounting, which in turn meant he couldn't steer the bike properly. All he could do was sit back and watch as Franco Uncini and Kenny Roberts swooped past, leaving him a disappointed third. He went one better in Belgium in a race which turned out to be of historical significance: Freddie Spencer, the future triple world champion, won his first Grand Prix; it was also Honda's first in 15 years (the last being Mike Hailwood's victory in the Canadian GP at Mosport in 1967). It was the start of an unparalleled run of dominance by Honda that continues to this day.

Sheene continued his good form by leading the Yugoslavian Grand Prix for a spell before eventually finishing third behind Uncini and Crosby. Roberts failed to finish the race, which allowed Sheene to pull level with him on points, but Uncini was still 20 points ahead of them both. At a time when bikes were still breaking down with alarming regularity, however, such a lead meant little, and

Uncini was due a non-finish. His luck couldn't hold out for ever, and the feeling was that it was still anyone's title. And with the next round being held at Silverstone, Sheene was confident he could redress the balance. After all, he was finally going to ride the elusive V4 Yamaha he'd been promised all season.

The week leading up to the 1982 British Grand Prix said a great deal about Barry Sheene's abilities when it came to setting up a motorcycle. He knew exactly what he wanted from a bike, what he liked and what worked for him. For reasons known only to the Japanese, Sheene was not allowed to take delivery of the V4 until the week before the British GP, even though there was a bike available – indeed, Crosby had already tested it. Sheene always wondered if things might have turned out differently at Silverstone had he had longer to get used to the machine. As it was, he took delivery of the bike at 9.30 a.m. on Monday 26 July, just six days before the British GP was due to take place. That allowed Sheene just three days of testing before official qualifying for the race started. It was never going to be enough.

On that Monday, Sheene rode the bike for the first time around Silverstone during free practice for the 500cc Grand Prix riders. He pulled in after just a handful of laps, bitterly disappointed with the way the Yamaha was handling, but at least he knew what had to be changed. The steering geometry needed to be radically altered. Sheene called Spondon Engineering in Derby and asked if they could alter the head angle of the chassis. They said they could, and that they would have the bike back to Barry by Tuesday evening.

Sheene's mechanics worked through Tuesday night to rebuild the bike, and Barry was out first thing Wednesday morning on near lap record pace: the changes had worked, so much for the chassis. Carburation and gearing alterations were next in line as the day wore on, and Sheene began to get nervous when by mid-afternoon the carbs were still flooding when the bike was started up. Time was running out, and there was so much left to do. The pressure increased.

Barry was unhappy about the amount of traffic out on the circuit, but if he wanted to finally win the one race that had eluded him throughout his career he knew he had to get out there and find a way through it all. It was his only chance. He slammed his visor down and headed out of the pit lane for just one last lap. It was a lap that would change his life.

Sheene's Silverstone crash has been well documented, but what is less well known is that Barry actually sued the circuit not only for being responsible for his injuries, but for effectively ending his competitive career. Having fought so hard to gain factory machinery once more, and despite having proved he was still a strong challenger for World Championship honours, Barry was never again given a top-notch bike. No manufacturer was going to hand out price-less machinery to someone on the wrong side of 30 who had been so badly injured that it was a miracle he could walk. Sheene estimated that the crash had cost him around £300,000 in medical bills and loss of earnings. He felt cheated. His mechanic, Simon Tonge, agreed with him. 'He was very unlucky not to win the championship in 1982. If he hadn't got involved in the shit fight with the V4 and just stuck with the square-four he might well have gone on to win it. He was riding really good that year. I think the V4 was a shit heap of a bike, but the engine was much more powerful than the square-four. Any new bike's going to be a handful until it's properly developed, and the Yamaha did become a proper bike, but not in that first year.'

Never before had riders from all classes been allowed out on a track at the same time, not to mention riders of such varying ability, from 500cc GP demi-gods to holiday club racers. Sheene also attacked the circuit for failing to have an adequate number of marshals on duty. Barry obviously felt he had a strong case, and, as it turned out, so did Silverstone. But the wheels of justice turn slowly, and it wasn't until 1987 that the case came to a head. Sheene told *Motor Cycle News* at the time, 'If I can take Silverstone to the cleaners, then I will.' In the end, after a protracted bout of legal wrangling, Silverstone's insurers settled out of court with a compensation fee rumoured to be around £350,000 – a significant sum at the time but small change compared to what Barry would earn in the ensuing years with his commercial property business.

But what price a career? Indeed, what price a job? After the Silverstone crash, Barry didn't have one. On 20 November 1982 he received word from Yamaha's president, Mr Koike, that his company no longer felt they had a place for him in their racing plans. Sheene was going to have to look elsewhere for a bike.

CHAPTER 8

CRUSADER

'I am filled with greater resolve to make the
racers' lot a far, far better one.'

Barry Sheene has done more for the sport of motorcycle racing than any rider before or since, and not just in terms of making it more popular. His role in the transformation in image of bike racing, making it more attractive to the general public, was an incredible achievement in itself, but even more important were the fundamental changes he helped instigate in terms of safety, which over the last few decades have probably saved scores of lives. On top of that, he helped negotiate better financial deals for all involved, and almost singlehandedly ushered the sport into a new era of professionalism. His efforts in these areas undoubtedly comprised Barry Sheene's greatest contribution to the sport he loved so much.

No Grand Prix motorcycle racer today would even think about racing on a circuit that had a dangerous surface or was lined with trees, nor would he contemplate riding if there were insufficient trackside marshals to warn of any dangers and to help clear up after a crash. Trackside medical facilities today are first class, and there are very specific rules in place dictating what should happen in the event of any number of potential hazards. No system is perfect and the current rules for modern Grand Prix racing are no exception, but standards have improved massively over the last quarter of a century and at least some of the credit for that has to go to Sheene for the pains he took to challenge organizers who appeared to be more concerned with making money than saving lives.

Sheene had ongoing battles with both the FIM (Fédération Internationale Motocycliste) and the ACU (Auto Cycle Union) throughout his career. The former controlled World Championship racing while the latter looked after British events and interests. Sheene made no secret of the fact that he thought FIM stood for 'Federation of Inconsiderate and Indifferent Morons', and he always maintained that British racing in particular had got where it had 'in spite of, and not because of, the ACU'. Naturally, Barry became public enemy number one with both organizations, but there was nothing either could do when he was elected as riders' representative to the FIM in 1977 and again in 1978. From the moment he accepted the position, Sheene was convinced he'd get a reputation as an 'international stirrer', but he couldn't have cared less; he was determined to get a better deal for both himself and his fellow riders, even if that did make him more unpopular with the sports' governing bodies than he already was. In *Leader of the Pack*, Barry described the thankless nature of his job as a representative: 'You could talk to them [the

FIM] at council meetings until you were blue in the face, but still they would not listen. They seemed to have made up their minds on every issue, however burning, before you even had an opportunity to express the views of the riders.'

After two years in the post, somewhat inevitably Sheene lost the backing of the ACU. He was forced from his position and replaced by the late Scottish sidecar racer Jock Taylor – who, incidentally, as a popular and intelligent man had Sheene's full backing and support. While he was still acting as representative, Sheene had argued that the Imatra track in Finland should be struck from the calendar as it was too dangerous, but nothing was done until, in a bitter irony, Taylor was killed there in 1982. Years later, Sheene's outrage at this senseless loss of life was still apparent. 'We had to race on a lot of circuits, for example Finland, the Imatra circuit, [that were] so dangerous it was ridiculous, but the Federation [FIM], being what it is, they had to get the riders' representative at the time killed there before they did anything about it.' Only after Taylor's death was the track dropped from the World Championship. In the most tragic of circumstances, Sheene was vindicated.

Sheene's battle to have the Isle of Man TT struck from the World Championship calendar has already been documented. He was also opposed to other natural road circuits such as Brno in Czechoslovakia and the Nurburgring, both of which were eventually dropped from World Championship racing thanks to pressure from Sheene and other riders. Barry was always quick to point out that he was not afraid of pure road circuits, he just felt that the new generation of bikes had outgrown them. 'It used to make me laugh sometimes when people would say, you know, "Oh, he's not a real road circuit racer," just because I hated the Isle of Man,' he said. 'But I used to like racing on road circuits [such as] Clermont Ferrand . . . the old Spa circuit, I always went quick there. Scarborough – you don't get much more of a road circuit than Scarborough. No, I liked road circuits, but it just got to the stage where bikes really outdated the road circuits and nowadays [it'd] just be ludicrous to race on the road.' As always, Sheene had his critics, not only among the ranks of the FIM and the ACU but also among traditionalists who enjoyed racing on the 'old' circuits and found modern, purpose-built GP tracks featureless. Sheene's response to that particular criticism went straight for the jugular: 'There is nothing more featureless than a corpse lying on a mortuary slab.'

Even on tracks that were deemed relatively safe – the term used is always 'relative' when relating to motorsport – Sheene pushed for improvements. He wanted to see more catch-fencing in place of straw bales and more impact-absorbent rubber in place of tyre walls. Today's air fencing is vastly superior to both. Such a safety net was unthinkable in Sheene's day, and it's another good example of how things have improved.

The effectiveness of improvements in safety standards can be directly measured by the number of riders seriously hurt or killed in any given period. It is noteworthy that of the six Suzuki riders from the late seventies – Sheene, John Williams, John Newbold, Tom Herron, Pat Hennen and Wil Hartog – three are dead and one was in a coma for three months. Only Sheene and Hartog made it through relatively unscathed. Just one decade later, Suzukis were being ridden by Kevin Schwantz, Alex Barros, Daryll Beattie, Scott Russell and Anthony Gobert, all of whom are still alive and well despite the fact that they probably racked up more crashes than Sheene and his team-mates.

Having suffered two monumental crashes, Sheene knew better than most about the dangers involved in his sport, although he never actually struck any tyre walls or lamp-posts during those two accidents. All the same, he knew many riders who were less fortunate, and their cases always provided him with inspiration. 'When I think back on the number of fellow riders who have been killed because safety standards are inadequate,' he said, 'I am filled with greater resolve to make the racers' lot a far, far better one.' And he didn't just mean riders who raced; Sheene also did his bit to promote safety issues for the road riders who made up a huge part of his fan base. In 1977 he began actively to promote the work of the Royal Society for the Prevention of Accidents (RoSPA) in a bid to reduce the number of motorcycle accidents on Britain's roads, which in those days of inadequate rider training was way too high.

A good example of Sheene's involvement in the improve-ment of safety measures and race coordination came at the Austrian Grand Prix at the Salzburgring in 1977. Barry, and many other riders, felt the trackside marshalling and medical facilities left a lot to be desired; they also pointed out to officials that the helicopter on stand-by was useless because it was too small to accommodate a rider on a stretcher. To make matters worse, the all-new AGV mobile hospital – the forerunner of today's state-of-the-art Clinica Mobile – could not actually be used because it was forbidden for foreign doctors to practise in Austria. The FIM declared that in their view the facilities were acceptable, so a stand-off between the riders and the organizers ensued.

When a multiple pile-up occurred during the 350cc race and the race was not stopped, Sheene rushed up to the organizers' office and urged them to red-flag it. When they finally did hold out the red flags, one rider was dead and several more were seriously injured. Furious at their inaction, Sheene and the other top 500cc riders refused to race even after they were offered double start money. As the supposed ringleader of the walkout Sheene was 'severely reprimanded' and issued with a fine by the FIM. He refused to pay it, as he refused to pay all his other FIM fines, and insisted he would take the matter to the European Court of Human Rights in Strasbourg were it to be pursued. Sheene knew he was running a real risk of losing his racing licence over the incident but he refused to back down. It was an issue he viewed as central to his own and his colleagues' safety. In the end, an internal appeal court overruled the fine and the clerk of the course at the Salzburgring was 'punished' with a suspension effective until the end of the year. Since there wasn't going to be another Austrian Grand Prix until the following year, it made absolutely no difference; he would be free to run the event again as if nothing had ever happened. It was the type of 'jobs for the boys' logic that Sheene so despised.

At the 1979 Belgian Grand Prix, he was again at the

Booze, fags and with James Hunt on a luxury yacht in Monaco harbour. You just know it's gonna be a good night.

Barry and Steph outside the Manor House at Charlwood. Parts of the house date back 700 years.

After winning the 1977 German Grand Prix, flanked by Steve Baker (left) and Suzuki team-mate Pat Hennen.

On his way to the fastest lap in Grand Prix history, at Spa-Francorchamps in 1977. His average speed was 135.06mph.

Lucky Seven. Barry cranks it over at the German Grand Prix in 1977, en route to his second world title.

Sporting his famous Donald Duck helmet during the 1979 Transatlantic Match races.

Playing to the crowd on his private Yamaha in 1980. Sheene remains unrivalled as a showman in motorcycle racing.

Shooting the breeze with American Dave Aldana in 1980. It was Sheene's worst-ever year in Grands Prix – he only finished 14th.

Chasing Kenny Roberts in the 1981 German Grand Prix at Hockenheim, ahead of Jack Middelburg and Randy Mamola.

On Kenny's tail again at the French Grand Prix. Sheene passed Roberts for fourth place.

Barry at Donington Park less than ten weeks after the Silverstone crash which so nearly killed him.

Back on a bike for the first time after the crash. Best friend Steve Parrish acts as a stabiliser.

'What more can I do?' Sheene was desperately frustrated with the below-par bike he had to ride in 1983...

...but he soldiered on and finished 14th in the world championship, equalling his worst-ever GP result.

Lining up alongside Keith Huewen in 1984. Huewen called Sheene a 'chief bull-shitter' while Barry reckoned Keith should have written a book on how to win friends and influence people.

On the gas, tucked in behind the screen, front wheel pawing the air. The Sheene machine at work in his last season, 1984.

Preparing for the 1984 South African Grand Prix with Eddie Lawson. Sheene finished third, his last-ever GP podium position.

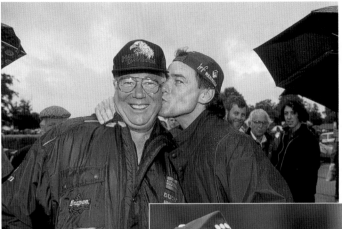

With his old mate and former rival John 'Moon-eyes' Cooper at Goodwood. The two remained great friends right to the end.

Like father, like son. Barry with his dad Franco in 1994. They were a team like no other.

Just for a laugh. Sheene transfers his famous number seven to a 100mph truck for a race at Donington Park after retiring from bike racing.

Racing a Toyota Celica in the 1985 British Saloon Car Championship. He came fifth in his class but quit at the end of the season.

Sheene the commentator. Interviewing Formula One star Nigel Mansell at the 1994 Australian Grand Prix.

With Damon Hill at the 1998 Goodwood Revival – Barry's first bike race for 14 years.

Barry with the love of his life, Stephanie, at the 2001 Australian Grand Prix.

Stylish to the end. Barry on his way to victory in the classic race at the 2002 British Grand Prix. Just days later he was diagnosed with cancer.

forefront of a stand-off with the FIM over a new track surface he and his fellow riders deemed too dangerous. It was pressure from Sheene in his role as riders' representative that had led to the resurfacing being carried out, but according to the leading riders it had not been successful: the tarmac was still oozing oil and it was therefore perilously slippery. Not wanting to disappoint the thousands of fans he knew would be turning up for the race, Sheene asked if the Grand Prix could be downgraded to an international meeting so that the riders could still put on a show without the pressure of having to ride flat-out for World Championship points. It seemed a logical and reasonable request, but it was declined by the FIM. The full-status Grand Prix went ahead – without any of the top riders.

On the face of it, it seems strange that Sheene didn't sign up to join the Association of Professional Riders when it was founded in 1977 to form a united front against race organizers on matters such as safety, money and conditions, but Barry wasn't confident that the riders would stick together when it mattered and preferred to flag up issues independently as and when they arose. While recognizing Sheene's efforts to improve conditions for riders, Mick Grant felt that at least in matters financial Barry chiefly had his own interests at heart. 'I think Barry probably helped with better safety standards,' he said, 'but he was a very switched-on guy, and when it came to money Barry looked out for Barry. If there was a spin-off [for other riders], it was coincidental.' He added, 'Barry's profile absolutely helped the sport, but in helping the sport he was actually helping himself – and that's not a criticism, it's an observation. Wherever he went he got publicity. I remember being at Paul Ricard once and he had George Harrison of the Beatles there. Living in London he sort of hung out with all these high-flying guys. I don't know of any Beatles actually going to Middlestown [Grant's home town].' John Cooper also attested to Sheene's financial acumen. 'He knew how to promote himself, unlike me. People like me agreed to ride for about £100, but Barry was having none of that. After he came back from his big crash at Daytona he demanded £10,000 to race at one particular track, but the owner said he wasn't going to pay it so Sheene rode somewhere else instead. Barry's thinking was that if he was going to bring 10,000 people through the gate at, say, £3 a head, then he had to be worth £10,000.'

In 1979, Sheene, frustrated beyond measure with what he saw as the uncaring attitude displayed by the FIM, agreed to be the frontman for the most audacious plan of all: the setting-up of a breakaway championship to be called the World Series. Forty of the world's top riders each put up £1,000 of their own money to fund the bid which would feature only two classes – 250cc machines and the premier 500cc class – to make the package more attractive to television companies and to make the sport more comparable to F1 car racing. It was a daring and revolutionary venture. Tracks that were considered too dangerous and countries that were too far away were to be struck from the calendar; instead, eight of the best tracks in Europe were to be included and prize money was to be vastly increased through better sponsorship. For the riders, it seemed the perfect scenario; for the FIM, it represented sheer rebellion, and the rebels had to be crushed.

Chief among those rebels was Sheene's arch rival Kenny Roberts – for once, the two actually saw eye to eye. Roberts, too, was a staunch campaigner for improved safety, organization and financial packages. From the moment he joined the European GP circus in 1978 he hadn't been able to believe how poorly organized and funded the championship was.

It would have been fascinating to see such a World Series in action, but in the end the plan was too ambitious and the FIM proved too powerful to overthrow. First of all they threatened circuit owners by saying that they would not sanction their tracks for the official World Championship if they supported the World Series; on top of that, riders who were expecting factory bikes started to get nervous that the Japanese might not support 'rebels' and would instead supply bikes only to riders competing in the official World Championship. Roberts, to offer just one example, was told by Yamaha that he had to ride in the FIM's championship. Roberts cannot be held to account for his employer's attitudes, but Sheene still blamed the riders for the collapse of the World Series. 'If we had stuck together, even if it meant a racing boycott, the manufacturers would have had no one to ride their machines.' There is an element of truth in this bold statement, but Sheene was being naive if he thought there weren't hundreds of other riders around the world begging for a chance in GPs. If motorcycle racing has taught us anything down the years it's that there are always new riders waiting in the wings to replace the old. In a sport with such a high mortality rate, there simply has to be a constant stream of new stars for it to survive.

The World Series might never have come to fruition, but it did have some positive and welcome knock-on effects including better financial packages and the removal of some of the more dangerous circuits from the GP calendar. Riders obviously need to be protected from the dangers of their sport as much as possible, but they also need to be paid in order to compete. Incredible as it may sound, Sheene and his fellow racers actually lost money competing in the World Championship, even into the eighties. Modern Grand Prix riders command multi-million-pound salaries, but Sheene and his colleagues used to race at a loss just for the privilege of picking up World Championship points. In 1982, for example, a win was worth around £3,500 while a sixth-place finish netted around £950. But in an era when mechanical breakdowns were a regular occurrence, there was every possibility that a rider could be leading a race right up to the last lap, suffer a breakdown and be rewarded for his efforts with the paltry settlement of £100. Even worse, should a rider crash in practice and be unable to race, he would leave the circuit with a standard fee of just £80. Sheene estimated that each round cost him in the region of £3,500 in fuel bills, hotels and expenses, so the farcical nature of the situation becomes evident. Riders were actually *paying* to risk their lives while others profited from their efforts. After all, someone had to be pocketing the gate money from hundreds of thousands of spectators, and it certainly wasn't the riders.

To compensate for these losses Sheene negotiated good financial deals to race in big international events, but that didn't stop him from continually trying to secure better deals for himself and his fellow riders for racing in the World Championship. And if he didn't feel he was being paid enough to race in any non-championship event, he simply wouldn't race, and that was that. Sheene had a very strong sense – some would say an over-inflated sense – of his own value; if he didn't consider he was being paid what he was worth, he wasn't interested. It was a policy that left many a burned bridge in Barry's wake.

If there was one man who personified the battle between Sheene and racing's various authorities, it was one-time chairman of the ACU Vernon Cooper. A man whose response to over 100 deaths at the Isle of Man TT was 'the throttle works both ways' was never going to see eye to eye with Sheene over safety issues, or, as it turned out, any issue whatsoever. It was almost inevitable that the two would come to loggerheads at some point. Cooper particularly incensed Sheene by claiming that 'after the big names have had their cut [of the money] there is often little left to share among the lesser-knowns'. Sheene took this remark as being aimed at him and he never wasted an opportunity for retribution. He voiced his hatred of Cooper in *Leader of the Pack*: 'It is acceptable for him to be a wealthy man and to live a life of luxury, but in his eyes, racers should be subservient peasants to whom he can successfully dictate and on whom he can foist his opinions.'

Sheene must have laughed louder than most when Cooper became the subject of Roger Cook's *Checkpoint* investigative programme (the forerunner of *The Cook Report*) in 1984. In an episode called 'Uneasy Rider', Cooper's abilities as head of the ACU came under heavy fire, and Sheene naturally had his say. Speaking of his former role as FIM riders' representative, he pointed out that he had been as welcome in the organization as 'a fart in a spacesuit'. He added that he'd 'always had a running battle with the ACU since my early days of racing', and inevitably that led to personal clashes with Cooper, of whom he had to say with regard to safety, 'If it comes to something that he's not in favour of then I would say the chances of it being accomplished are minimal.' Kenny Roberts was in total agreement with Sheene. He told Roger Cook, 'Vernon Cooper is in charge of the ACU and he is the one person that you absolutely know, when you go to him with anything about safety, he's gonna say no.' The programme ended, rather embarrassingly, with Cooper's wife fending off Cook on her doorstep and calling the police after Cooper changed his mind about being interviewed.

Barry's open attacks on the ACU didn't go unnoticed among his fellow riders, who respected the power he wielded. Ron Haslam was certainly in no doubt about Sheene's effectiveness when it came to bartering better deals for riders. 'He was absolutely perfect at doing interviews and dealing with the media. I was crap at all that and I didn't like doing it. Sheene was never scared to speak up, and that helped other riders a lot. Because he was a household name the authorities had to listen to him, whereas they didn't listen to the rest of us. Sheene could go on television and knock them down, so they were a bit scared of him, which was great for the rest of us when it came to getting things done in terms of getting better money and safety and stuff.'

It wasn't just safety issues and better money that Sheene pushed for; he was intelligent and broad-minded enough to realize that the sport's governing bodies should have been pushing for more television coverage of bike racing in an age when there was very little. Even back in the seventies Barry wanted every Grand Prix to be shown in full on mainstream television, a benefit Formula One car racing enjoyed. Only in 2003 did the BBC finally decide to televise every bike GP, though still nowhere near on the same scale as F1 racing.

Sheene was always at the forefront when it came to developing safety gear, too. He regarded himself as the first rider ever to wear protective knee pads inside his leathers – not to be confused with external knee sliders which protect a rider's leathers as his knee skims the tarmac (Sheene didn't own a leather suit with knee sliders until 2001). He had special pads made in Japan in 1976 which featured hard plastic on the outside for protection and soft foam rubber on the inside so that they were comfortable to wear and would help absorb any impact in that area. Sheene was convinced that during his huge Silverstone crash had his legs struck the handlebars just half an inch higher than they did, his knee pads would have helped protect him and his injuries would have been far less severe. Sewn-in knee protectors, still of a similar design, are now absolutely standard in leather suits, both for racing and road use.

Another Sheene innovation, which he initially developed

at home using three-quarter-inch foam, was the back protector – again, standard equipment nowadays. From 1976 he was involved with Italian bike-clothing specialist Dainese, and he would often ask them to develop specific items such as back protectors for him to wear. Later, he claimed that the firm's modern range of back protectors, which bent forwards but not backwards to help protect the spine while still allowing the rider to adopt a racing crouch, were based on his original ideas. He told *Bike* magazine, 'There was a chap who gave me a jockey's back protector in 1973 and that was the beginning. I modified it, formed some helmet visors onto a plastic plate, and made it so that it would bend forwards but not backwards. I made four or five prototypes then gave it to Dainese in 1977 and asked them to make it.' As a measure of how highly Sheene rated Dainese, he continued to wear the firm's leathers when racing classic bikes.

Sheene was also among the first group of riders to wear full-face helmets as opposed to the traditional helmet-and-goggles set-up that was prevalent when he started racing. He did start his career with a 'pudding bowl' helmet and goggles before briefly wearing a Bell Star open-face helmet, but he was among the new wave of riders to wear full-face lids, which are still worn today. He had a long-running contract with Italian firm AGV to supply his helmets, but when he got into classic racing he began to favour Japanese firm Arai. The firm responded to Barry's continuing popularity in 1997 by releasing a limited-edition Sheene replica, which was produced until 2001. Sheene owned a number of replicas for his personal use. When I rode with Barry through London for a feature for *Motor Cycle News* in 2000, I asked him why he had taped over his name on the back of his helmet. He explained that he didn't want people to recognize him, but revealed that the ploy had backfired recently. Having noted a rider passing him wearing a Sheene replica, Barry parked up and went about his business in a nearby shop. Within minutes, the rider with the Sheene rep came running into the shop shouting, 'I knew it had to be you! Who else would buy a Barry Sheene replica and then cover the name up?'

Sheene also explained at the time how the famous Donald Duck helmet had come about. 'My dad gave me a little plastic lid when I was five,' he said. 'It had a Donald Duck sticker on and the same gold surround, and I just kept the idea and developed it. Oh, and Donald Duck is cockney rhyming slang for fuck.' In the seventies, however, someone from the Walt Disney company, which owns all rights to the Donald Duck image, spotted Sheene's helmet and discovered that he hadn't obtained permission to exploit the image. When Sheene was asked to visit Disney representatives, he feared the worst. 'I thought I was in trouble, but they loved it, and from then on I've always been invited to Donald's birthday parties.'

One safety measure Sheene never took advantage of was earplugs, a fact he regretted later in life as his hearing was slightly impaired after years of racing extremely loud motor-cycles. Unsurprisingly, he once said that fitting silencers to race bikes was 'the best thing that ever happened in racing', though he did perform a complete U-turn on the issue in the last years of his life, repeatedly slating GP organizers for not allowing the new four-stroke bikes to run unsilenced like

Formula One cars. As he told *Bike*, in typically forthright manner, 'Whoever's final decision it was to do that is a complete and utter wanker and wants shooting.' Presumably he meant unsilenced bikes were good for spectators, as long as the riders themselves wore earplugs.

There are other, faintly comical but undoubtedly practical innovations Sheene brought to bike racing, such as wearing Marigold washing-up gloves over his racing gloves when it rained. It may sound wimpish, but racing gloves were not always waterproof, and having freezing-cold, wet hands meant reduced sensitivity when it came to a bike's controls. Of course, waterproof gloves are now widely available, should riders have any qualms about wearing bright yellow Marigolds. Another invention was cobbled together at an extremely cold Nurburgring, as Barry explained in *The Story So Far*. 'I dislike the cold on a bike more than anyone, so I rigged up a couple of lengths of car heater hose which ducted hot air up from the engine into muffs on the bars to keep my hands warm.'

The protective and practical capabilities of clothing aside, today's Grand Prix racer, indeed the Grand Prix paddock in general, has much to thank Sheene for when it comes to appearances. Pre-Sheene, almost everyone wore dull black leathers and very plain helmets. The celebration wheelie, now an intrinsic part of winning a race, was not often in evidence, and riders didn't have the luxury of motorhomes in which to relax between stints on their bikes. And no one even dreamt of beating the traffic by arriving at a circuit in a helicopter (though this is a luxury still cost-prohibitive to all but the most successful racers).

To greater or lesser degrees, Sheene can be thanked for all these innovations, and others. When one of his helmets came back from the painter's with his name emblazoned on the back, many other riders followed his (unwitting) lead and started to daub their own names on their lids, a practice which is still very much in evidence today. Barry also claimed to be the first rider ever to have raced with slick tyres when he tried out Dunlop's experimental slick during the 1974 Belgian Grand Prix. Again, slick tyres are now absolutely standard in dry conditions.

But if many of Sheene's innovations are now standard throughout the sport, not all of his predictions have come true. For example, he thought the future of Grand Prix motorcycling lay with the smaller-capacity 250cc class. Speaking in 1983, he said, 'The day is not far away, I believe, when racing classes will be restructured so that the blue riband category of the sport will be the 250cc. Advances in technology will allow design engineers to coax as much power out of the 250cc as they can from the 500.' In that, at least, he was correct: a modern 250cc GP bike produces around 120bhp, just 10 short of the 500cc machines of Sheene's era. But with the 1000cc four-stroke MotoGP series going from strength to strength, there seems little chance that the 250cc class will ever supersede it. In fact, it's very existence is in question as there has been much talk of a 600cc four-stroke feeder class supporting MotoGP.

Throughout his career, and indeed after his retirement from racing, Sheene helped many other riders, whether it was just with advice or to secure better bikes or sponsorship, even if at first some of them suspected his motives, as Ron Haslam explained. 'Early in my career I was crashing a lot and Barry told me that if I slowed down a bit I would end up going much faster. His advice makes sense now, but at the time I thought he was just scared of me as a rival and was trying to find ways of slowing me down. I ignored his advice for a while, but when I decided to try it I found Barry was right; I really did end up going quicker and I didn't fall off so much, which proved he really had been trying to help me.' Barry's mechanic Simon Tonge also testified to his avuncular altruism. The picture he painted was of a man who was extremely kind, loyal and free with his advice to those he liked and trusted. 'Barry offered me a job as his mechanic towards the end of 1981 and I ended up working for him until he retired in 1984. I was employed by Barry himself, not Suzuki, but then I worked for Suzuki after Barry retired. I was just a kid, just gone 18, and Barry treated me really well. He gave me a new motocross bike and let me drive his Rollers and big Mercs. He really did bring me up into adulthood really. Even though I was so young he trusted me completely because I had been working on bikes since I was 12 years old. We had a few disagreements, but I think they were all healthy and they were all forgotten within five minutes. He was good like that.'

After retiring from the sport, Sheene used his standing and experience to help and encourage many young riders, among them the 1993 500cc world champion Kevin Schwantz. Sheene was responsible for Schwantz's first ride on a 500cc Grand Prix bike when he arranged for him to ride one of his old 1984 Suzukis at the Mallory Park Race of the Year in 1986. Sheene had the bike removed from a museum and prepared in his own workshops. Better still for the young American, Barry arranged for him to earn £1,000 every time he won a race just for putting a DAF trucks sticker on his bike. Barry had seen Schwantz's performance in the Transatlantic Match Races and had been immediately impressed with the Texan, who later said, 'I forget how many races I won [it was actually four out of eight], but Barry Sheene was doing the TV commentary. After about the second or third day he came up to me and started talking to me, telling me that he would try and get me a ride on a 500.'

Often criticized, unfairly, by British bike-racing fans for deserting the sport when he moved to Australia, Sheene in fact kept up an active interest in racing and gave many young Australian riders a leg-up on to the international scene. Former World Superbike champion Troy Corser, for instance, burst on to the world scene in the mid-nineties with Sheene's recommendation. Now riding for Carl Fogarty's Petronas team in World Superbikes, Corser has said of Sheene, 'Barry was a really big inspiration for my racing and ultimately found me the opportunity to come to Europe, [enabling me to] start my racing career and be successful at what I always wanted to do.' Barry's last protégé was another Australian, Chris Vermuelen, who is currently riding in the World Supersport Championship on a Honda. Sheene called him 'the new Mick Doohan' and watched his progress with interest, although only time will tell if the youngster can ever match Doohan's awesome record of five straight 500cc world titles.

When Sheene's nephew Scott Smart took up racing, it seemed only natural that uncle Barry would help out. Smart is the son of Sheene's sister Maggie and his former rival Paul Smart, but when the couple approached Barry to ask for assistance, he refused. Sheene told *Motor Cycle News* that 'Scott went through a period where he was a real pain in the arse and I really didn't like him. He was arrogant, a legend in his own lunchtime.' Smart was forced to go it alone. He dropped out of a physics degree course to pursue his racing ambitions in 1994, when he entered a club race meeting at Brands Hatch, the same circuit where Sheene had made his debut back in 1968. Smart went on to win the 250cc British title in 1997, and to his credit secured a 500cc Grand Prix ride the next year, but he could only manage 21st place overall in the series on his under-powered V-twin Honda. Sheene thought this process necessary, believing that Scott should make his own way in life rather than being gifted rides because of who he is; until 1997, he hadn't even seen him ride. Later, the two of them buried the hatchet, and from that point on Barry offered to give any help or advice he could. Since 1998, Scott's career has been fairly chequered, though he bounced back in 2002 to finish second in the British Supersport 600 Championship. Smart does not seem to be destined to reach the levels of success his uncle did, but he's proud that he did things his own way. 'I'll always carry a label saying I'm Barry Sheene's nephew, but I want to be remembered as Scott Smart the racer and nothing else.'

With Sheene's acknowledged interest in helping out young riders, it was inevitable that talk of a team management position would come up at some point, and the rumours finally surfaced in 1997, although Barry was quick to quash them. *MCN* reported that there was talk of Sheene returning to set up his own big-money three-man team using factory Yamahas, but Barry soon put the record straight. 'When I gave up racing I always said there was no way I was going to come back, and I've kept my word. I've got a successful business in Australia and that's enough for me.' Apart from the occasional outing on his classic bike, Sheene did indeed keep to his word. It was the sport's loss, for the fact remains that no one has done more for the sport than Barry Sheene, and the results of his labours are still very evident.

CHAPTER 9

THE RACER: PART FOUR

'Without a decent bike there doesn't seem a lot of point. It's difficult to really get going.'

When Sheene rode onto the stage during the BBC's Sports Personality of the Year show in December 1982, there were lumps in many throats and not a few tears welling up in the eyes of viewers. It was the first time his adoring public had seen him back on a bike since the crash that should have killed him. He jokingly told host Frank Bough that the bike was 'the only way to beat the traffic', but keener observers were more interested in the name on the side of the otherwise plain white bike – Suzuki. Having established that Sheene would indeed be racing again in 1983, Bough finally asked about his team.

Sheene: 'I'm gonna ride for Suzuki, which is the company I rode for when I won both World Championships. I left them three years ago and now I've gone back to them, and I'm very pleased about that.'

Bough: 'And they're giving you full works team backing on it?'

Sheene: 'Yes, they're giving me all the help they can.'

Suzuki GB might have been giving Sheene all the help they could, but the Suzuki factory in Japan certainly wasn't. Sheene would be returning to World Championship racing on completely standard bikes after having worked so hard to gain full factory support from Yamaha. It must have been a devastating blow, but once again Sheene proved that he was not a quitter – as well as demonstrating yet again that he had indeed burned too many bridges with the Japanese over the years. Sheene was to be given two standard RG500 bikes to ease himself back into racing, but if he proved he was back to full fitness and capable of getting results, he would receive better bikes. At least, that was the plan.

The South African Grand Prix at Kyalami in February 1983 marked Sheene's comeback after his Silverstone crash of just seven months before. A fighting 10th place on a standard Mk V111 RG500 Suzuki proved to the world that he was still a force to be reckoned with, and an even more credible seventh place in the next round in France hammered home the point. It was enough to convince Suzuki that Barry deserved more support, and he was duly given an ex-Randy Mamola XR40 engine to replace his standard model. Sheene used it to good effect first time out in a round of the Shell Oils 500 Championship at Donington Park, where he finished second to his old mate Steve Parrish in what was, admittedly, a weak field by World Championship standards. Class field or not, Sheene was lucky to grab the second place as he'd suffered carburation problems; he complained that the engine had made little difference performance-wise. What he really wanted was one of the new aluminium chassis being used by Suzuki's factory-supported riders Randy Mamola and Franco Uncini.

One man not at all happy with Sheene's 'wish list' was his Heron Suzuki team-mate Keith Huewen. Huewen, from Woollaston in Northamptonshire, later became famous for his entertaining World Superbikes commentary on Sky TV, but in 1983 he was famous for his battles in the press with Sheene. Huewen, prone to being every bit as outspoken as Sheene, was infuriated that Barry had been given an ex-works engine when he had beaten Sheene both in the French GP and in a domestic race at Donington Park. Why was Sheene being shown such favouritism? Hadn't he had enough chances in the past? Racers are, quite naturally, extremely aggrieved when their team-mates are given superior equipment, but most manage to keep their grievances behind garage doors. Not Keith Huewen: he chose to tell the press just what he thought about Barry Sheene, and *Motor Cycle News* took full advantage of the juicy quotes. Huewen dubbed Sheene a 'so-called superstar and chief bullshitter', and although he later claimed to have been the victim of 'over-zealous journalism' he had made it clear that he was most definitely not Sheene's number-one fan. For once in his life Sheene took a more dignified stance and refused to become caught up in the public mud-slinging, saying only, 'Huewen should write a book on how to win friends and influence people.'

Sheene was given a full factory machine for the Transatlantic Trophy Match Races held at Donington Park over Easter weekend. However, it was a one-year-old machine, not one of the very latest 1983-spec bikes being raced by Mamola and Uncini. Still, it was a full factory bike nonetheless, and it looked like Suzuki were willing to uphold their promise to continue upgrading Barry's machinery so long as he kept notching up respectable results. Barry felt unwell throughout the Transatlantic weekend so he never really got the chance to put his new bike to full use – the string of mid-field finishes contrasted sharply with his five wins and one second place just a year before – but it was the Grands Prix where he really wanted to shine, and the German round at Hockenheim was going to be his first GP of the year on the factory bike.

Or so he thought. The bike had already been prepared for first practice when Sheene received a phone call from Suzuki's racing director Denys Rohan, who told him he couldn't race the factory bike and instead must revert to the production model. The decision was not Rohan's, it came directly from Japan, but that made little difference to Sheene who was understandably furious. There was little he could do about the situation, as Don Morley explained. 'Barry hated riding for Suzuki in the final years. There was still a lot of antagonism, but he didn't have a ride otherwise, and he knew it. By then it was humble-pie time. He just wasn't the same marketable commodity after his big Silverstone accident, but I think he did admirably under the circumstances.' No official explanation was given for the withdrawal of the bike, but most paddock pundits believed that Mamola and Uncini had exclusive rights to race factory Suzukis in the GPs, and that those rights were written into their contracts. That might well have been the case, but there is also the possibility that the top brass at Suzuki Japan were still unwilling to overlook Sheene's 'disloyalty' and public criticism of the firm in previous years and were now extracting a slow and indirect revenge. Dispirited and disheartened, Sheene made a bad start at Hockenheim and retired after failing to make the top 10.

If Suzuki were going to play games, then so was Sheene. He flatly refused to attend the Spanish Grand Prix in May, telling his employers that it was pointless even to turn up with the below-par bike he had. None of this political jousting between Sheene and Suzuki Japan was of much comfort to Suzuki's UK distributors, Heron. Barry was as big as ever in Britain, mainly thanks to his Silverstone crash and his new role as co-host on ITV's *Just Amazing!* Heron wanted Sheene to be out there grabbing headlines, preferably on the best bike possible, so after another bout of in-house wrangling Barry was eventually given permission to race the 1982 factory machine that had caused so much trouble. It appeared that his protest had paid off.

Sheene duly turned up a couple of weeks later at the Salzburgring for the Austrian GP and alternated between his standard bike and the factory bike during practice. Then, incredibly, after all the bickering over the factory machine, Barry opted to use his standard bike in the race, feeling that it was a better overall package. But at the super-fast Salzburgring he was only good enough to finish 13th – significantly, one place behind Keith Huewen, although both were rather embarrassingly lapped by race winner Kenny Roberts. It must have galled Sheene in particular to be lapped by the very man with whom he had been battling for the world title just one year earlier, but it was a measure of just how inferior his bike was compared to Roberts' Yamaha.

Another 13th place in Yugoslavia did nothing to lift Barry's spirits, and things got even worse in Holland in June when he had to retire with a smashed fairing after taking an unscheduled excursion into a Dutch ditch. Sheene was unhurt, but official HB Suzuki rider and reigning world champion Franco Uncini almost lost his life at the meeting when he crashed. Obviously dazed, Uncini crawled back onto the race track only to be hit on the head by a passing Wayne Gardner. His helmet came off in the horrific-looking accident, witnessed by millions of TV viewers. He eventually made a full recovery, but it was clear he would not be fit enough to race again for some time, which meant there were two full-factory Suzukis going spare. The burning question at the time was, who would get them?

Motorcycle racers never want to see any of their colleagues hurt, but they are realistic enough to take advantage of a bike that becomes available through another rider's misfortune. Sheene had been running in HB colours, but he was still not privy to the treatment, or bikes, Uncini had enjoyed before his unfortunate accident. With the British Grand Prix looming, Sheene's hopes of finally getting a full-on 1983 factory bike must have been high.

A bout of the flu ruled Sheene out of the Belgian GP, and then it was time for a return to the track which had so nearly killed him a year earlier. At Silverstone in 1983,

Norman Brown and Peter Huber were not so lucky. The two riders collided while Brown was touring back to the pits, and both lost their lives. It was a bad season for fatalities with three other riders having already been killed before the Silverstone round. Such statistics are a harsh reminder that motorcycle racing in the eighties was still a very dangerous occupation. Predictably, the press asked Barry if being at Silverstone brought back memories of his horrendous crash, but he told *Motocourse*, 'I hardly gave it a thought. Only when I saw the flag marshal in position approaching the left-hander [Abbey Curve], then I thought that if he'd been there a year ago it might not have happened.'

As things turned out, Sheene didn't gain promotion to official factory rider for the event; the honour went instead to Dutchman Boet van Dulmen, and Barry made no effort to disguise his disappointment. 'Without a decent bike there doesn't seem a lot of point,' he said. 'It's difficult to really get going.' But get going he did to finish a respectable eighth in the two-leg race, which was stopped and restarted after – too long after – the fatal accident involving Brown and Huber. Despite the fact that Sheene was never in the hunt for the lead, the crowd cheered him on like never before, wondering where courage like Sheene's came from. For them, Barry was a hero for just being there, back out on a bike again racing at breakneck speeds around a track that had so nearly claimed his life just twelve months earlier. The packed grandstands rose in unison every time he passed, and the track was completely mobbed on the slowing-down lap by tens of thousands of fans trying to get near their hero. World Championship contender he no longer was, but he was still Barry Sheene, a hero to millions.

Hero or not, Sheene's comeback year ended on a sour note with two non-finishes in Sweden and San Marino which left him 14th overall in the final World Championship standings – his worst position since that dire 1980 season on a private Yamaha. But if 1983 ended on a low, 1984 started on a fantastic high with what would prove to be Barry's last-ever Grand Prix podium finish.

Conditions were appalling for the opening round of the series in South Africa, but they suited Sheene down to the ground. In the wet, those with faster machines could not use their horsepower advantage; this levelled the field somewhat and gave Sheene more of a fighting chance on his underpowered Suzuki. In yet another of his oh-so-quotable quotes, Sheene once said of wet conditions, 'The advantage of the rain is that if you have a quick bike you have no advantage.' With his bike running on only three cylinders during the first lap, Barry was right at the back of the 18-man pack and was considering pulling out of the race when his Suzuki suddenly chimed on to all four cylinders. What happened next was pure Sheene magic. Carving his way through the pack, Barry set the fastest lap of the race and was lining up a pass on third-placed Didier de Radigues when his foot slipped off the footrest causing him to lose some ground. Undeterred, he got his head down once more, passed the Belgian rider and set about Raymond Roche in second place. It looked an impossible task, but on the very last corner he surprised Roche who, looking over his shoulder to see what the crowd were screaming about, was shocked to see one very determined Barry Sheene bearing down on him on the drag to the flag. Roche managed to hold his place, but with one more lap it might have been a very different story. It was a vintage and crowd-pleasing display from Sheene; he had proved that when all things were equal he was still capable of battling for podium positions.

A non-finish in Italy was followed by a dismal showing at the annual Transatlantic Match Races, held at Donington Park over six legs. Despite being captain of the British team, Sheene only managed a best finish of ninth place while his old rival Kenny Roberts celebrated his last appearance in Europe with a win in the final leg. It was another reminder of how far the gap between the two had grown. Even after retiring from Grands Prix, which he'd done at the end of the 1983 season, Roberts proved he was still capable of winning races while Sheene struggled to make it into the top 10.

In May, back in the GPs, Sheene took seventh place in Spain before having to suffer the humiliation of being lapped again, this time in Austria by Eddie Lawson, that year's eventual world champion. A 10th place in Germany was followed by a fighting fifth in France, which, in dry conditions at least, was about the best Sheene could hope to achieve against the plethora of vastly superior Hondas and Yamahas. The RG500 Suzuki was now a decade old and was, quite simply, outpaced. To make matters worse, Suzuki had withdrawn its direct support for Grand Prix racing so there was no chance of Sheene getting a full factory bike no matter how well he went. Instead, he had to content himself with a 1983 ex-Randy Mamola model. Mamola himself reflected on the demise of Suzuki as a GP force in the early eighties. 'The Yamaha V4 came out in 1982, and Kenny was the one who was really trying to develop that, and then of course Freddie Spencer won the championship with Honda in 1983 and raised the level so high that Suzuki pulled out. They just didn't have the budget to develop a V4 at that time, so they left racing until 1988, when they came back with Kevin Schwantz.'

Sheene at least enjoyed the benefits of a sweet-handling machine, thanks to the sterling job done by British chassis experts Harris Performance Products. Not only had they built Barry a frame for the RG, they had ingeniously devised one that allowed variable head angles so that Sheene could alter the steering geometry of the bike to his liking at different circuits. Harris also furnished Sheene with a variable rear suspension set-up, which again allowed Barry to claw back a little in handling of what he was losing in horsepower and through having to use second-rate tyres from Michelin, who no longer considered Barry one of their top riders.

Still he battled on, and he had another good finish in June in Yugoslavia; he was once again the fastest Suzuki in the field as he had been in France and South Africa. At Assen, a circuit which puts more emphasis on rider ability than sheer horsepower, Sheene looked set to have his best result since 1982. At one point he was running in second place behind Honda-mounted Randy Mamola, a near impossible feat considering the performance difference between the two bikes. And it was this very difference that was to be Sheene's undoing: on lap eight, he cruised to a halt with a broken con rod, the result of pushing his bike harder than it was capable of going.

A ninth place in Belgium didn't do Sheene's hopes for the British Grand Prix much good, but at Silverstone, with the help of a 17-inch rear tyre from Michelin – the first time he had been supplied with one – Sheene was as high as second place in Thursday's qualifying, although he ended up in sixth after the final session, praying for rain on race day. The heavens didn't open, but that didn't stop Sheene thrilling the crowds one last time. 'Rocket' Ron Haslam lived up to his nickname by getting another flying start off the grid to lead in the early stages, but Sheene was not far behind in second place. He stayed in touch with the leaders for 10 laps, riding the old Suzuki on the very limit as he had done at Assen, but again it proved too much for the outdated bike. When he felt a vibration coming from the rear of the machine he was forced to calm the pace and lost touch with the leading group. 'Every time I tried to go faster,' he said, 'the back end started pattering again.' Even so, Barry hung on to fifth place and came home to the biggest cheer of the day, his loyal fans still loving every result he could muster.

At times during that 1984 season Sheene showed flashes of brilliance, especially in August at Anderstorp – a track that had been as kind to Barry as Silverstone had been cruel – when he posted the fastest qualifying time, in the dry, on the Friday before the Swedish GP. During the race itself, however, Sheene was forced to take a very tight line to avoid the crashing Klaus Klein (who was later killed at the Ulster Grand Prix, another pure road circuit) and was thrown from his bike, knocking his knee and hip but otherwise emerging unscathed. At the San Marino Grand Prix in September he didn't even get a finish: unhappily, he lasted only eight laps at Imola before ignition problems robbed him of the chance to cross the line for one last time – though of course no one knew this at the time.

That meeting, some 15 years after his Grand Prix debut, and his overall sixth place in the 1984 World Championship marked the end of the GP career of the most popular rider in the history of the sport. Had Sheene himself known it was to be his last GP there would probably have been more of a fanfare and a bit of a party, but as it was, his last GP season simply petered out on a low note, plagued by the lacklustre machinery Barry had been forced to ride since leaving Suzuki in 1979, as his mechanic Simon Tonge explained. 'In 1980 he had that standard Yamaha which wasn't quick enough, then he started getting better stuff from the factory in 1981 before getting the good square-four in 1982 which was cool. But after the crash he was back onto production bikes again with the Suzuki just to see how he would go. In 1984 he did get some ex-Mamola engines but they weren't anything special. The Suzukis weren't any good at the best of times back then; they weren't the force they had been in the seventies.'

Sheene's bike might not have been competitive at a world-class level, but it was good enough on the domestic front where Barry took part in his last races. His final race win came at Oliver's Mount in Scarborough when he won the annual two-leg Gold Cup for a record fourth time. For

THE RACER: PART FOUR

Sheene it must have been just like old times as he battled once again with Mick Grant round the tree-lined circuit. In the first leg, Grant beat Sheene to second place with Suzuki rider Dave Griffith taking the win, but Barry won the second leg to take the overall victory from Griffith with Grant finishing third. It was the last time Sheene rode competitively at Scarborough, although he would return on many occasions to ride in parade laps, mainly because of his friendship with race organizer Peter Hillaby.

Barry's last-ever race was held at Donington Park on 22 September 1984, and, fittingly, it was a classic. The ITV *World of Sport* Superbike race was televised, and Sheene always seemed to have a little in reserve when he knew the nation was watching him. Donington was no exception, and the race turned into a breathtaking confrontation between Sheene and Ron Haslam. In the late summer sunshine, both riders swooped and dived under each other until Haslam looked like he had the race covered with a two-second lead over his rival going into the last lap. But in classic Sheene cat-and-mouse fashion, Barry gave it everything on the final tour and made up so much ground on Haslam that TV viewers were left wondering who had won the race as both riders crossed the finish line side by side. Haslam still has fond memories of the event. 'That last race was great. I looked at my pit board and thought I had him beaten on the last lap, so I backed off a little, but Sheene obviously still had a bit in reserve and he caught me sleeping on the line. We hadn't a clue who'd won it at first, it was that close.' Sheene himself was bubbling with enthusiasm when he spoke to the ITV camera crew straight after the race. 'Ron and I used to race together a hell of a lot, and it was just like 10 years ago, really good fun.'

The verdict went to Ron, who, being the sportsman and gentleman he is, would probably have handed the win to Barry had he known it was to be his last race. But as it was, no one knew, nor would they for several months, despite the fact that one publication had announced that 1984 would be Sheene's last season, much to Barry's annoyance. As far as the fans watching trackside and at home on TV were concerned, Barry Sheene had just proved yet again that he could cut it with world-class riders. Surely he'd do just one more season?

CHAPTER 10

WHAT IT TAKES

'You get on the bike, you wind it up, and you make sure you steer it in the right direction.'

There's a lot more to racing a motorcycle than meets the eye. Detractors of the sport will tell you that it consists merely of men on motorcycles going round and round and round the same stretch of tarmac without ever getting anywhere. For them, the only moment of light relief comes when there is a crash, the nastier the better. But it's easy to belittle any sport when you're unaware of what it truly entails. What is football but grown men kicking a pig's bladder around a field? And isn't cricket just a grown-up version of a game girls used to play at school? Grand Prix motorcycle racing, like any other sport played at its highest level, is a microcosm of the world itself, with all the expected ingredients, all the triumphs and defeats, the pains and jealousies, the money and lack of it, the bravery and daring, and so on. The crucial difference between bike racing and most other sports is that the competitors are quite literally putting their lives on the line every time they race. That's how much they love their sport. Call it fool-hardy, call it suicidal, but it is a truth. Of course, no racer wants to die, but neither is he willing to give an inch to a fellow competitor in his pursuit of victory, even if it does mean taking potentially unhealthy risks.

But it's not just on-track bravery that's required in the successful motorcycle racer – that's just a small, albeit extremely important, part of the overall picture. Anyone wishing to be a world champion will need to have highly tuned technical skills both for analysing bikes and develop-ing them; he will need to possess a strategic mind that can consider every possible course of action while he is actually racing a bike at 180mph; he will need to be fit and have enough endurance to last a one-hour race in temperatures well into the hundreds; he will need to have a high level of tolerance to pain, because he *is* going to get hurt; he will need to find sponsors to enable him to go racing; he will need to have the capacity to learn new tracks all over the world as well as to be prepared to travel all over the world, year in year out, long after the novelty of it has worn out; and the list goes on. Once all these factors are in place, maybe the rider can start thinking about his image and personality, and begin to plan a way to become the most popular rider in history. Not surprisingly, most racers find that their hands are full before even contemplating whether or not they are popular, and that suited Barry Sheene just fine. If everyone else was too preoccupied to enjoy the limelight, he'd just have it all to himself.

Sheene was, in many ways, the complete motorcycle racer with the ability to ride all kinds of bike, from 50cc two-strokes to 750cc four-strokes. Early in his career it was normal for GP riders to contest as many classes as possible simply to maximize their income through start money and prize money. By the mid-seventies this was less common as the differing Grand Prix disciplines became more specialized; the last notable exception was Freddie Spencer, who won both the 250cc and 500cc classes in 1985 – a feat never likely to be repeated. Sheene himself stuck to the 500cc class once he secured the RG500 Suzuki, although he did contest many non-GP races on a 750cc machine. But in the early years Barry raced whatever he could get his hands on. The list is impressive: TS125, TS250 and TS350cc two-stroke single-cylinder Bultacos; a three-cylinder 500cc two-stroke Kawasaki Mach One (on which he failed to finish an endurance race at Thruxton); a four-stroke 750cc Gus Kuhn Norton Commando with a Seeley frame; a 10-speed two-stroke RT67 125cc Suzuki twin; a Suzuki TR500 two-stroke parallel twin; a 50cc two-stroke Kreidler; a 250cc parallel-twin two-stroke Derbi; TZ250 and TR350cc Yamahas; a 500cc Seeley-Suzuki XR05; and a 750cc Seeley-Suzuki XR11.

Comparing riders of different generations has always been a largely futile and thankless task, but Sheene's ability to race, with great success, such a varying array of motorcycles was a tribute to his versatility. Few modern riders could make the switch from, say, a 125cc Grand Prix bike to a 1000cc Superbike and win on both, at least without a good period of familiarization. To the uneducated, it may appear that a bike is a bike and that the only difference is that some are faster than others. Not so. A rider carrying more speed into corners will have to change his braking points for every corner while remembering where his points are for another bike, should he be racing it the same day. Different bikes produce their power in different ways, so when and where Sheene could get on the power varied greatly from bike to bike. There is also a huge variation in weight between a 50cc and a 500cc bike, which affects handling, and on top of all that, tyres are of markedly different sizes from class to class. Riding a range of bikes requires an aptitude for adaptability today's riders no longer need, and therefore rarely cultivate. Sheene, although to a certain extent a product of his era, certainly had that ability. He remains the only rider to have won a Grand Prix on a 50cc bike and a 500cc machine.

But while modern riders may not need to race several machines at one Grand Prix meeting, they do need to be an awful lot fitter than the riders from Sheene's era, as triple British Superbike champion (and renowned fitness fanatic) Niall Mackenzie explained. 'The bikes are just so much more powerful now, and they're physically harder to ride because everything happens so much faster. The braking, grip and acceleration forces are a lot more now, so the rider's under a lot more strain. Even though the bikes from Sheene's era were heavier, gyroscopic forces helped you change direction, so that wasn't as much of a problem.' Sheene always maintained that he trained hard and was as fit as an athlete, and there can be no doubt that he punished himself vigorously when attempting to come back after his big crashes, but no rider who smoked several packs of cigarettes a day could truly claim to be totally fit.

Mackenzie believes the adrenalin rush experienced by riders during a race can often be enough to carry them through. 'Carl Fogarty always said he didn't train much, and Kevin Schwantz was the same in his earlier years, but they both won World Championships.'

Another factor Mackenzie believes is important is 'on-bike' fitness. By that he means that riding the bike in itself is a way of getting fit enough for the job in hand. Being 'bike fit' doesn't mean the rider is generally fit, it simply means that his body is accustomed to the very specific strains involved in racing, strains that cannot be replicated in a gymnasium. 'You need to be as good at the end of the hour as you were at the beginning,' Mackenzie added. 'Sheene wasn't carrying any extra weight, which would have helped him, and maybe he just had a natural stamina in hot conditions. As a rider, I had to try very hard physically to make things work, but some riders are more natural and don't have to expend so much energy.' Mackenzie's comments seem to be borne out by Barry's admission that he didn't 'have to take a deep breath to compose myself as I lean into a bend; the whole thing comes naturally to me'.

Sheene was photographed and filmed many times working out on his rowing and cycling machines at home, but he certainly didn't follow the strict training regimes of today's riders, which really only took off in the nineties, and he certainly didn't adhere to any strict carbohydrate-loaded diets. 'I frequently [have] eggs in some form for breakfast – scrambled on toast, boiled, poached, perhaps fried sometimes,' Sheene said. 'Two cups of Rosie Lee and a few cigarettes will set me up for the rest of the day.' At other times, Sheene's eating habits were little short of dangerous. In 1972, for example, he said he was 'going without food for long spells. This, I'm sure, led to the dizziness I was experiencing [at the time] and I didn't know whether I was coming or going.' Not an ideal position to be in when risking your life on a motorcycle. Even when Sheene did eat in those early Grand Prix days, it wasn't much. 'We still ate like hippies, a can of beans one day, maybe a frugal salad the next.'

However, by the time Sheene's family was accompanying him to Grands Prix, his mum Iris always ensured her son had plenty of home cooking to keep him going, a comfort Barry always enjoyed. 'It's important to line the stomach, no matter how pressing the need is to get to the track. Stamina has to be maintained, so I'll fuel the boiler with eggs, bacon, toast or whatever is available. A round of sandwiches at midday washed down with tea will be the only additional intake before the race.' Barry was certainly always careful not to take on too much liquid before a race as he never wanted to be in a position where he was bursting to go to the toilet just before the off, as happened before the 1980 French GP when he had to urinate in a tunnel in front of the main grandstand. Although not always a regular or healthy eater, Sheene always claimed that his eating style was of great benefit to him. 'I'm convinced my history of rapid healing is the result of eating good food full of the right nutritional ingredients,' he said. Given the shortcomings of his early diet, Sheene's statement may sound misguided, but he did later develop a taste for good food and drink, particularly Italian food and French wine, of which there was an abundance in his well-stocked cellar.

Healthy or not, Sheene proved to have incredible stamina during hot races, most notably in Venezuela where he won three GPs in a row from 1977 to 1979 in sweltering heat that severely affected his rivals' performances. Pat Hennen testified to this in the 1978 edition of *Motocourse*. 'In that heat, I just couldn't be quite that aggressive. Barry doesn't appear terribly fit for those sort of conditions. But he is. He rode past me and I couldn't hang on for more than a lap and a half. I had more or less the right combination for the conditions, but he had the stamina.' The 1976 Dutch TT was another good example. The 100-degree temperature took such a toll on the riders that sidecar race winner Hermann Schmid actually passed away after the race, though he was immediately revived. *Motocourse* noted that, though Sheene poured a bucket of cold water over his head after the race, he still looked 'fitter than most' after he'd won the event for a second year in succession.

To aid his natural stamina, Sheene always tried to ensure that he got a good night's sleep before a Grand Prix, and from 1975 onwards that meant in the best hotel available. At the beginning of his career, Sheene had roughed it like everyone else by sleeping in the back of a van. Then came the caravan in 1972, which at the time was seen as wanton luxury. He had, however, sampled five-star luxury on the few occasions when funds permitted it, as he explained. 'The Austrian organizers [in 1971] had reckoned my three rides were worth about £100, so Don [Mackay] and I checked into a swishy hotel in the mountains near the track the night before the meeting. It meant that we would be in reasonable physical shape for the big day. After the blow-out in the hotel, it was back to the back of the van and two cold sleeping bags. All the money had gone. There was about enough cash to buy fuel to get us to the next German round.'

After 1975, when Sheene could afford to pay hotel bills on a more regular basis, he found a comfortable bedroom to be as crucial to his race preparation as setting up his bike. For Barry, it was all about relaxing. 'When I go to bed the night before a big meeting,' he explained, 'often with half a bottle of wine inside me, my thoughts are miles away from racing. There are far better things to concentrate on. It is not until I get up in the morning that I start to allow the race to occupy my mind.' Sheene justified the expense of staying in top-class accommodation by remembering what he once had to endure. 'Ever woken up on a freezing-cold morning after spending the night on the floor of a van, competing for bed space with spare wheels, oil cans and tools? Droplets of moisture would cover the inner walls of the vehicle and you would climb out of a damp sleeping bag knowing the first race would be the rush across the paddock to beat everyone else to the normally appalling washing and toilet facilities.'

Even though he always stayed in five-star hotels when racing, Sheene still splashed out £28,000 in the early eighties on a luxury 30-foot motorhome just so he could have a base at circuits. At the time it was the most expensive the racing world had ever seen, and the vehicle was certainly a contrast to the caravan of the early days, but for Barry it was all part of keeping up his image, as well as affording him a luxurious and relatively tranquil bolthole. The motorhome and the hotel rooms allowed Barry to escape the often overwhelming atmosphere of paddock life where the only talk is of racing, where the sound of revving bikes and late-night parties can become too much.

It is easy to forget that bike racers have to travel the world every year in their bid for championship glory. For the millions watching at home, all the riders appear as if by magic in a different country each weekend with the touch of a button on the remote control. It is not so easy for the competitors. Travelling the world may sound glamorous, it may even hold an appeal for some riders when they are starting out, but the excitement soon wears off, especially as they rarely see anything other than an airport, a hotel and a race track no matter what country they are in. Incessant flight delays and cancellations eventually took their toll on Sheene, prompting him to drive to most European races in his Rolls Royce. This allowed him to stay another night in a hotel to celebrate when he won a race, and he could lie in bed the following morning without having to worry about catching a flight. Instead, he would set off at his own pace for the next country in the luxury of the Roller with all the time in the world to gather his thoughts away from the ever-present media scrum. And in 1981, of course, Sheene took his personal travel one stage further by purchasing the ultimate in private transport – a helicopter. As Sheene said, 'It's quicker [than the Rolls], far more relaxing and ends the constant risk of getting booked for speeding.'

Whenever he was at a race track, Sheene had to go through the same process as every other rider, famous or not. Practice was always the usual routine of setting the bike up to accommodate the nuances of whichever circuit he was riding. Gearing, carburation, suspension and tyre choice are always crucial to the outcome of a race, and Barry would work as hard as anyone else when it came to finding the correct race settings. It was a process that often annoyed him, simply because he often found his qualifying efforts had been in vain come the start of the race. Sheene struggled to push-start his machine because of his damaged legs; as the rest of the field disappeared from sight, he often found himself wondering why he'd even bothered to practise. Speaking about the 1984 South African Grand Prix, where his bike refused to fire up initially, he said, 'You work your nuts off over two days of qualifying, getting better and better, and then you sit on the line and push the thing and it doesn't start. You've just wasted two days. I might as well just have sat in the motorhome.'

With qualifying over, race day dawns, and the first thing Sheene always did was look out of his hotel window to check the weather. Never a fan of riding in the wet, Sheene was always very good at it, and in later years he came to relish the prospect as it was the only time his underpowered bikes had a chance of a good result. The 1984 South African Grand Prix was again a good example: Sheene stormed through to third place after being 20 seconds behind at the start of the race. Given the sub-standard nature of his bike, Sheene cited that performance as the best in his career.

After the compulsory warming-up lap, Sheene traditionally handed his bike to a mechanic to hold while he gave it the once-over, just to put his mind at ease that nothing was visibly wrong with the machine. Then there was little more to be done except wait for the flag to drop or the lights to change, depending on which system was in use. Barry had no particular preference for either, but he was wily enough to observe certain factors that would give him an advantage. With a lights system, for example, he would watch earlier races to try to determine how long the gap was between the red light going off and the green light coming on, as it varied from circuit to circuit. If the race was being started manually with a flag, Sheene keenly observed the starter, hoping he would give away slight gestures just before he was ready to drop the flag.

But, as the old racing saying goes, 'when the flag drops the bullshit stops', and Sheene's fame and popularity were of no use to him once things were underway. In a race, he was on his own for the best part of an hour, taking on the best riders in the world. He had to stand or fall by his own decisions and tactics, although Sheene always insisted that he never thought about tactics until the race had begun. 'I hardly ever spend time beforehand figuring out what my race strategy is going to be. Only in the thick of the action can a clear picture form of where certain riders in front demonstrate weaknesses, and you learn to remember the sections where they can be taken.'

Chip Hennen was well aware of just how much Sheene thought about his racing and how much others could learn from watching him at work. 'Barry taught my brother Pat a tremendous amount, and we watched him extremely closely. He was one of the most intelligent racers, if not the most intelligent racer, we ever raced against. He was just truly, truly amazing in his ability to map out a race track and to figure out what lines to take around it. He didn't have the natural ability that Pat and Kenny had, but that's because they had been racing since they were kids. Barry didn't have the advantage of that. But he was famous for winning races coming out of the last corner on the last lap of a race. He had learned how to get maximum drive coming out of a corner onto a straight so that he entered the straight going two or three miles per hour faster than the guy in front of him. A little later down the straight that translated into four or five miles per hour, meaning Barry could pass the next guy pretty easily.

'Barry's unusual cornering style was almost identical to the one Michael Schumacher uses today. At the slowest point of the corner, Barry would start to pick his bike upright and head as straight as possible for the edge of the track, trying to pick up as much speed as possible. He wouldn't finish the corner until he reached the edge of the track. At that point there was very little wheel spin, so he could lean the bike over a little more and turn the handlebars to complete the corner. It was really a very clever cornering technique, and I think it spoke volumes about his extraordinary intelligence. Barry was also exceptionally good at driving very deep into hairpin corners. Unlike everyone else, he used the braking power of the engine very effectively to help slow the bike down as he entered the corner. It was largely a function of how he geared his bike.

As he approached the corner and started to shift down, his engine was revving much, much higher than anyone else's, meaning his engine was working much, much harder in helping to slow the bike down.

'Especially at the races in the UK, where the tracks were generally fairly short, if someone like Barry was faster than Pat around a particular area of a track, Pat, Mike Sinclair [Pat's mechanic] and I would figure out what corner they were faster in and what they were doing that was different from what Pat was doing. By mid-1977, Pat had really learned all he could about Barry's cornering and braking tricks and had put them into practice with good effect. He was starting to finish ahead of Barry more and more often, and by the end of the season I think nearly everyone thought Pat was faster than Barry. Looking back, I'd say that Pat studied Barry's cornering and braking techniques and racing strategies more closely than any other rider. Though their riding styles were really very different, Pat incorporated all of Barry's unique cornering and braking techniques into his own riding style. At the end of the season Pat also started to work more on the PR, and again he, Mike and I were watching what Barry did.'

This is the side of motorcycle racing the casual observer fails to see; it is in fact a high-speed game of chess, each rider passing off dummy moves to fool another, allowing following riders to pass so they can be observed, slowing the pace to conserve tyres ready for a real fight in the last three laps, feigning a slow line through a corner to fool an opponent into thinking he can pass you, then closing the door on him. There is no end to the inventiveness of a good motorcycle racer, and everything must be done at speeds that would astonish the general public should they ever be lucky (or unlucky) enough to experience them. It is a fact that bike racing on television looks slow; the medium simply does not reproduce the impression of speed well. Anyone who has stood just feet from the track as the riders pass flat-out at 180mph will have some idea of the size of the task facing them and the level of skill required to perform it well. It's really not just a case of going round and round. There are other factors to consider too, such as positioning yourself in the pack through the first few crucial corners to avoid being knocked off by over-enthusiastic riders, and slipstreaming rivals – tucking in behind them to make use of the hole they are punching in the air, which in turn allows your own bike to gain a few rpm – down straights.

Even when a race was over, Sheene was still switched on enough to realize the popularity-winning potential of the slowing-down lap. After a victory wheelie over the finish line – commonplace now, but still a spectacle in Sheene's day – he would remove his helmet and play to the crowd as he toured round, waving and pulling the odd wheelie. It was a simple touch, but removing his helmet was another stroke of genius. One of the biggest problems with bike racing, as far as promoting personalities are concerned, is that they spend so much time hidden under crash helmets. Sheene always removed his at the earliest opportunity in the knowledge that every picture that was taken and every reel of film that was shot would show *him*, not a faceless helmet. The benefits of this kind of exposure were later judged to be of such importance to TV viewers that today, according to FIM rules, all GP racers must remove their helmets on the start-line.

Racing itself aside, another crucial part of a successful bike racer's make-up is the ability to attract sponsorship, and in that particular discipline Sheene had no peers. But like everything else about his racing, it was something he had to learn. In the beginning, he confessed, 'Sponsorship was something I knew nothing about. It never occurred to me that you could be given money for putting manufacturers' stickers on the machine's fairing. I was quite content to let companies such as Castrol, Dunlop and Champion advertise on my bikes if they were supplying goods, but I'd never thought about asking for cash hand-outs for displaying brand names for other people.' But Sheene proved a fast learner, and, as we know, went on to become the most marketable bike racer of all time; he could pick and choose the names he wanted to display on his bikes, leathers and helmet.

But a lot of hard work went in to creating Barry Sheene the marketing dream, and all of it was planned. In the early seventies, before he was well known, Barry sat down and had a long, hard think about sponsorship. Realizing that no one had heard of him and would therefore not be interested in sponsoring him, he set about making himself famous. 'I decided to be sensible and make an investment in myself. I did it by working hard at getting myself known. I did any TV or radio programme that came up, and I talked to anybody from any paper or magazine who wanted to interview me.' Sheene's Daytona crash was the icing on this particular cake, but he had already done a lot of the groundwork before the accident and many young riders today could still learn from his advice on making a name for themselves outside the sport. 'Back in the early seventies,' he added, 'I made a deliberate attempt to become known beyond the normal audience of spectators who followed racing. While other sports produced household names, motorcycle racing's heroes never received the exposure their feats deserved, and consequently there was nothing to awaken potential major sponsors to the fact that here was a good sport with the appeal to capture the imagination of all kinds of people, especially the free-spending young.'

For all kinds of people, Sheene did indeed fit the criteria of the complete racer. His skills on the track were enough to earn him two world titles, and his skills off the track earned him not only vast wealth, but a fan base of millions. Motorcycle racing entails more than meets the eye, and Sheene mastered every element of it like no rider before or since.

CHAPTER 11

NEVER SAY NEVER AGAIN

*'I enjoyed that. It seemed like I'd never
been away.'*

Barry Sheene had always intended to retire at the end of
the 1985 season at the age of 35, but, frustrated at not
being able to secure competitive motorcycles, he
announced his decision to hang up his leathers in January
1985 at a press conference at the Mayfair Hotel in
London. 'Since the [Silverstone] accident, it's been very difficult for me to get a competitive bike, or one competitive
enough to win the World Championship on,' he explained.
'Over the last couple of months I've been trying to get a
bike that I could win the World Championship on and I
couldn't get one, so I thought now was a good time to give
it up.' Sheene had toyed with the idea of racing for the
Italian Cagiva factory, but once again the plan went to
pieces when Barry learned he would not be allowed to run
the bikes from his own home because they were still in the
early stages of development.

With the sport's increasing emphasis on youth, it would

have been unusual for anyone of Sheene's age to be given the latest factory equipment, and despite his continuing popularity, Barry must have been well aware of the fact, no matter how much he might have wished it otherwise. Suzuki had withdrawn its factory involvement, leaving Sheene with no other realistic options, and there seemed little point in making up the numbers on a privately entered machine again. His time had come.

Sheene's retirement made the main news. He explained his decision to hang up his leathers and unveiled his plans for the future. 'I have a two-year contract with DAF trucks to race and promote their trucks, so I shall be going round different European race tracks to compete in that. And I'm also negotiating with a company to race saloon cars, but this is not to earn my living at, it's just something that's a little bit of fun.' Barry had become a father for the first time two months before he announced his retirement with the arrival of his daughter Sidonie, another factor that no doubt influenced his decision to retire. But rather than being bitter about not securing a competitive bike, he showed he had lost none of his sense of humour when he was asked by a *News at Six* reporter how his legs were: 'Oh, they're great. I wouldn't be without them.'

It was a time in Sheene's life that called for a measure of reflection, and among other questions put to him was, what was your greatest race? For the record, he listed his six most memorable battles for the 1990 FM Television production *Barry Sheene: Six of the Best*. In descending order, they were the 1975 Dutch TT, which was his first 500cc win; the 1984 South African Grand Prix, which marked his last ever GP podium; the 1977 Italian Grand Prix at Imola, simply because he'd always wanted to win in Italy but had until then been plagued by bad luck; the 1976 and 1982 Dutch GPs (he won the former and remembered the latter simply because it was held in pouring rain with all the riders' on slick tyres); and the 1979 British Grand Prix, which he so nearly won from Kenny Roberts on the very last corner.

But Sheene was not the sort to retreat from the spotlight, indulge in nostalgic reflection and fall back on his hard-earned millions, even though his retirement had been forced upon him a season earlier than intended. He had other fish to fry, and he wasted no time before throwing himself into new projects. He had already starred in his first (and thankfully only) movie, the dreadful 1984 flop *Space Riders*, alongside Gavan O'Herlihy, who had also featured in the 1983 Sean Connery Bond movie *Never Say Never Again* and *Superman III* and would go on to star in the 1988 George Lucas/Ron Howard movie *Willow*. But even O'Herlihy's involvement couldn't save the film, which was based around road racing and featured some spectacularly embarrassing crash sequences set to an eighties soundtrack by bands such as Simple Minds, Queen and Duran Duran. Barry was also one of three hosts – along with comedian and singer Kenny Lynch and actress Jan Ravens, who was later replaced by another actress, Suzanne Danielle – of a new ITV prime-time programme called *Just Amazing!*, which was effectively a hybrid of *Record Breakers* and *Game for a Laugh* that featured ludicrous stunts and moments of madness from around the world.

The first-ever episode, for example, featured a regurgitator, a surfing rabbit and a man attempting to fly across a river in a rocket-fuelled car. Sheene, as ever, was at ease in front of the cameras, although that wasn't always the case according to John Cadrick, the head of Fabergé's consumer products division when Barry started doing the Brut 33 TV ads. 'Barry's very good [on TV] now,' he said, 'but when he started doing talkies he was atrocious.' Still, showing typical determination to master any new skill that would ultimately benefit him, Sheene worked hard and before long had TV work mastered. *Just Amazing!* enjoyed a popular run on Saturday nights before being moved to Sunday evenings in 1984, where it eventually ran its course before the year was out. In 1986, Barry teamed up with The Who's Roger Daltrey to appear on (and win) *Driving Force*, a game show where celebrity contestants drove tanks, rally cars, trucks, fire engines and forklift trucks in timed stages and races.

Despite having these and other projects to keep him busy, Sheene still missed racing in his first year of retirement from the sport. 'It was pretty difficult in 1985 when I saw results and who was doing what. If times got difficult with some projects I was working on or whatever, I used to think, "If I was still racing it wouldn't be as difficult as this." But then in 1986 I got involved in a lot of different things and I didn't think about the racing at all.'

Sheene had vowed that from the moment he announced his retirement his decision would be final, that there was no way he would make a fool of himself by coming back for money and simply riding round at the back of the pack.

But this covered only motorcycle racing; he didn't say anything about cars or trucks. Truck racing was conceived in the United States (where else?) in 1979, but the first race in Britain didn't take place until September 1984 at Donington Park, neatly confirming the theory that Britain is America five years down the line. It was an instant and huge success, although initial crowds were drawn more out of curiosity than a genuine love for trucks.More than 80,000 people travelled to Leicestershire, blocking the nearby M1 motorway for five miles in both directions, to watch 40 massive 100mph trucks quite literally demolish the usually well-kept circuit. Among the drivers was Sheene. 'The reason I did the truck-racing thing was because I had advertising from DAF and they wanted me to get involved with it, so I did it, but it was never serious.'

Despite admitting to having lost his competitive edge, Sheene entered various truck races over the next few years, mostly to lock horns with his buddy Steve Parrish, who took the whole thing a lot more seriously and went on to win five European championships. For Sheene it was a bit of fun, although he did have several wins both in Britain and Australia, but after a final race in Australia in 1988 he hung up his truck-driving overalls alongside his racing leathers. 'I had burned my competitive [spirit] out as far as sport was concerned with the bike thing,' he reflected. 'I could never take anything seriously after that.'

Sheene's interest in four-wheeled racing actually went right back to 1973, when he tested a single-seater racing car at Magny-Cours in France. While at the track to race his bike, Sheene had got talking to the organizers of a car-racing school there and had a 'little wobble round after lunch' in one of the school's Renault-powered cars. It might have been a bit of fun initially, but things looked like they were getting a bit more serious in 1977 when John Surtees asked Barry if he would like a test drive in one of his Durex TS19 Formula 1 cars. Surtees remains the only man to have won World Championships on both two and four wheels: a seven-times motorcycling world champ, he also won the 1964 car Grand Prix World Championship before going on to become a successful car constructor. He arranged for Sheene to have his first drive in a Grand Prix car at Brands Hatch in August 1977 during a private mid-week session away from the glare of the media. With his car-mad pal George Harrison looking on, Sheene completed 70 laps of the short Indy circuit and, despite having faulty brakes, came within 2.9 seconds of the lap record – an impressive performance, even if it didn't overly excite Barry. 'It was no major problem to achieve that fast time,' he said later, 'and the experience, although enjoyable and requiring immense concentration, did not stimulate me to the point where I felt I just had to switch to four wheels.' But he had at least been encouraged enough to consider racing a Surtees in the Aurora series, a British championship for F1-spec cars, in 1978, as well as defending his world bike title and racing in the *MCN* British Superbike Championship – a commitment his contract with Suzuki obliged him to fulfil. It was all too much, however; there were too many date clashes and Sheene was forced to shelve the idea, at least for 1978.

He maintained links with the car-racing world. He had already become good friends with James Hunt through their mutual Texaco sponsorship, and when he met Arrows designer Tony Southgate at the Spanish bike Grand Prix in 1978 he struck up an immediate friendship that led to a test in Riccardo Patrese's car, once again with a view to contesting the Aurora series. Sheene eventually tried out the Arrows at Donington Park that September, but spun out after only eight laps, damaging the car too badly to be able to continue. Realizing that these things happen in motorsport, especially on cold tyres as Sheene's were, the Arrows team arranged another test at Silverstone on 1 December. Sheene was instructed to take things easy, to familiarize himself with the car rather than go out chasing lap times, and that's exactly what he did, completing almost a full Grand Prix distance without any problems. The fact that he was seven seconds off regular Arrows driver Jochen Mass's best times should have been irrelevant, but the press, always on the lookout for a more sensational angle, slated Sheene's performance and claimed he had no ability on four wheels. Ultimately, it wasn't Sheene's talent or lack of it that put paid to him racing an Arrows in 1979, it was purely down to cash. Sheene's agents, Championship Sporting Specialists, were ultimately unable to find the £300,000 sponsorship package Barry needed to fund an eight-race season and the project collapsed, despite the fact that Sheene had managed to negotiate a new contract with Suzuki that would have allowed him to race cars as well as bikes in 1979.

Unable to fund a full season of car racing, Sheene accepted an offer to race in a round of the BMW County Saloon Car Championship at Ingliston near Edinburgh.

Driving a fuel-injected BMW323, Barry set pole position and won the race by eight seconds. It should have been enough to convince him that a career in car racing was worth pursuing, but the effect was actually the opposite. Speaking in 1983, he said, 'When I passed that chequered flag, my car-racing career was over. While it was mildly enjoyable, I knew in my heart that the world of bikes was where I really belonged. I am a motorcycle racer, and cars are not for me.'

Despite these sentiments, after his retirement from motorcycle racing it was indeed to cars that he turned, this time for a full season in the Trimoco RAC British Saloon Car Championship, the forerunner of today's popular British Touring Car Championship. Sheene signed up to race a 2.8-litre Toyota Celica Supra in the 1985 series with sponsorship from Hughes of Beaconsfield. 'In 1985 I drove for Toyota,' he said in an interview for FM television, 'and I put my heart and soul into that, but the car got written off. I was okay at it, you know, pole position and I was up the front to begin with, then the car got written off. I got hit from the back and then T-boned at about 130mph, and the next car they built just wouldn't go within two and a half seconds a lap of the original car, which was set up by a guy called Wynne Percy. So after that I lost interest, if you like, and at the end of the year I decided to forget saloon car racing.'As Sheene pointed out, his results were encouraging at times, two thirds at Thruxton and Silverstone and a fourth at Brands Hatch the season's highlights, but a spate of mechanical problems ruined any chance of a decent championship challenge. He retired with accident damage at Oulton Park, Thruxton and Silverstone (two of the circuits that hosted two rounds of the series that season), suffered gearbox problems at Donington Park and electrical problems at Snetterton, and was forced out with ignition trouble at Brands Hatch. With only six finishes from a 12-round championship, he ended the season fifth in his class – Class A for engine sizes of 2501cc to 3600cc – and 12th overall.

In July 1985 Sheene also raced a Toyota Celica in the Spa 24-Hour endurance race with Belgian co-drivers Michel Delcourt and Pascal Witmeur. The trio managed 107 laps before suffering engine problems serious enough to put them out of the race. It was won by emerging Formula 1 star Gerhard Berger, who remained a friend of Sheene's until he passed away. But after 1985 Sheene turned his back completely on car racing for 16 years. Only in 2001 did he, along with five-times 500cc world champion Mick Doohan, decide to race on four wheels again, in the Targa Tasmania rally. The six-day Targa event covers nearly 1,400 miles over 54 stages, and in 2001 more than 300 cars took part. Sheene drove a Mercedes four-wheel-drive ML55 and finished in 76th place, which was better than Doohan who crashed out while lying in 13th place and damaged his car too badly to continue.

The rally was just a bit of fun for Sheene, and easy to get to from his home in Queensland where he'd emigrated in 1987 (Barry had discovered that ever since his 1975 Daytona crash his bones ached in cold, wet conditions, whereas heat helped to soothe the pain). It was a laid-back lifestyle that suited him well, as he told Thames Television in 1990. 'One of the lovely things about living over here is that, having a young family, I can spend so much time with them. I take my little girl to school in the morning and I can go and pick her up from school. I spend a lot of time with my family. There's no sort of typical day for me. Normally I get out of bed about 6.30 in the morning, go to the gym, then go to the office to see if there are any faxes from England or anywhere in Europe. If there are, I sit down and answer them. By that time there will have been a couple of phone calls, and maybe I'll have to go to Sydney or Melbourne. Obviously I miss a lot of things about England; I had a lot of good friends there, but we still stay in touch. My phone bill costs an arm and a leg 'cos I'm forever phoning people up. As I said, I didn't leave England because I didn't like it; I love England, and I had tremendous support over there. The reason I came to Australia was for health reasons, and it's a great way to bring a family up.'

Always an astute businessman, Sheene had long been a believer in investing in bricks and mortar as a surefire winner when it came to making cash, as former Grand Prix star and three-times British Superbike champion Niall Mackenzie knows to his cost. 'I met Barry at a function in 1986 when I'd just signed with Honda to race in Grands Prix. Barry told me to invest everything I had in property in London. I thought he was a bit off the mark with that one, but with London prices the way they are now it shows how wrong I was.' Sheene took advantage of his knowledge of the property business when he moved to Australia by buying commercial properties and renting them out. It started on a small scale, but by 1999 Sheene estimated that his business, which by that time had grown to the point where he was renting out massive office blocks, was worth more than £10 million – not bad going for a man who didn't even have a bank account of any kind until he was 22 years old.

Though his hugely successful property business was his main source of income, it wasn't by any means the only one. Sheene also signed a deal to work for Australia's Channel 9 commentating on car and bike Grands Prix, as well as Indy cars and pretty much anything else the station wanted him to cover. Barry also netted some healthy contracts to appear in TV adverts for Shell and Daewoo which were to make him a household name all over again, but this time on the other side of the world.

Barry's parents, Frank and Iris, made the move to Australia along with their son, but Iris sadly passed away as the result of a brain tumour in 1991. It was a devastating loss for Frank and Barry; the family had always been close, and Barry's parents had been a key ingredient in his racing success, always on hand to offer support and advice not just to Barry but to anyone in the paddock, as John Cooper recalled. 'The Sheene family was always a nice, friendly family. Franco, Iris, Maggie, Barry, even his uncle Arthur used to go to all the races. They always made everyone feel very welcome. I'd go to their barbecues at the circuits and they'd come to mine. Barry was always a very good family man, he always enjoyed his family being around him.' Barry was never shy when it came to admitting his devotion to his family. 'I love my family,' he said. 'I just think that people who look after their parents and like their parents are nice people.' Frank found life in Oz difficult after Iris passed away; all his friends and memories were back in England, and he often flew home to stay with his daughter Maggie in Maidstone, Kent, during the racing season to meet up with old friends before jetting back to Australia for the winter.

In 1996, Barry signed up with Channel 10, again to commentate on motorsport but also to co-host the station's *RPM* motorsports programme. Happy with his status as a celebrity presenter, he signed up for another six-year stint in 2001. In 1996, few people held out any hope that Sheene would become the focus of the programme himself by racing a bike again, but in 1998 the seeds were sown for a racing comeback when Barry was invited to take part in the Assen Centennial Classic event between 8 and 10 May. Organized by Ferry Brouwer of Arai helmets, the meeting brought together the largest number of world champions and historic machines ever seen. It took two years of planning to get riders such as Sheene, Giacomo Agostini, John Surtees, Geoff Duke, Phil Read, Jim Redman, Kork Ballington, Luigi Taveri and Randy Mamola together along with many of the actual machines they had won their world titles on.

Forty-five thousand nostalgic spectators turned up to witness the once-in-a-lifetime event where 'races' were staged as reliability trials, the bikes being too old, too precious and in some cases too fragile to be raced properly. Sheene clearly enjoyed himself riding the Suzuki XR14 he had won his first 500cc GP on in 1975, a machine now owned by English collector Chris Wilson. Barry said, 'It's fun to see all the old people again, see some old faces and have a laugh. I've had a lot of fun and a couple of great hangovers, and that's what it's all about.' But when he was asked if the experience had made him want to reach for the throttle again, Sheene replied, 'Not really. Not at all, in actual fact.'

He must have had a change of heart at some point, then, because four months later he found himself lining up for a 'real' motorcycle race. The venue was the Goodwood circuit in West Sussex, and the event was the Goodwood Revival meeting, being held to celebrate not only the circuit's reopening but also to mark the 50th anniversary of the first-ever race there in 1948. Sheene was close friends with the Earl of March, whose grandfather had founded the 2.4-mile Goodwood circuit. The earl had spent some years securing the rights to hold racing on the historic track again, and by 1998, with John Surtees' help, he had arranged a vast array of more than 300 famous cars and bikes to be piloted by some of the most successful drivers and riders in history. Sheene drove a classic 1962 Manx Norton in a 'demo' race alongside 29 other pre-1966 (the year the circuit closed) motorcycles. He said at the time, 'I've renewed my race licence for the event, but I don't think you'll see me riding under the red mist. It will be a good day out for a lot of people and I just want to have fun.' Another star name on the classic bike grid, as well as the car grid, was 1996 Formula 1 car world champion and close friend Damon Hill. Hill, a former bike courier and bike racer himself, also rode a Manx Norton after securing

tentative permission from his F1 team boss Eddie Jordan.
'I am really looking forward to lining up on a classic
Norton at Goodwood,' he enthused. 'To race against a
boyhood idol like Sheene is a dream come true.' But he
added that he was under strict instructions not to crash.
'Eddie Jordan has told me that if I hurt myself he'll oper-
ate on me himself, without anaesthetic.' Hill told *F1
News* that Sheene himself was as keyed up as he was. 'He
is getting all excited about racing against Damon Hill,
which I can't understand as he was my big hero when I
was growing up.'

The Lennox Cup event's two legs were Barry's first-
ever races on a British single-cylinder bike, as well as his
first motorcycle races since 1984, and some 80,000 spectators turned up to witness his return. In the first leg
Sheene rode swiftly but steadily and finished a close
second to Mick Hemmings' McIntyre Matchless but
ahead of Malcolm Clark's Matchless G50, demonstrating that he had lost none of the old magic after so many
years away on a bike that was completely unfamiliar to
him. Hill set off way down the field but finished a
respectable 10th after clawing his way back through the
pack. The second leg was held without Hill, who was
preparing for the following TT car demo, but that didn't
stop Barry enjoying himself once again. The race turned
out to be a close battle won by Hemmings by less than a
second from Clark, with Sheene completing the podium
in third place. It wasn't a fairy-tale comeback, in fact it
wasn't a comeback at all, as Barry insisted, but he'd had
a good scrap against men vastly more experienced in the

nuances of classic bike racing, a discipline as unique as any in motorcycle racing.

By the time of the 1999 Goodwood meeting, Sheene was in no mood to settle for podium finishes even though the weather was atrocious and he had nothing to prove to anyone. In heavy rain, he toyed with the leaders in both legs of the Lennox Cup before clearing off and winning with ease, arms outstretched above his head as he show-boated across the line, the overall winner of the cup for the first time and looking every bit as flamboyant as in his seventies heyday. Hill rode again too, and was third fastest in Friday's practice, but he opted just to wobble around in Saturday's wet race rather than risk falling off and injuring himself. Sheene had had to apply a little more effort in Sunday's race, as he admitted: he'd woken up with a terrible hangover after an 'enthusiastic' drinking session the night before.

By January 2000, it was obvious that Sheene had been well and truly bitten by the classic racing bug and had decided to extend his racing activities by taking part in a major classic event at Phillip Island in his adopted home-land, his bike having been shipped over from England by its builder, Fred Walmsley. Barry dominated the event with two wins. Even after suffering a non-finish in one race, he claimed the Phillip Island classic crown, his first 'title' since quitting the sport he had made his own.

Sheene's classic race bike was no less a work of art than his former Grand Prix bikes. It wasn't an original Manx Norton – production of those stopped in 1962, and genuine spares were extremely difficult to find –

rather a modernized copy with improved performance and handling to match. For example, Sheene's bike pumped out 66bhp compared to the 50bhp of the original bikes, and it weighed 108kg compared to 140kg. The bike was built by Lancastrian tuning guru Fred Walmsley, who has been building Nortons for five years using parts manufactured from original Manx Norton patterns by Andy Molnar's Stainless Engineering company. Such are the levels of technology and handcraftsmanship used that it costs £25,000 to build just one bike. But so impressive is the final result that 2002 World Superbike champion Colin Edwards, an unexpected enthusiast, ordered one as soon as he saw it on display. Sheene's bike was identical to the one ridden by John Cronshaw, who won the 2002 European Classic Bike Championship, and it was as good as anything else out there, though it still had to be ridden hard and well. Colin Breeze raced against Sheene on classic bikes several times, and he can testify to how hard classic racers ride. 'I don't know what the top speed is on these kind of bikes, but they aren't slow. It's really intense racing, and the corner speed on a classic is quicker than on some modern bikes. I don't know why, but I can drive round the outside of modern 600cc bikes on my Norton. They're not the old heaps of shit that some people think.'

Breeze first encountered Sheene on-track at the British Grand Prix in 2000 where both men raced in the classic support races. He testified to Sheene's popularity and acceptance within the paddock. 'Everyone in the classic racing paddock was pleased to see Barry there; he was good for the image of the whole thing. There was no jealousy because Sheene's bike wasn't really any better or worse than the other top bikes, so he didn't have a massive advantage. It was still a very good bike, though; I raced it at Cadwell Park in 2002 after my own Norton broke down.'

While he was in England during that summer in 2000, Barry agreed to help me 'test' a Cagiva Raptor and MV Agusta F4 for *Motor Cycle News*. It was the first and only time Sheene had ridden on the road with a journalist for a photoshoot, and he did it mostly as a favour to his friend of more than 30 years Claudio Castiglioni, president of MV Agusta. Barry also helped promote Castiglioni's bikes in Australia through an advertising campaign for Australian Cagiva and MV Agusta distributors the Paul Feeney Group. He also attended the launch of Cagiva's Raptor at the Milan bike show in 1999, and, as usual, had a battery of ready-made quotes available for the press. He told *MCN*, 'The V-Raptor is fantastic. It's beautiful, like a woman – except it does everything you want it to.' Sheene was given the MV and the Raptor by Castiglioni, and they were kept at a friend's house in London for his use when he visited the capital. He had ridden both during their developmental stages and professed to be a big fan. The MV was, he claimed, better than any of his old race bikes in terms of handling and useable power. Sheene was never a big fan of riding on the road – he never had any real need to be – but as congestion in the capital city increased he found it was the only way to get around. He once claimed in *Bike* magazine that the furthest he had ever ridden on public roads non-stop was from central London to Biggin Hill airfield in Kent, a distance of no more than 40 miles.

Still, he never lost any of his magic on a race track, as he proved yet again at Donington Park in 2000. Barry retired from the first International classic race with engine problems, but in the second leg, after a very close battle, he came back to finish second to Steve Tomes on a similar machine, setting the fastest lap of the race in the process. It was the highest finish of any British rider at the Grand Prix meeting and a reminder to all that Sheene was, and remains, the last Brit to win a 500GP and a GP world title. It seemed that even after 16 years of retirement he still couldn't help but overshadow the new generation of British riders. He told *MCN*, 'I enjoyed that. It seemed like I'd never been away. But this isn't a new career for me. This was my fourth race in 16 years so I don't think it marks a comeback.' After the race, Tomes backed up Breeze's testimony that classic bike racing is as fierce as any other discipline of the sport and confirmed that Sheene was as tenacious a contender as he ever was. 'He is the toughest competitor I've come up against in this series. He wasn't just riding around, he was racing really hard.'

Sheene, like everyone attending the British Grand Prix that year, had been shocked just one week earlier by news of the death of 26-times TT winner and five-times Formula 1 world champion Joey Dunlop at an obscure race in Tallinn, Estonia. Never a fan of the TT, Sheene had nonetheless a very high regard for Dunlop, as he explained to Ulster Television. 'I hate the bloody Isle of Man, but his achievements there are dumbfounding, I mean absolutely stunning, when you think of a guy of his age, or any age, achieving so many victories. He [was] just a lovely, lovely bloke.' Sheene told me how in 1996 Dunlop had inspired him to stop smoking – eventually, that is: after several relapses he had finally kicked the habit by 2000 – when the two met at Scarborough Bike Week. 'I'd tried to give up three times and couldn't manage it, and it was annoying me that I couldn't stop. Then I saw Joey and he'd managed to stop. I thought, "Right, that's it – if Joey can quit, so can I." I was devastated to hear of his death. He was a wonderful bloke.' Barry got a chance to pay his respects at the Irish Motorcycle Show in Belfast in 2000, when he and Mick Doohan presented Joey's widow Linda with the Road Racer of the Year award. Sheene attended the show again in 2001, mainly due to his friendship with organizer Wallace Rollins, whom he had met in 1971 when he raced at Bishopscourt in Northern Ireland.

Sheene lost his Lennox Cup title at Goodwood in 2000. After scoring two wins the year before, he suffered a non-finish with a seized engine before saving something from the weekend with a second place in leg two of the event. But for this inveterate racer there were always the Phillip Island classic races to look forward to, though in early 2001 Sheene courted controversy when word got out that he was receiving $8,000 a day in appearance money. Decades earlier Sheene had upset race fans and promoters with his high salary demands; now he found himself once again having to defend his reputation through his column in *Bike* magazine. 'Some people used to say I was mercenary – money this, that and the other. Well, that's a lot of shit. I certainly didn't earn any money out of racing at Donington [in the classic events] and at the end of both the races I got the same feeling of "wow – that was good" as I did in the seventies and eighties. The reason I used to hang out for the right price back then was because that was what I was worth.'

If Bazza was up to his old tricks again on the financial front, he certainly brought back some memories on the race track too when he showed he had lost none of his penchant for crashing. Sheene needed a four-hour stint in hospital after a 100mph highside at Hayshed corner in his final race of the weekend at Phillip Island. He said, 'The bike hadn't been running well all weekend, so I wasn't going to stick my neck out. It just locked up, and as I peeled into the turn it spat me over the top. I got a decent whack on the head. I had a headache like you wouldn't believe, but I'm all right.' Sheene was kept in nearby Cowes Hospital for observation, but later released. He was also forced to relinquish his Phillip Island crown after finishing second in the two earlier races, both times behind Craig Morris on a 1960 Manx Norton.

Sheene's accident was further proof that top classic bike racers nowadays hold nothing back, a point on which Colin Breeze was insistent. 'Classic racing used to be sort of polite and "after you, sir", but there's none of that any more; it's proper racing, and the machines are very evenly matched. Whenever I raced with Sheene I had the most horrific run of bad luck, but we whizzed round in practice together and the guy hadn't lost anything. He still knew what he was doing on a bike.'

Sheene had fully recovered from his crash by the time of the 2001 British Grand Prix, but he had been experiencing other health problems that almost prevented him from racing. As a result of a sinus virus there was doubt over whether or not Barry would be able to start in Saturday's race, but at the last minute he decided to give it a go. No one watching could have guessed there was anything wrong with the black-clad figure on the number seven bike as he battled for the lead with John Cronshaw, who was mounted on an identical Fred Walmsley Norton. The two were clashing fairings from the very first lap, and Sheene looked capable of winning the race had he not suffered carburation problems when exiting slow corners. 'I was losing 50 yards out of that corner [the Melbourne hairpin] every lap. It didn't seem to pull the gearing and it felt like it gave a cough each time I got back on the throttle. But I still enjoyed the race, especially since I felt so sick before the start.' Despite his problems, Sheene managed a creditable fourth place, and after Walmsley changed the Norton's gearing and checked over the engine he was ready for battle again on the Sunday after the Grand Prix classes had run their races.

With all due respect to classic bike racing, it doesn't usually hold the attention of a modern Grand Prix crowd, most of whom usually leave the circuit before the classic race starts. That wasn't so when Barry Sheene was involved. British fans, still starved of a winner in GPs, stayed on in their thousands to cheer the man who had inspired many of them to watch a motorcycle race in the first place, and in the summer of 2001 they weren't disappointed. Sheene had a terrific battle with series regular Sandro Baumann, finally barging his way past into the lead at Redgate corner on the very last lap of the race. 'I didn't expect to win, but it was so much fun to race with Sandro,' he said later. 'I kept missing gears and even touched a kerb, which lost me a lot of ground, but I was just able to get back in front going into the last lap.'

One thing about modern racing rules that Sheene found useful was that they demanded a clutch start. In Sheene's day, the rider had to push his bike and bump-start it, a process Barry found extremely difficult due to his shattered legs. It was not until three years after his retirement, in 1987, that the rules were changed to allow for clutch starts, where the rider sits astride his machine, which is already running, and simply lets the clutch out. 'Since I started racing my classic bike,' Sheene said, 'my mate Mike Farrell – an ex-speedway guy who tells me how to race a classic bike – has shown me how to do clutch starts. Ever since then I've had some really good starts, and it's a lot easier than I ever thought it would be. Why the bloody hell couldn't they have had clutch starts when I was racing?'

A record 123,000 spectators crammed into Goodwood on 15 and 16 September 2001 to soak up the atmosphere of racing's past and to watch Sheene repeat his feat of 1999 by winning both legs of the Lennox Cup. The first leg was a thriller, with Barry dicing it out in a five-man group comprising veteran classic racer Bill Swallow on an Aermacchi 408, Mick Hemmings on a McIntyre G50, and Tim Jackson and Duncan Fitchett, like Sheene, on Manx Nortons. With two laps to go Sheene outbraked both

Hemmings and Jackson into Woodcote then forced the same move on Swallow on the very last lap to win the race in vintage style. He took no such last-minute chances in the second leg and held a two-second lead over the same four men right to the chequered flag. The Lennox Cup was his once more.

There were no wins for Barry in his by now annual meeting at Phillip Island in early 2002; instead he had to content himself with three second places, although he did set a new classic lap record. Another second place was the best he could manage at Eastern Creek, another Australian circuit, shortly afterwards. But he was in no mood to disappoint when he arrived in mid-July at a blazing-hot Donington Park for the classic races held, once again, as part of the British Grand Prix weekend. Despite suffering from a sore throat which was the first symptom of his cancer, Sheene was in good form and even managed to inspire Niall Mackenzie for the second time in his life. 'I met up with Barry at the Grand Prix for the first time in ages,' Mackenzie explained, 'and he tried to convince me to have a go at classic bike racing. I must admit, I think he's succeeded. Barry got me to sit on his Fred Walmsley-prepared Manx Norton and he told me how much of a buzz he got out of racing old bikes. I might just give it a go in the future. I'm certainly tempted. If I do go classic racing, it will be the second time that Barry's inspired me to race after I saw him as a youngster.'

Before the race, Sheene had attended a press event held in London's Leicester Square to honour 500cc world champion Valentino Rossi. Rossi has come closer than anyone in bike racing to achieving the same level of popularity Sheene had, and he's very much like Barry in that he has always been a bit of a prankster, is popular with women, and is generally an all-round colourful character – merits of which Sheene wholeheartedly approved. 'He's such a lovely bloke,' he said, 'and is so good for the sport. He's just a good laugh, a really nice kid. The spin-off is it's incredibly good for motorcycle racing.'

The International Classic Association's (INCA) championship series was held over five rounds in 2002 at Donington, Misano in Italy, the A1 Ring in Austria, Oschersleben in Germany and Autodrom 'Most' in the Czech Republic. The series, which for 2003 has been granted full World Championship status, was eventually won by John Cronshaw on an FWD Molnar Manx, the same bike as Sheene's, but at Donington Park, the only round Sheene entered, it was Barry all the way. The first leg was held on the Saturday after GP qualifying. Again largely because of Sheene's attendance, a big crowd opted to stay on to watch the race rather than take the chance of making a quick exit from the circuit. Sheene took advantage of the bad luck that befell several of his competitors – front-row qualifier Colin Breeze's bike gave up the ghost on the sighting lap, race leader Lea Gourley retired with carburettor problems, and Glen English fell back to third place after losing his rear brake when he had been in the lead – to take a massively popular victory. In front of the majority of the 60,000 GP fans on Sunday, Sheene once more made it a clean sweep as the leader Gourley was again forced to retire. Once in front, Barry made a clean break and romped home to celebrate in typical fashion by removing his helmet and riding a lap of honour to the deafening blasts of thousands of air horns – not a sound he was familiar with from the seventies. His two wins were enough to place him fifth overall in the INCA championship by the end of the season, even though he had competed in only one of the five rounds. It was a fitting victory for a man who was not feeling his best.

By the time the 2002 Goodwood meeting rolled around, news of Sheene's cancer had broken and many feared it would be their last ever chance to see him race. As a result, more than 80,000 fans attended the meeting. Sheene was prepared to talk about his illness with the press in his usual witty manner, and other than the fact that he'd already made an announcement and that he looked quite gaunt, no one would have guessed there was anything wrong with him at all. He spent hours chatting to fans in the bike paddock, far removed from the upmarket car paddock where stars such as Stirling Moss, David Coulthard, Damon Hill and Murray Walker enjoyed first-class hospitality. Not Sheene; he mingled with his adoring British public, knowing it might be his last opportunity. Despite the fact that he was tiring by mid-afternoon, Sheene stuck it out and didn't allow a single fan to go home disappointed. As he told *MCN*, 'If people can be bothered to come over and be nice to me, the very least I can do is give them some of my time.'

No one had really expected Barry to make the gruelling trip to attend Goodwood, but as usual everyone had underestimated his determination. He told *MCN* shortly before the event that he was 'not going to let anybody down'. But because he had committed only at the last minute, his usual Manx Norton wasn't ready and he had to make do with a replica, also built by Fred Walmsley but not up to the same spec. Indeed, Sheene complained that it was 20mph slower than Wayne Gardner's Matchless G50, also prepared by Walmsley, but it wasn't going to stop him trying his hardest. To make matters worse, Barry blew up an engine in the first lap of practice.

Gardner set pole, but Sheene was only fractions behind and two epic eight-lap races looked to be on the cards. Neither rider disappointed in the first leg as they circulated almost in unison, Gardner edging the win by just 0.011 seconds after a near collision with Sheene at the final chicane. Freddie Spencer never figured at the front of the race, having taken his ride on an ex-John Surtees MV Agusta cautiously for fear of damaging the precious machine, but vastly experienced riders including John Cronshaw and Bill Swallow were left behind the Sheene steamroller.

For a man battling cancer, Barry had put on a terrific display both in the paddock and on the race track, but he really got the tears flowing on Sunday with a fairy-tale victory in the second leg. He had to battle his way through the field from a sixth-place start to get into contention with Gardner, and eventually passed him to win by 0.156 seconds and secure the most popular and emotional victory of the meeting. And it was all topped off by Sheene winning the Lennox Cup for the third time thanks to his aggregate times over the two races. Not even cancer could stop Sheene from being a winner, and he was obviously overwhelmed by the whole experience. 'It's fantastic to win here,' he said. 'This weekend has been just unbelievable.

The fans have been fantastic, incredible.'

His draining weekend over, Sheene faced up to reality and flew back to Australia to begin the toughest battle of his life.

CHAPTER 12

CANCER

'It's another battle to be won, and I plan to do it my way.'

Media release from Barry Sheene
Friday, 23 August 2002

On 22 July I was diagnosed with cancer of the oesophagus and upper stomach. Although this is a complete pain in the arse, it happens to a lot of people, and a lot of people get over it. I will do everything within my power to beat this thing. I and my family would appreciate privacy at this time so I can get on with fighting this in my own way. At this time I feel there is nothing more for me to add, and I thank all my well-wishers for their thoughts.

This is how Barry Sheene shocked the racing world and beyond with the news that he had developed cancer. As with all cancers, the exact cause remained unknown, though smoking, drinking and genetics must have played a part. For anyone who had ever heard of Barry, there seemed to be a terrible irony in the fact that he had survived so many horrific motorcycle crashes only to be struck down with the most dreaded of diseases.

Sheene had begun to feel unwell early in July 2002, complaining of a sore throat. Eating became increasingly difficult, and he soon found he could swallow food only if he had a glass of water with which to wash it down. It was the first tangible symptom of the cancer in his oesophagus, part of the alimentary canal linking the pharynx to the stomach. Sheene was later prescribed a special isotonic drink to help lubricate and soothe the pain in his throat. He had visited doctors for tests before flying to England for the classic bike races held as part of the 2002 British Grand Prix, but he didn't learn the awful truth until he returned to Australia. Steve Hislop was among the first to realize that all was not well. 'I was supposed to be doing a chat show and dinner evening with Barry and [fellow superbike racer] Paul "Marra" Brown on 2 August at the Winter Gardens Hotel in Cleethorpes, Lincolnshire, but shortly beforehand Paul phoned and said it was cancelled because Barry had a perforated ulcer or something. We didn't realize it at the time, but that was the first sign of his cancer.'

The news of his illness was broken to Sheene in no uncertain terms, as he explained to Australian newspaper *The Age*. 'I had an endoscopy, and when I came round from the anaesthetic I got dressed and went into the doctor's office. "Bloody 'ell, Baz, it's cancer," he said. Best way to tell me. Straight out with it.' But no one takes the news that they have cancer lightly, and Sheene was quite naturally 'knocked for six' by the massive shock of his diagnosis, according to his best friend Steve Parrish.

Initially, Sheene shared the news only with Parrish and his closest friends and family before deciding to release a statement to the world's media. The day after that, messages of encouragement started to flood in to his Queensland home. But Barry had a further announcement to make, which shocked almost as much as the first: he was going to reject orthodox chemotherapy treatment and invasive surgery and seek alternative cures for his cancer. He explained his reasons to Sue Mott of the *Daily Telegraph*, saying that he simply didn't believe in chemotherapy. 'Anybody I've ever known who's had it has been, basically, completely destroyed,' he said. 'I can't let someone put an IV drip in my arm and inject me with poison. I've seen friends of mine after chemo. They look like dead people who can still talk.'

Sheene had always done things his own way, and his approach to cancer was going to be the same – on his own terms, and in the way he thought best. The first method of treatment he signed up for was the Breuss diet developed by the Austrian-born naturopath Rudolf Breuss, born in 1899. The treatment involved following a strict diet of liquidized organic vegetables including carrots, celery, beetroot, potatoes and Chinese radishes, the theory being that if cancer is starved of the protein it feeds off, it will die. Sheene followed the diet for three weeks, after which time his weight had dropped from 11 stones (154lb) to nine and a half (133lb). He also lost three and a half inches of muscle off his already slight chest. It wasn't the first time Sheene's muscles had been eaten away. A week after his Silverstone crash he'd admitted having 'no desire to eat anything, and consequently, as my body had to live off something, my muscles began to reduce. My chest is normally 42 inches. When I left hospital, it was down to 38.'

Before Breuss died in 1991, he claimed that his method had cured as many as 45,000 people over a 30-year period and that it enjoyed a 96 per cent success rate. Leading oncologists took a very different view, insisting that there was no scientific evidence that the treatment worked; indeed, they went further, claiming that the diet actually put the patient at risk of malnutrition. Sheene certainly admitted to feeling weak and a bit 'iffy' after three weeks of the Breuss treatment. When he started eating some solids again, albeit still only vegetables, he felt even worse. It wasn't until he began eating more substantial dishes, though still low in alkaline, that he regained some strength.

In the *Sun* newspaper, Dr Richard Sullivan, head of clinical programmes at Cancer Research UK, warned that Sheene could be gambling with his life by choosing alternative treatment. Sullivan pointed out that over 100,000 people were successfully treated for cancer every year by orthodox means, and that facts about cancer cures and survival rates can only be obtained when they 'come out of hard evidence, as opposed to anecdotal evidence'. He added that, while complementary therapies could have a role in alleviating some symptoms, he 'wouldn't bet [his] life on it'. Conventional practitioners do indeed support some alternative treatments alongside scientifically proven methods such as chemotherapy and surgery, but not as sole methods of treatment. Sheene, however, defended his decision to follow the Breuss diet, saying, 'I did it to clean my system out and give my immune system its best shot,' though he admitted the side-effects were a bit worrying. 'Because I didn't have any fat, it just ate my muscles. It ate three inches off my chest in 10 days.'

As news of Sheene's cancer spread, messages of support came in from everyone involved in bike racing, even from old rivals and recent adversaries. At the Czech Grand Prix in August 2002, Kenny Roberts spoke for the whole paddock when he told *Motor Cycle News*, 'We were all very shocked when we heard the news today. I just hope they have caught the illness in the early stages. Barry was always a great fighter and I'm sure he will fight just as hard again.' Even Carl Fogarty forgot about his recent war of words with Sheene and his threat of legal action against him when he heard the news. 'Despite all the stuff that's happened this year,' he said, 'I am very sad to hear this news. If Barry can show half of the bravery he did when he came back from the injuries he sustained in his racing career, then he must have a good chance.' Another British rider, Jamie Whitham, was better placed than most to offer Sheene advice as he had won his own battle against cancer of the lymph nodes back in 1995, although he'd opted to endure conventional chemotherapy treatment. 'When I was sick, Barry was really supportive. I will do anything I can to return the gesture. Beating cancer is all about having a positive frame of mind, and that shouldn't be a problem for someone like Barry Sheene. I mean, he's Barry Sheene isn't he!' Ron Haslam added, 'Sheene has broken just about every bone in his body and still got back on the track, and that shows the determination of the man. If it's possible for him to get over it, Barry Sheene will do it.' Troy Corser, the 1996 World Superbike champion, has always been grateful to Sheene for the help he provided in kick-starting his international racing career. He too paid tribute to Sheene's determination and wished him well. 'The diagnosis of throat cancer is obviously very worrying for Barry and everyone around him, but medical treatment is incredible these days, and coupled with his strong personality, if anyone can get through this it's Barry. This isn't the first challenge he's had to face in his life and I'm sure he can beat his illness as he has every challenge before.'

In October, Barry's wife Stephanie persuaded him to put in an appearance at the Australian Grand Prix to cheer himself up and see some old mates. Barry piloted himself and his son Freddie on the five-and-a-half-hour flight down to Phillip Island. Everywhere Sheene went he was mobbed, not just by fans but by all the world's top riders who wanted to wish him well. When he was paraded around the circuit in an open-top car, he got a bigger ovation than the hugely popular world champion, Valentino Rossi. Sheene insisted he was 'feeling fine apart from this cancer', but the effects were beginning to show. He looked gaunt. That didn't stop Barry meeting up with Rossi and his old sparring partner Angel Nieto for a meal a few days before the race, and his optimism about beating cancer remained high, as he told reporters, 'My whole life I've spent as an optimist, and I'm not going to start being a pessimist now.'

Sheene was clearly overwhelmed by the messages of goodwill being sent from around the world in the form of emails – by October he'd received more than 20,000 – comments on the website, conventional letters and, for those lucky enough to meet him, warm words in person. 'You cannot believe the compassion,' he remarked. 'It brings tears to your eyes. People write to me and say, "I'm praying for you." It's just fantastic. If support is going to do it, then I've got it beat already.'

Putting his faith in alternative treatments was one thing, but Barry surprised people yet again by announcing that he was ultimately putting his faith in God. Never known to be overly religious, Barry had become convinced that a higher force had saved his life many times in the past and might do so again. 'I believe in God,' he said. 'When you think of the accidents that I have got away with, then there has to be someone looking after me. You can't be that lucky all the time.' But Sheene didn't want to push his Maker too far, as he explained in *Leader of the Pack*. 'Although I regard myself as a Christian and do believe in God, I didn't pray in hospital [after the 1982 Silverstone crash] when there was some doubt over the future of my legs. I reckon He looked after me in the crash, but I'm not such a hypocrite as to get on to the guy only when I'm in need of outside help. I don't mind admitting I prayed for [Formula 1 drivers] Niki Lauda and Didier Pironi when they had bad smashes, but I don't do it any other time, so why should I contact Him only in moments of personal distress? God helps those who help themselves . . . and God help those caught helping themselves!'

After putting the Breuss diet to one side, Sheene jetted off to Mexico for a consultation at a clinic that specialized in natural cures. He also planned to visit China and Kuala Lumpur for further consultations, although he did not openly discuss the details of these trips. He vented his growing anger and resentment at the disease in his monthly column for *Bike* magazine. 'It's such a shit disease. I've said to other people, there is no way I want to give it any credibility. It's a shit thing, and I don't want to give it any space in my life.' Sheene's *Bike* column was ghostwritten by deputy editor Mick Phillips, and Barry was highly amused by an incident that took place while Phillips was trying to compile the column for the February 2003 issue. Knowing that Sheene was staying in a hotel in Perth while undergoing further treatment, Phillips called the establishment only to be told, 'I'm sorry, but Mr Sheene is no longer with us.' The receptionist merely meant that Barry had checked out and gone home, but Phillips presumed the worst. It is testament to Sheene's courage and sense of humour even in the most dire circumstances that he 'cracked up with laughter' when Phillips related the tale to him.

But there were darker moments to deal with too, and one of the toughest tasks for Barry was telling his children about his illness. He explained how harrowing it had been to the *Daily Telegraph*. 'Telling them was the hardest part. It was horrible. I was a little economical with the truth, but I did tell them basically what was happening. It was terrible and incredibly touching at the same time.'

In November 2002 Sheene's employers, Channel 10, had

told him not to worry about his TV commitments and instructed him just to focus on getting better. That was when Barry decided to submit himself to a course of treatment at a specialist clinic in Perth run by British cancer specialist Dr John Holt. Holt has dealt with more than 7,000 cancer patients in his career and claims a high rate of success for his 'microwave' treatment, which although not recognized as an orthodox treatment is still a lot more technically advanced than the Breuss diet. The theory behind microwave therapy is to deprive cancerous cells of their only energy source, glucose, thereby sending the cancer into remission. Sheene was given a daily injection of a glucose-blocking agent, Cytotoxic, combined with a radioactive tracer that isolated the cancerous cells from any glucose supply and highlighted the location of the cancer. He was then bombarded with ultra-high-frequency (UHF) radiowaves that heated the cancer cells in a bid to make them temporarily inactive. Microwave or 'radiowave' therapy differs from more conventional radiotherapy in that it utilizes different frequencies of radiation and cannot be concentrated in a narrow beam. Sheene described the experience of being bombarded all over with UHF waves as like 'being in a microwave'. By this stage he was seemingly taking great delight in flying in the face of convention, saying of his microwave course, 'The doctors disapprove of it so it must be all right.'

Barry was subjected to this treatment three times a day, Monday to Friday, for what proved to be three gruelling weeks. Part of the reason he chose microwave treatment was that the side-effects were far less severe than those created by chemotherapy, which caused hair loss and skin problems as well as possible damage to many vital internal organs such as the brain, the lungs, the liver and the kidneys. Even so, Sheene reported feeling sick after each injection, and over the three weeks of the treatment he felt 'tired and lethargic'. Nearly five months after his diagnosis, cancer was really beginning to test Barry Sheene's will.

After completing this initial course of treatment, Barry returned to his luxurious home on the Gold Coast to spend Christmas with his family. There he spoke to Bob McKenzie of the *Express* about his battle with cancer and explained again why he would never have chemotherapy or surgery. 'I would rather die. I have always had a good quality of life. I don't want to have something a lot worse, which is what would happen if I had the other treatments.' He added, 'You don't give in to something like this, you fight it. But I don't think "Why me?" Definitely not. Not one day. I wake up every morning to get on with life, not to hang around feeling sorry for myself.'

Yet Sheene's search for a successful alternative cure was proving increasingly futile. In early February 2003, he announced that the microwave treatment had not been successful and that undergoing further sessions would be of no benefit. Instead, he vowed to continue his search for other solutions. He told *MCN*, 'I have to admit I'm not feeling particularly great at the moment. I just permanently feel sick. I've been feeling like this pretty much since the middle of November [2002], and I can tell you that feeling sick 24 hours a day is not pleasant. It isn't nice not wanting to eat anything at all.' Despite feeling so bad, Barry was adamant that he was not on his last legs amid increasing rumours that he was losing the fight. He refused to divulge any information about how long doctors had given him to live when he was first diagnosed, claiming that he didn't pay any attention to medical opinion where timescales were concerned. He cited his recovery from the Silverstone crash in 1982 as an example. 'I was told I'd be in hospital for three months, and I was out after three weeks.'

By mid-February Sheene was being joined by close friends and family. Steve Parrish was among them. After spending a week with Sheene, he told the *News of the World*, 'He's tired, and weaker than he's ever been in his life, but he is still the Barry Sheene I know. But how long he has got to live I have no idea. Barry is positive he is going to beat it. If you are this ill, you're not going to say, "It's got the better of me and I'm going to roll over." That isn't Barry.'

Sheene was now struggling to keep down the small amounts of food he was eating and was visiting hospital every three days to have fluid drained from his body. He was offered the honour of being flag marshal at the Formula 1 Australian Grand Prix but was too ill to leave his home. On Friday 7 March, he was admitted to hospital because he was unable to sleep at home. Three days later he lost what had been the toughest battle of his extraordinary life.

Media release from the family of Barry Sheene
Monday, 10 March 2003

Barry Sheene, Britain's 500cc motorcycle world champion in 1976 and 1977, who has been resident in Australia for many years, died today after a brave battle against cancer. Sheene, aged 52, passed away in hospital on Queensland's Gold Coast at about 2 p.m. Queensland time. He is survived by his wife Stephanie, daughter Sidonie (18) and son Freddie (14). A private family funeral will be held later this week.

Sheene had faced cancer like he had faced every other challenge in his life – in his own way. Tragically, this time it wasn't enough. His brave attempts to seek out natural cures over a period of some eight months ultimately failed, but he maintained his fighting spirit until the very end, as his nephew Scott Smart explained to ITV news cameras. 'His determination and that vigour for life was still there throughout the whole of the problem, and he continued fighting.'

Sheene's death made headline news virtually everywhere. Even in death he grabbed more column inches than any other motorcycle racer could ever have done, and the tributes simply poured in as friends, colleagues, former rivals and complete strangers unanimously attested to the unique contribution he had made to the sport of motorcycle racing.

Kenny Roberts, who was in touch with Barry right up to a week before his death, told *The Times*, 'I could not have had a greater rival when we went into battle. He spurred me on, and I wouldn't be where I am today without Barry.' Carl Fogarty paid the ultimate tribute: 'Barry Sheene packed more into his 52 years than most people would have put into 100. He was the inspiration for millions, the guy who made motorbike racing famous.' Steve Parrish summed up the feelings of millions when he said, 'If good wishes could have made Barry survive, he'd be sitting on a boat with a gin and tonic in his hand now.' Sheene's former Suzuki team-mate Keith Huewen was another to mourn Barry's passing, despite the fact that the two hadn't always seen eye to eye. He told the *Daily Mirror*, 'We have lost the boss. He was a global ambassador for motorcycling. His fame, fortune and legend go beyond everyone.'

Barry's old friend Murray Walker was one of the first to speak about the tragic news, both on television and in the national press. 'Barry Sheene was not only one of the most brilliant motorcycle racers who has ever lived, he was a lovely man [too]. He was brilliantly cheerful. He had a core of steel.' In the *Daily Mirror* he added, 'Few men make the impact on life that Barry did, and his passing leaves an unfillable void.' Another name forever associated with Sheene, boxer Henry Cooper, Sheene's co-star on the Brut 33 adverts, was also quick to pay tribute. 'They talk about fighters being game,' he said. 'I remember watching him having a crash at 100mph, getting a bruise as big as a football, and the next day he was ready to shoot the [Brut] commercial.' George Best was never a rival of Sheene's on a race track, but he certainly was when it came to dating the most number of glamorous models in the seventies. He told *MCN* that Sheene was 'an absolute legend, the glamour boy of the era', and added that 'he'll be greatly missed. My thoughts go out to his wife and kids. What a sad day.' Former F1 world champion Damon Hill told news crews that Sheene had 'exuded an enormous personality, an effervescence, and a completely daring attitude to everything'.

The *Daily Mail*'s Ian Wooldridge thought Sheene 'one of the most glorious mavericks' he had ever met, while the *Sun* reminded its readers that 'horrific high-speed crashes that almost destroyed his body could not even dent his spirit. Men like Sheene are a rare breed – he'll be sadly missed.' The *Daily Star* added its own warm words, acknowledging that Sheene was 'one of the most glamorous British sportsmen of the past century', and the *Daily Mirror* bemoaned the fact that 'someone who so celebrated life did not deserve to die so young'. Sheene was even mentioned in the House of Commons: Sports Minister Richard Caborn referred to him as 'a sportsman of the highest order'. But if ever a measure were needed of Barry's standing in UK sport, it was provided by Prime Minister Tony Blair who, despite being preoccupied with the looming war against Iraq, said, 'It's very sad to hear of Barry's death. He made a huge contribution to his sport and our thoughts are with his family.'

Sheene's passing marked the end of an era for motorcycling and motorcycle racing. It is unlikely that anyone will ever have such an impact on the sport, and beyond, again. Small comfort though it may be to those mourning his passing, especially his loving wife and two beautiful children, it will always be at least partly reassuring to remember that Barry Sheene MBE lived every single minute of his tragically foreshortened life to the absolute maximum. He could have had no regrets. Barry Sheene, in the end, was not invincible as so many had thought, but his legacy certainly is.

CHAPTER 13

A STAR WITHOUT EQUAL

*'It can't be underestimated what Barry Sheene
has done for British motorcycling.'*
KENNY ROBERTS

If awards are a measure of achievement and popularity, then
Barry Sheene had good reason to feel proud. Chief among
his collection was his MBE, a rare honour indeed for a
motorcycle racer, but one which has also been bestowed
upon Carl Fogarty and the late Joey Dunlop, among others.
Both Fogarty and Dunlop, incidentally, finished ahead of
Sheene in a poll carried out in 2001 at the NEC bike show in
Birmingham to establish Britain's all-time biking icon, but it
is worth remembering that Dunlop, sadly, had been killed
the year before the poll and Fogarty, who won the accolade,
had been forced into retirement the same year. Barry was
also voted *Motor Cycle News* Man of the Year an incredible
five times, a record that stood for almost two decades until
Carl Fogarty was awarded his sixth gong in 1999.

   MCN further honoured Sheene in 2001 with a Lifetime
Achievement award, an honour that had only previously

been conferred on such names as Evel Knievel, John Surtees and Willie G. Davidson of Harley-Davidson fame. Sheene said the award was 'very nice and much appreciated' but was unable to attend the ceremony. Steve Parrish collected it on his behalf as Sheene thanked the audience via a telephone link from Australia. *MCN* ran a story the week after the ceremony paying tribute to Sheene's contribution to motorcycle racing and motorcycling in general. 'The *MCN* Lifetime Achievement award recognizes outstanding individuals. Named after Dave Taylor, a tireless campaigner for motorcycling, the award is given to someone who has touched our lives in a unique way. And few people have touched us like Barry Sheene. Sheene transformed the face of British bike racing and became a household name almost overnight. He is without doubt a legend in his own lifetime.'

In what turned out to be a busy year for honours, Barry was also officially recognized in the Grand Prix Hall of Fame: he was inducted during the Australian Grand Prix at Phillip Island alongside 1987 world champion Wayne Gardner, joining such racing luminaries as Giacomo Agostini, Wayne Rainey, Mick Doohan and his old foe Kenny Roberts. Barry seemed genuinely delighted finally to be placed among so many legendary names. 'When you look down the list of other riders,' he said, 'it is a great honour to be included. Racing is still my passion and my life and it is still great to be involved,' though he later added in *Bike* magazine, 'I went to the ceremony, but in reality Geoff Duke and John Surtees should have been the first people in there.'

The Segrave Trophy is awarded in honour of Sir Henry Segrave, a war hero and world land-speed record holder who was killed on a Friday the 13th in 1930 while attempting to break the world water-speed record. The memorial trophy recognizes outstanding achievements on land and sea or in the air and has been bestowed upon men such as Richard Branson, Stirling Moss, Donald Campbell, Jackie Stewart and Damon Hill. Sheene was the recipient of the award twice, in 1977 and again in 1984, for his services to biking and his World Championship achievements.

But of all the accolades and all the hundreds of trophies Barry was presented with, perhaps the best tributes came from those who knew Sheene best – his fellow riders and colleagues from the world of motorcycling. Some of them might have had their differences with Sheene over the years, but none denied the positive effect he had on the sport of motorcycle road racing over the years. 'He might have enjoyed a playboy lifestyle,' Ron Haslam remarked, 'but when he was on a bike Sheene was dead serious about his racing and he was one of the cleanest racers I've ever ridden with. He would beat you fair and square and never pulled any dirty tricks. He'd shut the door on you and he was forceful, but never dirty, and he'd always give you plenty of room. He was really safe on the track.' Kenny Roberts echoed those sentiments. 'Despite our rivalry, there was never anything dirty or malicious between us. You could not have wished for a better rival than Barry, and when we were racing together it really was a great period for motorcycle sport. It can't be underestimated what Barry Sheene has done for British motorcycling.'

Randy Mamola, Sheene's replacement in the factory
Suzuki GP squad after he left to ride Yamahas, totally
agreed with Roberts. 'Barry Sheene gave more to the sport
than many ever will. He was one of those guys who was
liked everywhere, in the English-speaking world and in
France, Spain and Italy, because he spoke those languages.
To me that was great to be so well liked, and Barry gave
back to everybody everywhere. People who didn't know
the sport recognized Barry because of his personality.
There are some racers who will always be just racers. Alex
Criville [1999 500cc world champion] will always be a
racer because he didn't have the same kind of personality,
and that's what made Sheene – his personality.'

Mick Grant, one-time figurehead for those race fans
who were not so fond of Sheene but a man who never had
any personal differences with Barry himself, also recognized that there was something a bit special about his old
rival. 'Charisma is a very difficult thing to define. I mean,
Joey Dunlop had charisma, even though none of us could
understand a single word he said for the first half of his
career. Hailwood had charisma, too. It comes in a lot of
different shapes and forms, but Barry had it, there's no
question about it.'

It wasn't just the riders who benefited from the extra
exposure Sheene brought to bike racing; there were many
others working in the sport who noticed the benefits.
Photographer Don Morley acknowledged that 'Sheene was
the best thing since sliced bread for us journalists and photographers. All our earnings shot up. I mean, I was selling
pictures to women's magazines, daily papers, you name it.

It was like a phenomenon. He was bloody good for business and bloody good for the sport. He was the first rider to become a household name. People like Phil Read were great riders, but no one outside the sport had heard of him. I did the pictures for the Brut 33 adverts, and what other motorcyclists could have modelled for that? There was a very noticeable surge in the popularity of motorcycling when Barry came along. We could do with that surge again now.' Morley added that Sheene 'had a wicked sense of humour as well, and you could guarantee he would always come out with something that would leave you breathless. He was brilliant, there was no question about it. It was great for photographers to have a colourful rider to shoot after so many years of shooting black leathers and dull-coloured bikes. When Sheene came along in his brightly coloured leathers and helmet on well-painted Suzukis, it was manna from heaven.'

Chip Hennen, despite all the differences his brother Pat had with Barry, paid tribute to Sheene's universal appeal. 'I think everyone loved Barry Sheene, quite frankly. I don't think I ever met a single fan who didn't respect or admire him. They held him in very high esteem.' Even riders from another generation who never raced head to head with the man himself are aware of what they owe to Barry Sheene's popularity. Steve Hislop might have made his name on the TT circuit Sheene so despised, but he still feels the sport in general is indebted to Barry. 'He raised the profile of the sport dramatically in the seventies, and in such a nice way. He was a woman's man, he brought big-name sponsors into the sport, and he was even able to model the products on TV, something you can't imagine many riders doing now. He was controversial and very outspoken, but in a nice way; he got away with it, unlike some riders today who just sound arrogant.'

With so much emphasis having been put on Sheene's character and non-racing activities over the years, it's easy to forget just how much he achieved as a racer. Two 500cc World Championships, 19 500cc Grand Prix victories, three 125cc Grand Prix wins and one 50cc GP victory; 19 pole positions, 18 fastest laps and a total of 52 podiums at GP level. He remains the only man to have won Grands Prix in both the 50cc and 500cc classes, and it shall always be so, the smallest GP class having been abolished in 1983. Barry also won the European Formula 750 Championship, was five times *MCN* British Superbike champion, five times Shellsport 500 champion and twice British 125cc champion. It's unarguably an impressive record. It would no doubt have been more impressive had Sheene not suffered so many serious injuries.

Barry was an extremely intelligent and self-motivated racer, as Chip Hennen explained. 'I think Pat was on a par with Barry intelligence-wise, but I used to sit down and tell Pat that racing is a thinking-man's sport, so if there was a problem we should sit down and think about it. Barry didn't have anyone telling him that, but he did it on his own. He was a thinking-man's racer. And he certainly did more for the sport than any other racer did; much more than Mike Hailwood did, certainly more than Giacomo Agostini did. What he did in promoting the sport is a lesson to everybody else. Pat and I had many conversations at night time in the paddock with Kenny Roberts and Kel Carruthers [Roberts' chief engineer] about how to promote the sport and how to promote riders, and in that sphere there were some exceptional things about Barry. I don't think we will ever, in our lifetimes, find anybody to excel in the way he did. I think Barry Sheene is probably the most exceptional racer I've ever met.'

Barry knew that his fame was down to winning races, and that he could never have been so popular and successful had he been just an average rider. 'That's why he got to where he was,' explained his former mechanic Simon Tonge. 'Barry didn't get there just from being a good self-publicist, although he was much better at that than any of his contemporaries. At the end of the day, he was really fast on a bike.' Indeed, it's one subject every rider who ever raced with Sheene agrees on: on the track he was clever, hard, safe and quick. Mamola again: 'There was a group of guys I always raced with, and Barry Sheene was in that group. With a group of riders who you race against like that, you have to have respect for them. There are certain guys you have respect for on the track but not off it, but Barry was one I respected both on and off the track.' Chip Hennen still sounds amazed today when he recollects just how good a rider Barry could be on his day. 'He was extremely fast at his home circuits like Mallory Park. If he wanted to, he could go faster than anybody else on that track. It was absolutely incredible how quick he could go when he put his mind to it.' Pat Hennen, who had a grand-stand view as Barry's team-mate, agreed wholeheartedly. 'He was a rocket ship, especially on the circuits he knew well, like Brands and Silverstone, and European circuits like Assen. He was definitely a class act, as well as quite a performer. Whenever he came to a circuit, he didn't just arrive, he always made an entrance. He and Stephanie always arrived in style, in his Rolls Royce or in a helicopter.'

It was this very capacity to combine track success with off-track marketability that made Sheene the star he was, as his old friend and early rival Chas Mortimer recounted. 'Barry was always very good at publicity and in dealing with the public – they've always associated with him. I would say that Barry was a tremendous communicator with the public and with the press. He clearly always had an amazing amount of ability. There were a lot of other people at the same time who had the same amount of ability, but Barry was always very good at publicity. That's not sour grapes – it's meant to be a compliment.'

For the public at large, motorcycling was Barry Sheene and Barry Sheene was motorcycling. He was quite simply the only name from the sport almost universally recognized outside it, as John Cooper explained. 'If you stop anybody in the street and ask if they've heard of Barry Sheene, more than likely they'll say yes. If you asked them if they'd heard of John Cooper, they'd say no! Barry promoted himself exceptionally well and he was always liked. He'd always sign autographs and he would speak to people. He just had it weighed up.' This appeal to the non-motorcycling masses was one of the reason's why Suzuki's racing director Denys Rohan wanted to re-sign Sheene for the 1983 season. 'He was *the* man for promoting the motorcycle product, not only to the enthusiast,' Rohan said. 'If you put his photograph in front of the average man or woman who was going to buy a moped, he'd be instantly recognized. He is the only racer who falls into that category.'

When Sheene announced his retirement, Peter Clifford, a former journalist who now runs the WCM Grand Prix team, wrote a glowing tribute for the 1985–86 edition of *Motocourse*, which he edited at the time. It read, in part, 'It would be difficult to overestimate the contribution Barry Sheene has made to motorcycle racing. More than anyone else he has brought racing to the attention of the general public. If he gained a great deal in financial terms from being a successful rider, then the sport gained far more, and Sheene paid for his success with a considerable amount of pain.' It was a fitting and honest accolade. Sheene did make a lot of money from racing, but he also increased the profile of the sport to such a high level that everyone eventually felt the financial benefits.

Barry was born an honest fighter, and remained one to the very last. Unfortunately, his final enemy did not harbour the same chivalric code. Though he died too young, in truth he was lucky to live as long as he did considering the catalogue of monumental crashes he suffered, as well as the fact that he spent 16 years tearing around some of the world's most dangerous circuits. Cancer might have taken Sheene away from his family, friends and fans, but it can never take away the legacy he left to us all. We must treasure it, respect it, celebrate it and nurture it for present and future generations who will never be fortunate enough to witness in action the most famous motorcyclist who ever lived.

BARRY SHEENE

MAJOR CAREER RESULTS

1968

Venue/Race	Class	Place
Brands Hatch	125cc	DNF
	250cc	3rd
Brands Hatch	125cc	1st
	350cc	1st

1969

Venue/Race	Class	Place
Brands Hatch Hutchinson 100	250cc	4th
Snetterton Race of Aces	350cc	2nd
	125cc	2nd

125cc British Championship: 2nd

1970

Venue/Race	Class	Place
Brands Hatch Hutchinson 100	250cc	4th
Snetterton Race of Aces	500cc	DNF
Montjuich Park	GP125	2nd

125cc British Championship: 1st
250cc British Championship: 3rd

1971

Grands Prix	Class	Place
Salzburgring	125cc	3rd
	250cc	DNF
Isle of Man TT	125cc	DNF
	250Prod	DNF
Assen	125cc	2nd
Spa-Francorchamps	125cc	1st
Sachsenring	125cc	2nd
	250cc	6th
Brno	50cc	1st
	125cc	3rd
Anderstorp	50cc	4th
	125cc	3rd
Imatra	125cc	1st
Monza	125cc	3rd
Jarama	50cc	2nd
	125cc	3rd

GP125 World Championship: 2nd
GP50 World Championship: 7th

Major national and international meetings

Mallory Park	125cc	1st
	250cc	1st
	350cc	1st
Mallory Park Post TT Meeting	500cc	2nd
Silverstone 'Grand Prix'	125cc	1st
	250cc	1st
	500cc	2nd

125cc British Championship: 1st
250cc British Championship: 2nd

1972

Grands Prix	Class	Place
Nurburgring	250cc	DNF
	350cc	DNF
Clermont Ferrand	250cc	DNS
	350cc	DNS
Salzburgring	250cc	4th
Imola	250cc	DNS
	350cc	DNS
Anderstorp	250cc	DNF
	350cc	DNF
Montjuich Park	250cc	3rd

Major national and international meetings

Snetterton Race of Aces meeting	250cc	1st
	350cc	1st
	500cc	2nd
King of Brands	500cc	1st

1973

Grands Prix	Class	Place
Rouen	F750	DNF
Imola	F750	DNF
Clermont Ferrand	F750	1st
Anderstorp	F750	3rd
Hameenlinna	F750	2nd
Silverstone	F750	DSQ
Hockenheim	F750	4th
Montjuich Park	F750	2nd
Imatra	GP500	DNF

Formula 750 European Champion

Major national and international meetings

King of Brands	750cc	1st

MCN British Superbike Champion
Shellsport 500 Champion

1974

Grands Prix	Class	Place
Clermont Ferrand	500cc	2nd
Nurburgring	500cc	DNS
Salzburgring	500cc	3rd
Imola	500cc	DNF
Assen	500cc	DNF
Spa-Francorchamps	500cc	DNF
Anderstorp	500cc	DNF
Brno	500cc	4th

GP500 World Championship: 6th

Major national and international meetings

Daytona 200	750cc	DNF
Imola 200	750cc	5th
Silverstone 'Grand Prix'	750cc	1st
	500cc	1st
Mallory Park Race of the Year	750cc	1st

MCN Superbike Champion
Shellsport 500 Champion

1975

Grands Prix	Class	Place
Salzburgring	500cc	DNS
Hockenheim	500cc	DNF
Assen	500cc	1st
Spa-Francorchamps	500cc	DNF
Anderstorp	500cc	1st
Imatra	500cc	DNF
Brno	500cc	DNF

GP500 World Championship: 6th

Major national and international meetings

Daytona 200	750cc	DNS
Magny-Cours	F750	1st
Anderstorp	F750	1st
Silverstone	F750	1st
Mallory Park Race of the Year	750cc	1st

Formula 750 European Championship: 2nd
MCN British Superbike Championship: 3rd

1976

Grands Prix	Class	Place
Le Mans	500cc	1st
Salzburgring	500cc	1st
Mugello	500cc	1st
IOM TT	500cc	DNS
Assen	500cc	1st
Spa-Francorchamps	500cc	2nd
Anderstorp	500cc	1st
Imatra	500cc	DNS
Brno	500cc	DNS
Nurburgring	500cc	DNS

GP500 World Champion

Major national and international meetings

Brands Hatch	Trans	2nd, 3rd
Mallory Park	Trans	1st, 3rd
Oulton Park	Trans	3rd, 13th
Daytona 200	F750	34th
Imola	F750	3rd
Chimay	500cc	1st
Brands Hatch Hutchinson 100	750cc	1st
Mallory Park Race of the Year	750cc	2nd

MCN British Superbike Champion
Shellsport 500 Champion

1977

Grands Prix	Class	Place
San Carlos	500cc	1st
Salzburgring	500cc	DNS
Hockenheim	500cc	1st
Imola	500cc	1st
Paul Ricard	500cc	1st
Assen	500cc	2nd
Spa-Francorchamps	500cc	1st
Anderstorp	500cc	1st
Imatra	500cc	6th
Brno	500cc	DNS
Silverstone	500cc	DNF

GP500 World Champion

Major national and international meetings

Brands Hatch	Trans	2nd, 2nd
Mallory Park	Trans	4th, 3rd
Oulton Park	Trans	1st, 11th
King of Brands	750cc	1st
Snetterton Race of Aces	750cc	4th

MCN British Superbike Champion
Shellsport 500 Champion

1978

Grands Prix	Class	Place
San Carlos	500cc	1st
Jarama	500cc	5th
Salzburgring	500cc	3rd

Nogaro	500cc	3rd
Mugello	500cc	5th
Assen	500cc	3rd
Spa-Francorchamps	500cc	3rd
Karlskoga	500cc	1st
Imatra	500cc	DNF
Silverstone	500cc	3rd
Nurburgring	500cc	4th

GP500 World Championship: 2nd

Major national and international meetings

Brands Hatch	Trans	1st, 2nd
Mallory Park	Trans	3rd, 14th
Oulton Park	Trans	13th, 3rd
Chimay	750cc	1st
	500cc	1st
Snetterton Race of Aces	750cc	1st
Imola	Nations Cup	1st, 1st, 2nd
		3rd, 1st, 1st

MCN British Superbike Champion
Shellsport 500 Champion

1979

Grands Prix	**Class**	**Place**
San Carlos	500cc	1st
Salzburgring	500cc	12th
Hockenheim	500cc	DNF
Imola	500cc	4th
Jarama	500cc	DNF

Rijeka	500cc	DNF
Assen	500cc	2nd
Spa-Francorchamps	500cc	DNS
Karlskoga	500cc	1st
Imatra	500cc	3rd
Silverstone	500cc	2nd
Le Mans	500cc	1st

GP500 World Championship: 3rd

Major national and international meetings

Brands Hatch	Trans	1st, 1st
Mallory Park	Trans	1st, 2nd
Oulton Park	Trans	DNF, DNF
Donington Park	Nations Cup	1st, 1st, 1st 1st
Oulton Park Race of the Year	750cc	2nd

MCN British Superbike Championship: 6th

1980

Grands Prix	Class	Place
Misano	500cc	7th
Jarama	500cc	5th
Paul Ricard	500cc	DNF
Assen	500cc	DNF
Zolder	500cc	DNS
Imatra	500cc	DNS
Silverstone	500cc	DNF
Nurburgring	500cc	DNS

GP500 World Championship: 14th

Major national and international meetings

Brands Hatch	Trans	4th, 16th
Mallory Park	Trans	8th, 5th
Oulton Park	Trans	DNF, DNF
Mallory Park Race of the Year	750cc	2nd

1981

Grands Prix	Class	Place
Salzburgring	500cc	4th
Hockenheim	500cc	6th
Monza	500cc	3rd
Paul Ricard	500cc	4th
Rijeka	500cc	5th
Assen	500cc	DNF
Spa-Francorchamps	500cc	4th
Imola	500cc	2nd
Silverstone	500cc	DNF
Imatra	500cc	DNF
Anderstorp	500cc	1st

GP500 World Championship: 5th

Major national and international meetings

Brands Hatch	Trans	7th, 15th
Mallory Park	Trans	6th, 3rd
Oulton Park	Trans	1st, DNF
Mallory Park Race of the Year	750cc	2nd

MCN British Superbike Championship: 6th

1982

Grands Prix	Class	Place
Buenos Aires	500cc	2nd
Salzburgring	500cc	2nd
Nogaro	500cc	DNS
Jarama	500cc	2nd
Misano	500cc	DNF
Assen	500cc	3rd
Spa-Francorchamps	500cc	2nd
Rijeka	500cc	3rd
Silverstone	500cc	DNS

GP500 World Championship: 5th

Major national and international meetings

	Class	Place
Brands Hatch	Trans	1st, 1st
Mallory Park	Trans	1st, 2nd
Oulton Park	Trans	1st, 1st
Hockenheim	500cc	1st

MCN British Superbike Championship: 9th

1983

Grands Prix	Class	Place
Kyalami	500cc	10th
Le Mans	500cc	7th
Monza	500cc	9th
Hockenheim	500cc	DNF
Jarama	500cc	DNS
Salzburgring	500cc	13th

Rijeka	500cc	13th
Assen	500cc	DNF
Spa-Francorchamps	500cc	DNS
Silverstone	500cc	9th
Anderstorp	500cc	DNF
Imola	500cc	DNF

GP500 World Championship: 14th

Major national and international meetings

Oulton Park	Trans	8th, 7th
Snetterton	Trans	4th, 6th
Brands Hatch	Trans	5th, 8th

Shell Oils 500 Championship: 7th
MCN Masters Championship: 12th (only two rounds entered)

1984

Grands Prix	Class	Place
Kyalami	500cc	3rd
Misano	500cc	DNF
Jarama	500cc	7th
Salzburgring	500cc	10th
Nurburgring	500cc	10th
Paul Ricard	500cc	5th
Rijeka	500cc	7th
Assen	500cc	DNF
Spa-Francorchamps	500cc	9th
Silverstone	500cc	5th

Anderstorp	500cc	DNF
Imola	500cc	DNF

GP500 World Championship: 6th

Major national and international meetings

Donington Park	Trans	10th, 11th, 9th, 11th, 9th, DNF

ITV World of Sport Superbike Challenge: 6th
Motor Cycle News Masters: 12th=

MAJOR CLASSIC BIKES RACING RESULTS

Venue/Year	Class	Place
Goodwood, 1998	500cc	2nd, 3rd
Goodwood, 1999	500cc	1st, 1st
Phillip Island, 2000	500cc	1st, 1st, DNF
Donington Park, 2000	500cc	DNF, 2nd
Goodwood, 2000	500cc	DNF, 2nd
Phillip Island, 2001	500cc	3rd, 3rd, DNF
Eastern Creek, 2001	500cc	3rd, 3rd
Donington Park, 2001	500cc	4th, 1st
Goodwood, 2001	500cc	1st, 1st
Phillip Island, 2002	500cc	2nd, 2nd, 2nd

Eastern Creek, 2002	500cc	5th, 4th, 6th, 2nd
Donington Park, 2002	500cc	1st, 1st
Goodwood, 2002	500cc	2nd, 1st

KEY TO ABBREVIATIONS

GP = Grand Prix
F750 = Formula 750 European Championship
Prod = Production bike
MCN = Motor Cycle News British Superbikes
Trans = TransAtlantic Challenge series
DNS = Did not start
DNF = Did not finish
DSQ = Disqualified

SELECT BIBLIOGRAPHY

Donaldson, Gerald, *James Hunt: The Biography*, CollinsWillow, 1994

Fogarty, Carl, with Neil Bramwell, *Foggy*, CollinsWillow, 2000

Harris, Nick and Clifford, Peter, *Fast Freddie*, Motor Racing Publications Limited, 1986

Hilton, Christopher, *Two Wheel Showdown*, Patrick Stephens Limited, 1994

Lawrence, Mike, Taylor, Simon and Nye, Doug, *The Glory of Goodwood*, Virgin Books, 1999

Motocourse: 50 Years of Moto Grand Prix, Hazleton Publishing Ltd, 1999

Motocourse 1976–1977, Hazleton Securities Ltd, 1976

Motocourse 1977–1978, Hazleton Securities Ltd, 1977

Motocourse 1978–1979, Hazleton Securities Ltd, 1978

Motocourse 1979–1980, Hazleton Securities Ltd, 1979

Motocourse 1980–1981, Hazleton Securities Ltd, 1980

Motocourse 1981–1982, Hazleton Publishing, 1981

Motocourse 1982–1983, Hazleton Publishing, 1982

Motocourse 1983–1984, Hazleton Publishing, 1983

Motocourse 1984–1985, Hazleton Publishing, 1984

Motor Cycle News Annual '75, Patrick Stephens Limited and *Motor Cycle News*, 1974

Marriot, Andrew, *The Sheene Machine*, Pelham Books, 1979

Peck, Alan, *No Time to Lose: The Fast Moving World of Bill Ivy*, Motor Racing Publications Ltd, 1972

Scott, Michael, *Barry Sheene: A Will to Win*, Comet Books, W.H. Allen & Co. Ltd, 1983

Sheene, Barry, with Ian Beacham, *Barry Sheene: The Story So Far*, Studio Publications, 1976

Sheene, Barry, with Ian Beacham, *Leader of the Pack*, Queen Anne Press, Macdonald & Co. (Publishers) Ltd, 1983

Magazines
Bike, Biking Times, F1 Racing, MCN Sport, Motorcycle Racing, Two Wheels Only

Newspapers
Daily Express, Daily Mail, Daily Mirror, Daily Telegraph, Evening Standard, Guardian, Mail on Sunday, Motor Cycle News, Motor Cycle Weekly, News of the World, Northern Daily Mail, Sun, The Age (Australia)

INDEX

BARRY SHEENE

Mott, Sue 285
movies 18, 257
Mugello (Italy) 130–1, 173
Multi Coloured Swap Shop 18, 91
musical career 27
MV Agusta 52, 110, 272, 280

Newbold, John 137, 155
News of the World 156, 293
Nieto, Angel 50, 51, 60, 61, 62, 155, 288
Nixon, Gary 101, 108, 155
Nogaro (France) 173
Northern Daily Mail 150
Norton
  Gus Kuhn Commando 241
  Manx 13, 267, 269–70, 274–7, 280
Nurburgring (Germany) 32, 177–8, 205, 233

O'Herlihy, Gavan 257
Oliver's Mount 58, 148–51, 194, 206, 236–7
Oulton Park, Cheshire 152, 159, 184, 263

Parkinson 18, 27, 90–1, 147, 151
Parlotti, Gilberto 58, 62
Parrish, Steve 'Stavros'
  1977 Suzuki team-mate 139–40, 144
  1982 Donington Park 124
  1983 season 226
  BS cancer 285, 293, 295
  BS Lifetime Achievement award 300
  mechanic 117
  rider rivalries 155, 158, 166
  truck racing 259
  Yamaha T-Shirt stunt 169
Patrese, Riccardo 261
Paul Ricard (France) 111–12, 140–1, 189, 192–3, 210, 233

Percy, Wynne 262
personality 151–2, 175, 302
Phillip Island 269, 273–4, 277, 288, 300, 321
Phillips, Mick 290
pilot's licence 83
playboy image 71–83, 139–40, 148, 154, 247
popularity problems
  fans 147–54
  manufacturers 167–9, 192
  media 147, 153
  rider rivalries 154–67
Prodigy 94
property
  Australia 26, 86, 223, 264–5
  Charlwood 66, 85, 88–9, 152
  London 89
public relations
  agents 93
  image 73, 90, 102, 147–8, 152–4
  self promotion 95, 137, 161, 169, 188, 210, 252–4, 306

radio 90, 91–2
Ravens, Jan 257
Read, Madeleine 156
Read, Phil
  1976 season 129, 130–1
  classic racing 266
  Frank Sheene as mechanic 23
  Isle of Man TT races 58
  rivalry 155–6
  Rolls Royce 77
  World Championship 125
records 18, 141–2, 272, 277, 304
religion 289
Rijeka (Yugoslavia) 180, 198, 230, 234
road circuits 58–9, 149–50, 155, 205–6
Roberts, Kenny
  1978 season 171, 173, 176–8, 194
  1979 season 179, 180, 181–3

332

PHOTOGRAPHIC ACKNOWLEDGEMENTS

The Publishers would like to thank the following for their permission to reproduce copyrighted photographs in the plates sections 1–16:

Action Plus 15bl
Brian Moody/Scope Features 3tl
Don Morley 2t, 5tr, 5b, 7(all), 8(all), 10c, 10b, 11(all), 12(all), 13(all), 14bl, 14br, 15tl, 15tr
Express 16br
Hulton /Corbis 1t
Hulton 1r, 4c
LAT 15br
Mirror 5tl, 6bl, 6br
Nick Harris 6t
PA 3b, 4b
Popperfoto 1l, 3tr, 4t
Rex Features 2c, 2b 10t, 14t
Sutton Images 9, 16tl, 16tr, 16bl